1975

may be kept

SOUTH WEST:
The last frontier in Africa

SOUTH WEST:
The last frontier in Africa

ESCHEL RHOODIE

 TWIN CIRCLE PUBLISHING CO., INC.
1776 BROADWAY, NEW YORK, N.Y. 10019

In association with

VOORTREKKER PRESS, JOHANNESBURG, SOUTH AFRICA

Introduction by the Rev. Daniel Lyons S.J., with a Preface by General S.L.A. Marshall.

2A

TABLE OF CONTENTS

LIST OF ILLUSTRATIONS, MAPS AND TABLES

PREFACE

Many years ago in the course of my work as a soldier and writer, I discovered pretty much on my own that the one thing more difficult to refute than a final truth is an utter absurdity.

My relatively brief but also intense experience with South West Africa and with the case before the International Court, whereby the future of the territory was continued in jeopardy, therefore taught me no new lesson except that a rule which applies in the simpler affairs of life, where person deals with person, also holds good on a global scale in contentions between nations or between peoples or between pressure blocs that disregard national boundaries.

It is inordinately difficult to convince anyone who has not been there that South West is a land of such enchantment, natural wonders and unique human problems as to beggar description by such a book as this. To persuade them that it is a land of calm, good order and steady progress when conditions there are formally charged with being a menace to the peace of the world is simply impossible. But if these are tasks beyond me, I would still rather attempt them than try to explain how the case against South Africa concerning the mandate for South West has won such wide acceptance and credibility in world opinion. Nothing is proved by this phenomenon except that if a thing is said often enough and loud enough, it will become believed. But then, we have known that for a long time.

Certainly if I were to repeat or to underscore what the author has said and do nothing else, my witness in this preface would become boring. What seems to me important above all is to impress Americans with an understanding that South West is not like our land, its problems, economic, cultural and racial, are in little or no way comparable to our own, and to attempt to judge what goes on there by what we do and by the standards we set for ourselves is wrong and hypocritical. That is doubly true in an era when we are anything but united concerning our own standards. So toward putting it gently that all perspectives are different, and that we reflect here on a strange land with a unique variety of peoples, many of them as firmly set in their tribal ways as are our reservation Indians, I simply quote from my notebook the story of a sentimental journey taken in South West.

Runtu, the main station in the Okavango country, is high on the south bank of the river of that name which bends like an oxbow as it courses eastward. From the rim, the view to the westward is most impressive, as to the sweep and hospitability of the valley, the volume and gentle fall of the river and the resulting opportunity afforded man. It does not take an engineer's eye to see that this water, properly conserved and turned toward the land on either side, would make the valley enormously productive all year around, promoting a food surplus far beyond the needs of the area population which is relatively sparse even for South West.

As things are, the water of the Okavango is almost wholly wasted. Some miles to the south of the Caprivi

Strip the river empties into the marches of Betchuanaland (Botswana). Its utilization around the Runtu region is according to what the tribesman want, and what they will stand for, which is not according to what civilization considers a proper use of natural resources. There are only about 32,000 tribesmen in the Okavango district. A few hundred of them are centred immediately around Runtu, where the commissioner, D. J. F. Maree, holds forth. This is the site also of the leper colony which has about 200 members who live communally in a native-type but modernly served and sanitary facility. As in all such colonies, sex is a main avocation and problem.

The Okavango people are divided into five tribes, Kuangari, Sambiu, Mbundza, Dziriku and Mbukshu. Males who want employment for wages find it in road work paid for by the state. The roads are still greatly primitive, though in dry weather the countryside is traversable without them. The natives work in fortnightly shifts, from which they get enough pay to provide for the family for one month.

During the past several years there has gone on at Runtu, under Maree's direction and urging, a token experiment in irrigation and crop diversification. About 15 acres along the river bank several miles east of the station were set aside. Water is pumped out of the Okavango to serve the tract. The first difficulty was to get volunteers who would believe that the experiment could be made productive, and that if any worthwhile crops resulted, they would be beneficiaries. Maree had decided to seed with mealies, kaffircorn, millet, tobacco,

Indian jute, peanuts and sugar cane. Resistance was broken for this one group after Maree agreed that, to protect themselves, they would be allowed to plant their usual crops on their own plots, spending only part of the time on the project next to the river. Due to drought, they had to work harder than usual in their own gardens. So less work was put in on the river-bank irrigated farm than had been planned. But the drought became so intense that their own plantings largely failed, while on the other hand the small community project flourished abundantly.

The influence of this one success is now radiating widely, and there are requests for other limited, local projects of the small pump variety from other groups elsewhere along the river. But this still falls far short of getting tribal and chieftainship approval of large-scale reclamation. Maree believes that it can be done only by this gradual method, taking one step at a time. This, though for the past several years the off-river mealie crop has been an almost total failure.

As to the raising of cattle and the improving of stock through selective breeding, the station is getting almost 100 per cent acceptance from the tribesmen, though touching a Bantu's cows is a most sensitive of all matters. I would judge that the Okavango people, as is true of the Bantu in general, have an economy based fundamentally on cattle wealth with products of the soil being marginal in their scale of values. That somewhat explains the start. There are definite limits to how much may be done at one time when the problem is one of transforming the mores of a people through persuasion and experiment towards winning voluntary co-operation.

The authority of the chief remains the dominant consideration in winning popular support for any reform measure. The influence of the witch doctor is still a force with which to reckon, though some of the witch doctors now submit themselves to hospital care, and back up the immunization programmes and field extension of other medical services which in the Runtu region are generally successful. Malaria control does not have the same geographical obstacles to contend with around Runtu as in Ovamboland.

I called at Vungu-Vungu, the hospital there, the mission station and the school. My chief contacts were Father Hartmann, head of the Catholic mission serving the Sambiu tribe, and Chieftainess Muengere, a woman of about 60 who runs tribal affairs. She was quite reserved and carried herself proudly, though replying to most questions with monosyllables. She obviously wished to be interviewed and her restraint when we discussed programmes (which she endorsed uncritically) came, I would judge, from the assumed dignity of her position. Dealing with me was as if she were dealing with an inferior.

Recruitment of students for the grade schools around Runtu is not necessary. Unlike among the Caprivi people they accept the idea in the determining numbers, and there are more eligible applicants than there is available space. With few exceptions, the teaching is done by Bantu from the same tribe. Pupils — boys and girls —

wear European clothing provided by the mission authority and about half of the kids go barefoot, though they are supplied with shoes.

* * *

"Money is not worth cattle."

That almost epigrammatic sentence, uttered by Chief Martin Chilongo who is head of the Ondongo tribe of the Ovambo people, reflects the difference between the European and Bantu scale of values almost precisely. Chief Martin is relatively a wealthy man. He measures his power and influence in terms of thousands of head of livestock and has no intention of changing, regardless of what reforms and other paths to prosperity become fixed on Ovamboland. His sense of well-being is determined by the size and shape of his herds.

We had gone to his kraal, Ontoneigo, for an audience. With me were F. A. J. J. du Preez, the senior Bantu affairs commissioner, H. S. van Niewenhuizen, my escort, and Julius, the Ovambo interpreter. Ontoneigo is about 15 miles from Ondongua, the main town of Ovamboland, and is a far-spreading establishment, a veritable maze of native huts and interlocking native fences, without civilized embellishments. Though the engagement had been long set, we were kept waiting in the sun outside the kraal for 65 minutes. The Chief had to attend certain preliminaries, the dressing of self in Western clothes, including tan shoes fresh from the box, and the summoning of his councillors who were prostrate before him when we at last saw him.

Then there was another thing: the Chief is an addict of strong Angola beer, smuggled across the border. Two empty bottles were beside him where he squatted on the ground and he was sipping at a third when we entered. He continued, making no offer to share. If he acted a bit potted, it did not make him less happy. Following the usual amenities and small talk, we discussed business of a kind. How are things going? Are your people fairly content? What's the state of public health? What more do you need? That sort of general question.

The prolonged drought had been broken by great rains coincidental with my arrival in South West. Some of the previously dry stream beds were running floods out of Angola. The young Ovambos were busy with improvised seines trekking small fish from the muddy waters. Everywhere the land was green. Crop prospects were better than in several years, though it was too late to save the mealies. All of these things, between burps, the Chief reflected upon.

Then he concluded: "The schools are good. But give us more. More schools, more medicine, more dams. More. More."

The construction of a pipeline from Oshakati to Ondangua at a cost of about $500,000 was right then being completed. Work was also going on a 60-mile canal between Ombalantu and Oshakati. The main purpose of this construction from the border southward is to convey and store the flood waters so that much of Ovamboland will have insurance against drought. Ultimate costs of the completed system are estimated at $7,500,000. Whether it is wholly a practical project, the unique nature of the Ovambo terrain considered, is a good question.

There was also opening, not far from Ondangua, a 500-bed hospital to take care of Chief Martin's people. For none of these good works were the tribesmen paying anything. It was when talk turned toward the hospital that Niewenhuizen asked the indelicate question. He said: "They will need much beef and the hospital is far away from any other source of supply. Will you be willing to sell some of your cattle to us to help meet the hospital's requirements?"

That's when the Chief bridled. He asked: "Do you think I'm a fool? You have many cows in South Africa. Use them. Money is not worth cattle."

On that note the conversation died, though my wonderment at South West went on and on. I found less tension there than in any land I have visited. Not one person was in jail among the tribes. There were only 12 police in Ovamboland, six in the whole Kaokoveld; not one weapon was in evidence anywhere. People smiled and waved when the Landrover sped by. The commissioners' homes were unguarded. One felt quite safe walking about at night, without escort. Still, I hear voices at UN say: "We must change all of that; it is bad, very bad." What sense it makes, I'd like to know, I'd really like to know.

S. L. A. MARSHALL.*

Dherran Dhoun,
Birmingham, Michigan.

* GENERAL MARSHALL is one of America's leading military writers and strategists. During World War II he served as Expert Consultant to the Secretary for War and later as Chief Historian for the European theatre of the war. After World War II he was entrusted with various missions by the Department of the Army and the Department of State particularly in connection with the Korean war and the war in Vietnam. He is the author of numerous works on military matters. General Marshall was an expert witness in the South West Africa case before the International Court of Justice.

INTRODUCTION

SOUTH WEST AFRICA: THE LAST FRONTIER IN AFRICA

South West Africa is a country the size of Texas. Most Americans know very little about it, yet it has recently been a hotly debated subject at the United Nations and front-page news in almost every newspaper in the United States. Only two books have appeared on South West Africa in America the last ten years. Neither one has provided the background needed. A good book on the subject was almost more than we could hope for. But here it is, the book that provides the answers.

Dr. Rhoodie is a white African, with roots that go deep into African soil. His forefathers have lived there since 1659. He first worked as a journalist in Johannesburg and later served as press attaché for his country in Canberra, Washington and New York. A careful scholar, he is a contributer to *Collier's Encyclopedia,* and is currently doing a 1,000 page documentary entitled *Africa: A Political History.*

Like the Gaul of old, all of Africa is divided roughly into three parts. The first is northern Africa, Arab country. The second is central Africa, comprised of non-white states. The third is southern Africa, which is largely governed by people of European descent. In the words of the late Dag Hammarskjold in Cape Town: "But this is not Africa. This is Europe."

The subject of South West Africa is so charged with emotion in America that anyone who adopts an anti-United Nations line is considered a "segregationist". Yet since it is linked with a threat to world peace it needs to be discussed. A former German colony, it was placed under South African administration by the League of Nations at the end of World War I.

The greatest mistake we make in regard to southern Africa is to compare the native African to the Negro in America. They have little in common except the colour of their skin. The tribal languages and customs of the African make him much more like our Indian.

Our first instinct is to disregard his tribal background. Nothing could be more false or artificial. Who would "integrate" our Indians by destroying tribal loyalties and mixing them together? How would the Indians react to it? Unless we favour this, unless we are convinced that this would help the Indians of North America, we should hesitate to try it on the African continent, a place about which we know so very little.

There is no progress to be made by disregarding the language barrier and ancient customs and traditions that divide the various peoples of South West Africa. A perfect solution to such a racial problem exists neither in Africa nor in America.

There is no substitute for considering the facts. To say that Dr. Rhoodie worked harder in gathering his material than he did in writing a 500 page doctoral dissertation would be an understatement. In his knowledge of South West Africa he hardly has a rival. Let us see what he has to say.

DANIEL LYONS, S.J.*

New York, 1967.

---

* DANIEL LYONS is President of the Free Pacific Association, New York, a Member of the Strategy Staff of the American Security Council, Washington, D.C., and co-author of VIET-NAM CRISIS.

The shifting sands of the Namib Desert —
the oldest desert in the world.
Some of the dunes reach a height
of close to a 1,000 feet.

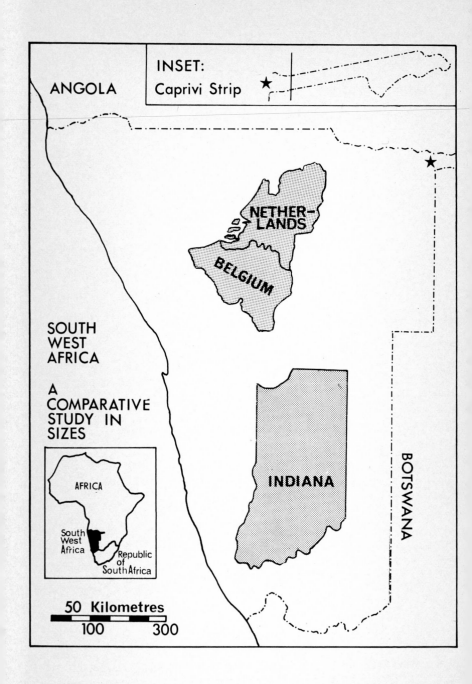

INSET:
Caprivi Strip

ANGOLA

NETHER-
LANDS

BELGIUM

SOUTH
WEST
AFRICA

A
COMPARATIVE
STUDY IN
SIZES

AFRICA

South
West
Africa

Republic
of
South Africa

INDIANA

BOTSWANA

50 Kilometres
100   300

1

THE DISPUTE ON SOUTH WEST AFRICA

Low on the Atlantic coast of Africa where the Benguella current races northward from Antarctica towards the Horse Latitudes of the tropics, there lies a land which can rightly be called the last frontier in Africa — if not in the world.

Of all the regions of Africa, South West Africa is the least known and its problems and complexities the least understood. It has been mentioned in the Security Council of the United Nations as part of the "threat to world peace" posed by South Africa's policy of apartheid; it has also been the subject of a five-year dispute before the International Court of Justice at the Hague[1] with the Black African states ranged on one side and the White controlled Republic of South Africa on the other. Yet the real conditions of existence in this territory and its complex socio-economic problems have received scant attention in the world press. Indeed, even in America there exists only two fairly recent books dealing with this huge slice of virtually uninhabited territory.

Although it is twice the size of California, America's most populous state, or as large as France and Italy combined, it has a population of only half a million or about 1.6 persons per square mile — *forty* times less than the State of Pennsylvania in America. United Nations demographic sources described it as one of the least populated territories in the world. In view of the grossly overpopulated state of so many countries of the world, this is a fact of no mean significance.

For many years people referred to the territory as "The Nameless Land" for this remote place does not have a name — only a rather cumbersome geographical designation — South West Africa. Outside South West Africa, even in South Africa, its big and prosperous neighbour, people know or care little about this deeply fascinating and, despite its generally cruel exterior, hauntingly beautiful land. It is inexplicable that people generally know as little of this territory, which has so often been the subject of discussions in the General Assembly of the United Nations, as they do of the surface of the moon.

---

1. Also known as the World Court.

On closer examination there are all the reasons in the world why political scientists, botanists, students of archaeology, historians, ethnologists, economists and even the man in the street should find South West Africa a most fascinating subject for discussions or study. For many people in Southern Africa its political future will have a direct bearing on their own country's progress and stability, notably Angola, Botswana, Rhodesia and South Africa.

Because of its fascinating contrasts and bizarre phenomena, the territory has also much to offer those who prefer to do their investigations or research on the spot. One cannot help feeling that in this land the vanished centuries have contributed to an aura of mystery which completely envelopes one. It is beyond the human mind to comprehend a period of 200,000,000 years — the approximate age of the large number of fossilized trees lying in the Huab Valley of South West Africa. One hundred and fifty million years ago the now extinct dinosaur left an incredibly clear track of footprints, showing all three toes, on a bank of sandstone on a farm in South West Africa bearing the almost unpronouncable name of Otjihaenemaparero.

The Namib Desert which covers a large area of this land contains the highest sand dunes found anywhere in the world, some reaching a height which would almost dwarf the Eiffel Tower in Paris, the spire of the Chrysler Building in New York or the Hertzog Tower in Johannesburg. The Namib is one of the oldest deserts in the world. The Welwitschia plant found here, lives for

3

more than 2,000 years — a living prehistoric object. On the other hand it is also the home of a "golden mole" only seen for the first time as recently as 1963. It is the home of a snake which, unlike its brethren elsewhere in the world, prefers not to slither *forward* on its belly but to move *sideways* in a series of jerky motions. By day it buries itself in the sand with only its eyes, situated on the point of two periscopes, protruding above the surface — a natural submarine lying in wait of its prey. A touch of Picasso is lent by the three-eyed gecko.

Except for the wiry Bushman, remnants of the stone age, whose language consists of less than a few dozen clicking sounds, all of the dozen different races and nations living in South West Africa to-day are relatively newcomers. Paradoxically and illogically, however, the impression is easily gained that the human race may have had its origin here.

Scientists know of a mysterious race which lived in the territory for centuries, chiselling strange marks on the rock cliffs, and then disappearing without leaving any sign of their origin. The rich variety of prehistoric rock paintings in South West Africa has prompted visits from many famous ethnologists. One drawing in particular — the mysterious "White Lady" of the Brandberg — is today the subject of ardent scientific speculation. The famous French scientist the Abbé Breuil drew attention to the fact that the fifteen inch high rockpainting displays startling similarity to murals found in Egypt and Crete. Could the "White Lady" possibly have been painted by an initiate of the Palace of Cnossus? If so, further intriguing events are conjured up about the territory for the age of the rock painting has tentatively been set at about 2,000 years.

The history of the non-White people now living in South West Africa was one of genocide and chaos. During the one hundred years preceding administration of the territory by Germany and later South Africa, the minority groups waged an incredible struggle for survival.

Here in South West Africa dwell, among others, the Damaras, the Namas, the Hereros, the Ovambos and Okavangos and also people of European descent. They speak different languages and are poles apart in traditions, customs and culture.

The development of this inhospitable and arid land into its present state of peace and prosperity is nothing but an epic of civilization — due to a large extent to the loyalty which the territory instilled in the breasts of those people of European descent who tamed the land and, with their skills, knowledge and enterprise, brought to life its trade and industries. What the inhabitants have achieved in the conservation of water, their most precious commodity, is simply incredible. In fact the use and conservation of water in South West Africa sets an example for arid areas all over the world whether it be in Saudia Arabia or in the Gobi Desert of Asia.

The nature of the territory, its mountains, deserts, rivers, fauna and flora, presents a kaleidoscope which is extremely fascinating, even to the layman. There are sand dunes which "sing", lizards with semi-transparent bodies and web-toed feet which enable them to "swim" in the shifting desert sands. The coastline is probably the most inhospitable to be found anywhere in the world barring the icy shores of the polar regions. The coast has no fixed "line" of position. Because of the actions of currents and waves it is constantly shifting. It has well deserved the name *Skeleton Coast* and wrecks of large ocean-going vessels have been discovered way inland, riding the dunes like some ghostly ship. Even the trees in the territory, unlike trees elsewhere, do not simply die. In dying the camel thorn tree falls gradually to the ground, slowly folding its branches around the trunk. This may be due to the gradual "baking" of the branches by the blistering hot sun, but to the inhabitants the trees fold their branches to hide their tragic death from inquisitive eyes — a quaint fiction, no doubt, but one thoroughly in keeping with the strange aura of the territory.

From the preceding pages it can be concluded that South West Africa is a land which could mean something to everyone, whether in its dramatic history, its rare phenomena, the striking landscape or the diversity of its people. Even then, there is now far more to South West Africa to capture the attention. South Africa's control and administration of the territory has long been the subject of Afro-Asian criticism in the General Assembly of the United Nations. This criticism did not cause world-wide interest. Because of the World Court's decision, however (which captured the headlines in the newspapers of Europe, Africa and the Americas), the international status of South West Africa is likely to become the subject of intense debate in the capitals of the world before the year 1967 has drawn to a close. The principal reason is the refusal of the Afro-Asian states to accept the decision of the World Court. This amounted to an order that no individual state or group of states has the right to interfere in South Africa's administration of the territory. The Afro-Asian states not only publicly denounced the decision but immediately began threatening extreme political action, including force of arms to get the United Nations to destroy South Africa's right of authority over South West Africa.

Tucked away behind their desert, inhospitable coastline and hostile mountains, the people of South West Africa may be a lonely lot but because of this politically immoral (and decidedly illegal) action of the Afro-Asian states, their future will remain a major international headache, the outcome of which could determine Southern African history for a long time to come. There are good grounds for this prediction. For one, South West Africa is seen as the lever by means of which the African states, in concert with the Communists, would seek to upset the Republic of South Africa itself. That the Republic is the most advanced, prosperous and stable country on the whole African continent and the only country in Africa whose allegiance to the Free World is unquestionable, is of no concern to them; that it is not only best equipped to promote the general welfare of all of South West Africa's peoples but, as *proved* before the World Court, having more success in this field is considered to be equally irrelevant. Their *only* concern appears to be the absence of a one-man-one-vote system and the fact that White South Africa hold the reins.

Before expanding somewhat on the preceding theme it should also be remembered that South West Africa itself is not a rich country and is, therefore, not being coveted by South Africa for its wealth. For many decades it was thought utterly unlikely that the territory could yield anything of use to mankind. The very face of the territory contributed to this belief. It is harsh and forbidding, bleak and hostile. Here and there endless sand dunes stretch in parallel lines for miles on end with only a few thorn trees and melon-like creepers to be seen. Other areas resemble a cosmic strip mining operation with fissures and canyons gouged out of the earth. Along the coast giant dunes are cloaked in fog and frequently torn by fierce and blinding sand storms. Inland there are ranges of barren hostile mountains devoid of any tree cover or vegetation and extinct volcanoes. One, a non-active gas volcano, the Geitsigubib, as it is called by the Nama people, was used by America's Smithsonian Institute as a heliometric station for many years until shortly before World War II. The big rivers in the north lie on the boundaries of the territory and while there are some grassy plains to be found as well as hidden valleys and gorges where fountains of water flow from the earth, the fact remains that the area is geo-physically desperately poor and arid.

Under the generally appalling surface much of which enjoys a rainfall of less than two inches a year and sometimes none at all for several years, does lie some wealth. Like the Sahara Desert now giving up its hidden treasure of oil, the desolate and waterless plains of South West Africa also contains deposits of minerals but it is exceedingly difficult to develop because of the inhospitable climate, the lack of water and the vast distances from railheads and ocean ports. Today something like a million carats of diamonds are mined here every year; the territory is a major source to the West of germanium, vital for the production of transistors, and other metals and minerals. However, without the highly skilled workers provided by South African companies for the exceedingly deep-level mining, these operations, the principal source of revenue for the territory, would never have been possible. The vast distances involved would have made it impossible for any country except neighbouring South Africa to develop its mineral potential at all.

It is evident therefore, that it is not the so-called "riches" of South West Africa which have now made it a hot news item. It is the twenty-year struggle by hostile countries in the United Nations to force South Africa to hand over the administration of the territory to the United Nations and which culminated in the protracted dispute before the World Court at the Hague. Liberia and Ethiopia, on behalf of the Black African states[2], had accused South Africa of wilfully oppressing the people, of

2. Their legal expenses were borne by a special fund set up by the organization of African Unity and to which all Black African states and some Arab states contributed an annual amount.

militarising the area, of attempting to incorporate South West Africa and even of committing genocide.

The African states, openly supported by the Communist countries, made no attempt to disguise the fact that they expected the Court to hand down an adverse decision for South Africa. They had hoped that this would have led to a Security Council attempt to end South Africa's administration of the former mandated territory and, since the Court's decision in the case is binding, would thereby have been virtually assured of the support of the big powers without whom the United Nations is powerless. When shortly after the World Court's setback of African hopes, there took place an abortive "invasion" of the territory by terrorists from Tanzania, armed with Russian and Chinese weapons, South Africa knew that a new phase in the territory's history had begun. Her opponents knew that international law would not serve their purpose. Henceforth political pressure and aggression would be employed.

South West Africa was originally inhabited by only the nomadic Hottentot and the stone age Bushmen. Many centuries passed before the arrival of the Hereros, Ovambos and others. In 1484, almost five hundred years ago, the first White men set foot ashore. They were the Portuguese. In 1884 Germany's statesman-warrior, Otto von Bismarck, proclaimed the territory to be under German rule. On July the 9th, 1915, soon after the outbreak of World War I, German troops in the territory surrendered to the South African forces led by

General Jan Christiaan Smuts — later a Field Marshal of the British Empire and the author of the preamble to the Charter of the United Nations. Thus South Africa's presence was established in South West Africa by military conquest, as part of the Allied war effort against Germany. The mandate was confirmed upon South Africa by the League of Nations in 1920.

Although the term "Mandate" had been used before in regard to certain international relationships, it first acquired a special meaning in International Law when the Mandate System of the League of Nations was instituted. This system originated, together with the League, from the peace settlements effected after World War I. As Quincy Wright remarked: "This system, like most other political innovations, was not a product of disinterested juristic thought nor of detached scientific investigation but was a compromise invented by the Versailles statesmen (the Allied war powers) to meet an immediate political dilemma".[3]

The dilemma which required resolution by compromise involved, briefly, a clash of views and aspirations within the ranks of the Allied and Associated Powers relative to the future of territories and colonies conquered from enemy powers during World War I. South West Africa apart, similar situations obtained in respect of other territories conquered and occupied by other Allied and Associated Powers. These included, inter alia, the former German colony in New Guinea, which was occupied by Australia; that in Samoa, by New Zealand;

---

3. Wright, Q.; *Mandates Under the League of Nations, 1930*, p. 3

the German islands in the Pacific Ocean north of the Equator, by Japan; and various German territories elsewhere in Africa, by Great Britain, Belgium and France. Further north, various portions of the Ottoman Empire were in Allied occupation.

During the war, secret treaties and agreements were made between some of the Allies whereby their respective claims to various occupied territories were to be recognized in the event of an Allied victory. And the British Imperial War Cabinet decided in March, 1917, that her three Dominions, Australia, New Zealand and South Africa should be allowed to annex the abovementioned occupied territories, adjacent to their own, namely, German New Guinea, German Samoa and German South West Africa respectively.

On the other hand, certain proposals for international control of conquered colonies, some of them even relating to all colonies, were also made during the war years.

In 1918, G. L. Beer, historian, and adviser to President Wilson of the United States of America, connected such proposals with others then current for the establishment of the League of Nations. He proposed a Mandate System for Mesopotamia and certain of the German colonies, urging that the administration of these areas should be entrusted to "different States acting as mandatories of the League of Nations".[4]

---

4. Beer, G. L. *African Questions at the Paris Peace Conference,* edited by L. H. Gray (1923), p. 431.

Beer considered, however, that the Mandate System could not be applied to South West Africa, and recommended that this region be "incorporated in the Union of South Africa".

The United States of America was not a party to the secret treaties and agreements mentioned above; *she entered the war after most of them had been concluded.* At the termination of the war, President Wilson strongly advocated a policy of 'non annexations'; and he went to the Paris Peace Conference determined to secure application of the proposed Mandate System, in an extreme form, to all ex-enemy colonies and possessions. His proposals, as contained in his drafts of the Covenant, included that the League would be vested with complete authority and control, that it would be *entitled* (not obliged) at its discretion to delegate to a State or 'organized agency' powers to act 'as its agent or mandatory', and also that by reason of an appeal from the people of the territory the League could substitute some other State or agency as mandatory. In keeping with this conception, his Third Draft proposed that the expenses of Mandatory Government would, if necessary, be borne by all the Members of the League.[5]

From the above, the makings of conflict at the Paris Peace Conference will be manifest. There was fairly general agreement that a Mandate System was to be established. The controversy concerned the contents of

---

5. Vide particularly paras. I, II and III of his Second Draft, as amended by his Third Draft: Baker, R. S.: *Woodrow Wilson and World Settlement.* (1922-23), Vol. III, pp. 108-10, 126-29.

such a System, and particularly the peoples and territories to which it was to be applied, especially since there was general recognition of the wide differences between the various peoples and territories concerned, ranging from, on the one hand, developed societies to, on the other, people still living in the Stone Age, such as in New Guinea.

The main elements of the compromise finally embodied in Article 22 of the Covenant (The System of Mandates) are rendered clear by the preceding historical background. As was commented generally by M. Rappard, Secretary and subsequently member of the Permanent Mandates Commission of the old League of Nations: "The terms of the compromise were obvious: President Wilson succeeded in preventing annexation; the conquerors in retaining their conquests".[6] More particularly, in return for the concession that all German Colonial possessions be brought into the Mandate System, President Wilson had to abandon certain of the extreme aspects of his proposals concerning League supremacy and control and the consequent payment of expenses of Mandate administration by League Members. All Mandatories were to be States, not 'organized agencies'. The Mandates were to be allocated by the Principal Allied and Associated Powers *(not the League)*, and at any rate in the case of certain Mandates the allocation 'would have

6. Rappard, W. E. 'The Mandates and the International Trusteeship System,' *Varia Politica* (1953), p. 182.

14

to be to the adjacent claimant States'.[7]   The relationship
between the League and Mandatories was in each case
regulated by a Mandate instrument, the terms of which
were *assented* to by the Mandatory and would normally
require its *consent for alteration*.[8]   (In view of this particular situation, many legal experts concluded from the
World Court's 1966 decision that unless South Africa
agreed to any changes in its administration, she could not
legally be forced to do so and now has a free hand in the
matter, particularly since the League no longer exists.)
All this was very far removed from Wilson's envisaged
free League discretion to appoint and change Mandatories.
Again in the case of certain Mandates, the Mandatories
were to have powers to administer the territories 'as
integral portions' of their own.   *And there would be no
objection to eventual amalgamation that could naturally
result from such administration, if agreed to by the
inhabitants.*   At the Peace Conference President Wilson
himself stressed that "It was up to the Union of South
Africa to make it so attractive that South West Africa
would come into the Union of their own free will . . .
It successful administration by a mandatory should lead
to union with the mandatory, he would be the last to
object . . . " and later he said that "if South Africa

7. Vide Lloyd George's statement on 30th January, 1919, Para. 6
   supra. It is a most important point that South Africa did not
   obtain its Mandatory powers from the League of Nations.
   The mandate was *allocated* to South Africa by the Allied
   Powers at the Versailles Peace Canference.   The League of
   Nations merely acted as an international rubber stamp when
   they "confirmed" the Mandate.

8. Vide Art. 7 of the 'Mandate for German South West Africa.'

managed South West Africa as well as she had managed her own country, then she would be married to South West Africa."[9]

The operative article in the Mandate of South West Africa (Article II) provided: "The Mandatory shall have full power of administration and legislation over the territory subject to the present Mandate as an *integral portion* of the Union of South Africa, and may apply the laws of the Union of South Africa to the territory, subject to such local modifications as circumstances may require."

In 1921, the military government in the territory was replaced by a civilian authority whose major executive officer was an Administrator. He was initially assisted by an advisory council and later, with the granting of a limited measure of self-government in 1925, by an Executive Committee and a Legislative Assembly elected from among the White population. The Bantu nations in South West Africa retained their particular system of government consisting of village elders, counsellors and chiefs.

The South African Parliament passed in 1925 an Act granting a Constitution to South West Africa, under which the White residents (then estimated at 15,000) were given a large measure of local autonomy. Considerably more control has since been delegated, but the South African Parliament remains the supreme legislative body for the territory and South Africa's government retains ultimate executive power.

---

9. For. Rel. U.S.: *The Paris Peace Conference, 1919*, Vol. III pp. 741-42, 788.

Called Mukorob, "the finger of God",
this a well-known landmark near Keetmanshoop.

Not the Rhineland but an old German Castle in Windhoek, South West Africa — the Auas Mountains form the background.

The current Legislative Assembly, consisting of a member from each of the eighteen electorial districts, has authority over taxation in respect of the White population. But it does not have power over mining rights (or taxation of mining revenues), communications facilities (including railways, harbours, mail, telephones, telegraph and aviation), currency and banking, police or the administration of justice, customs or immigration, and the public service. Even those measures entrusted to the Legislative Assembly are subject to a semi-veto power held by the Administrator — who is appointed by the Republic of South Africa.

The South African government and Parliament have retained the welfare of the non-White population of the territory as their special concern. Legislation concerning non-White affairs is enacted by the South African Parliament and promulgated through the proclamation of the Administrator.

The territory is administered through seventeen magisterial districts in which the magistrates (judges) exercise some executive as well as judicial functions. Three territories — Ovamboland, the Kaokoveld and Okavangoland — are under the direct control of the South African Department of Bantu Affairs and, together with a fourth (the Eastern Caprivi), are governed from Pretoria.

In short, South West Africa *remains largely a trust in fact as well as in name.* For although local autonomy has been granted to both Whites and non-

Whites, South Africa continues to handle the bulk of
its domestic and foreign affairs.

When the League of Nations collapsed just after
World War II, South Africans took it for granted that the
Mandate had also lapsed. The Communists and Afro-
Asian members of the United Nations thought otherwise,
maintaining that the United Nations was the "successor"
to the old League and that they had the right to supervise
the administration of South West Africa. Because of
the uncertainty that had thus been deliberately fostered
in the United Nations on its international status, South
West Africa has proved an excellent "loophole" through
which the Afro-Asian nations could attack South Africa's
administration of South West Africa without directly
infringing the "domestic jurisdiction" provision of the
United Nations Charter.[10] Liberia and Ethiopia assumed
the role of accuser. Ethiopia and Liberia at the time were
thought to be the only African countries with a definite
"standing" in the case since they — along with South

---

10. Article 2 Paragraph 7 of the United Nations Charter specifies
that: "Nothing . . . shall authorize the United Nations to
intervene in matters which are essentially within the domestic
jurisdiction of any state or shall require the Members to
submit such matters to settlement under the present Charter."
Despite this provision, the United Nations has repeatedly
dabbled in South Africa's domestic affairs, including its
domestic policy of apartheid and the provisions governing
its minority Asian population. For an excellent compilation
of United Nations action on these issues (as well as South
West Africa) see Eric H. Louw's *The Case for South Africa*,
Macfadden, New York. 1963.

Africa — were the only African members of the League.[11]

The other Afro-Asian nations, seeking a "legitimate" excuse to intervene in South Africa's domestic affairs, always considered South West Africa only as a means of getting at the throat of South Africa. Here, according to their view, was a *legal* way of meddling without actually infringing the national sovereignty provisions of the Charter. Here, ran the argument, the "international community" had a right to intervene, especially if South Africa had defaulted on its obligations under the original mandate. In fact, they asked the Court to rule that the United Nations had the same legal right in respect of South West Africa as the League of Nations had.

When the case was introduced in 1960, South Africa objected that the Court had no jurisdiction to rule on the question. It argued that the Mandate had never been a treaty or convention "in force", at least since the demise of the League of Nations. The International Court decided by the closest margin ever — eight votes to seven — that South Africa had accepted its jurisdiction by ratifying the United Nations Charter and ruled in 1962 to hear the case.

In January 1963, the late South African Prime Minister, Dr. H. F. Verwoerd, announced that South Africa would file a counter-memorial before the International Court so that its case would not go by default. He emphasized that the decision to participate in the Hague proceedings should not be construed as implying

---

11. The World Court, in its 1966 judgment decided that the two countries in fact had no standing at all.

that South Africa recognized the Court's jurisdiction over the matter. It was a matter of refusing to let South Africa's case go unheard.

The case was the most protracted dispute ever heard by the World Court and the record of the oral proceedings alone was sufficient to make up *twenty* good-sized novels.

At first Ethiopia and Liberia relied on charges against South Africa which had been repeated in the United Nations for years on end. Reduced to its essentials the original charges against South Africa were that it acted in bad faith towards the inhabitants of South West Africa by applying policies designed to oppress, suppress or exploit them. It amounted to a violation of the fundamental obligations conferred upon it by the League of Nations. South Africa denied that the system of separate development of the disparate races in the territory was harmful to the inhabitants. On the contrary. South Africa contended that it was beneficial and that abolition of the existing distinctions and differential development, as proposed by Ethiopia and Liberia, would destroy the character of the various ethnic groups — a form of cultural genocide — and deprive them of the fundamental right of protection against loss of identity.

Ethiopia and Liberia fared badly in the case before the World Court, at least as far as the original charges were considered. After South Africa had produced a battery of prominent witnesses from the United States, Great Britain, South Africa and South West Africa and submitted documented facts to support its case, sufficient to fill ten good-sized books, Liberia and Ethiopia *abandoned* their charges of bad faith and oppression of the inhabitants including a host of other allegations, such as militarization of the area and genocide, annually voiced at the General Assembly of the United Nations. Liberia and Ethiopia were finally forced to state that for the purposes of the court case they *accepted* all South Africa's averments of fact. This changed the whole factual basis of the case and was such a dramatic *volte face* on the part of the accusing countries that South Africa could consider its name cleared in court on the various charges of oppression and maladministration.

The substitute charge which Liberia and Ethiopia then levelled against South Africa was that by its policy of differential development, South Africa was violating an as yet unwritten *international norm of non-discrimination* set by the *international community*.

This international norm, so they contended, prohibited discrimination or differential development in any form, irrespective of whether it was in the best interest of the inhabitants or not. This last aspect was considered to be irrelevant; simply by violating the so-called "norm" South Africa had, in the eyes of the African states, violated its sacred trust to the inhabitants of the territory.

It is not necessary at this stage to elaborate upon the nebulous base of this charge or the objectives of South African policies in South West Africa, that is set forth in the last chapter. What is of fundamental importance is that by abandoning their earlier charges (almost word by word the same as those parroted by the other Afro-Asian states at the United Nations whenever the subject of South Africa came up for discussion) the accusing countries i.e. Liberia and Ethiopia, backed by the Communist Bloc, the Asian and African states, actually threw into the lap of the court a charge which it was not originally asked to judge upon. It did not have factual evidence about socio-economic conditions in South West Africa or questions of oppression, etc., as its basis but undiluted ideological argument for one-world, one-law, one-norm of international and domestic conduct. The Court was in fact asked to rule on a completely abstract political ideology — almost in the realm of religion. By this act Ethiopia and Liberia attempted to force the Court into the role of a political court and not one of international law. In fact they hoped to turn the court into an ideological debating chamber similar to the General Assembly of the United Nations.

What Council for Liberia and Ethiopia was hoping for was not a judgement on merit, but one of racial ideology as expounded by the Afro-Asians at the United Nations. With virtually every continent embroiled in racial trouble and the world on a wave of liberalism which refuses to recognise fundamental differences existing between races and nations (or the merits of differential development under conditions favourable for such development), they virtually begged the court to parrot the line of the Afro-Asian majority at the United Nations.

Like almost everything else about South West Africa therefore, the International Court case, from the beginning, was not what it appeared. It really signalled the beginning of a new and more refined campaign against White-controlled South Africa and its "fifth province" South West Africa.

To South Africans it was always evident that behind the South West Africa case there was far more than a pious desire of two undeveloped and poverty stricken Black states, Liberia and Ethiopia, to better the lot of the non-White in South West Africa — particularly since they knew that the non-White races in South West Africa were so much better off, economically and otherwise, than their own population. (It was almost comparable to a situation in which Fidel Castro accused the United States of oppressing the Cuban refugees in Florida.) Although they had been indignantly evasive before the Court on this point, there was no practical reason why they should have initiated the proceedings. They had no direct contact and cultural, economic or other ties with South West Africa. Liberia and Ethiopia's acceptance of the body of the factual evidence provided by South Africa also underlined the fact that the standard of progress in South West Africa was as high or higher than in these two countries.

The question arises why they had brought this case before the Court.

The fact is that the South West Africa case was na ordinary law-suit, but the culmination of a long and persistent baseless campaign of abuse and vilification of

South Africa and its administration of South West Africa. (For supporting evidence see Chapter V, pp. 210 — 215.) The campaign was waged in the international political arena, particularly at the United Nations. The *volte face* of Liberia and Ethiopia, however, proved conclusively that they were unable to substantiate their original charges of oppression and bad faith. It provided South Africa with the opportunity to prove in court that the attacks on South Africa were part and parcel of a political campaign and not based on facts. The objective of the campaign is to establish Black rule over the whole of Africa, including South West Africa and ultimately the Republic of South Africa. The South West African case was merely one facet of the operation. To its instigators, represented in the South West Africa case by Liberia and Ethiopia, this campaign assumed the aspect of a "holy crusade" of modern times, to "liberate" the people of South West Africa from conditions said to be worse than slavery. There was a direct link between this campaign and the case before the Court. Records of the United Nations and resolutions adopted by the Organisation for African Unity proved the point. Liberia and Ethiopia were only nominal parties to the proceedings. In actual fact they were appearing in a representative capacity. Their legal costs were being paid by the O.A.U.[12] (The reader is referred to *The Paper Curtain,* Voortrekkerpers, Johannesburg, 1967, for a detailed examination of the crusade to "liberate" South Africa and South West Africa and its motives.)

---

12. Organisation for African Unity.

Against this background the proposal by South Africa for an *on the spot* inspection by the Court was obviously made to place at the Court's disposal every means of enlightenment that could contribute to objective evaluation and adjudication of the situation. South Africa argued that African reality had to be seen in order to be grasped effectively. It was virtually impossible for visitors from outside the African Continent to view and evaluate well-being and progress in an African territory such as South West Africa fairly, and in proper perspective, unless they had been able also to assess comparable standards in other African territories. Otherwise perspective might quite unconsciously be warped by the introduction of European, American or Asian standards to an African context. South Africa, therefore, argued that inspection of achievements and standards in Liberia and Ethiopia could assist the Court considerably in evaluating the policies and practices followed in South West Africa. In this way the Court could form a general impression of comparable standards of material and moral well-being and of social progress in the respective countries. Apart from a visit to Liberia and Ethiopia, it was also proposed that the inspection should include one or two other sub-Saharan territories in Africa, at least one of which should formerly have been under Mandate or trusteeship. South Africa offered to shoulder all expenses for this inspection visit.

It is a matter for the record that Liberia and Ethiopia strenuously *objected* to this invitation terming it unnecessary, cumbersome and unwarranted. This action on their part spoke more than 10,000 pages of ideological argument.

From a political point of view, why is South West Africa so important to the world's power blocs?

In the *first* instance the territory has frontiers with the Portuguese overseas province of Angola, and with the Republic of South Africa itself. For this reason it is considered an ideal base by the Afro-Asian nations for operations against the "colonial" powers of Portugal and South Africa. These long borders are all but indefensible since they cut through largely unsettled country, some of it desert wastes. The boundaries were drawn in the latter half of the 19th century by imperialist-minded European powers who gave little thought to the slicing up of tribes and even nations of politically naive peoples who, to this day, wander freely across international frontiers as if these had never existed. Lines drawn on a map mean nothing to them. The very map itself holds no meaning for them.

The eastern arm of the territory, the Caprivi Strip, thrusts halfway across the continent and forms a barrier to access from Equatorial Africa to the south. The Strip also locks Botswana in the embrace of the White Western-controlled south. (A few hundred yards of contiguous border between Zambia and Botswana — formerly Bechuanaland — form the only "corridor" not controlled by the southern states.) So far, geopolitical realities have dictated a policy of moderation on Botswana and its leaders. Its Prime Minister, Seretse Khama, publicly confided to American journalists in June, 1965, that his country would not be allowed to serve as a base for subversion against its southern neighbours. Perhaps in less constricted circumstances the policy of Botswana would be more in line with the policies of the White-baiting states of Central and West Africa. But in the foreseeable future, its actions will be moderated by its position between South West Africa, South Africa and Rhodesia and its dependence upon South Africa for economic survival. Political independence but with economic co-operation has, therefore, been the policy expressed by Prime Minister Khama ever since.

Liberia and Ethiopia were under orders from the Organization of African Unity to press the case against South Africa, not for the sake of the people of South West Africa but in order to set up a neutralist state, a sort of "people's republic" in South West Africa in which the electorate would vote once and then never again as happened in so many other African states. This "neutralist" or "non-aligned" state right next to South Africa would serve as a basis of operations for Black Africa's "army of liberation" against the richest prize in all of Africa.[13] It was no chance remark on the part

---

13. The Constitution of the Organization of African Unity representing thirty-six Black African and Arab states provides for regular contributions by member states to the establishment of an "army of liberation" to be sent south against Rhodesia or South Africa. This provision is not only a direct violation of the Charter of the United Nations but it signals the determination of the Organization for African Unity states to openly instigate trouble for South Africa. It is perhaps the best example of what a real threat to world peace means.

of ex-President Nkhrumah of Ghana when he said that Africa required the wealth of South Africa for the development of all Africa — a barely masked example of Black imperialism. One can imagine world reaction if the Russian leaders stated that they required the wealth of Western Europe for the development of the Communist Bloc!

In the *second* place, South West Africa is, globally speaking, strategically well placed. South West Africa forms a large segment of the vital Cape of Good Hope sea route which dominates the South Atlantic shipping routes. In the event of a breakdown in the Suez Canal route, the shipping lanes around the southern tip of Africa would be the fastest way from Europe to the Near and Far East.

During the Suez crisis of 1956, British and other shipping was compelled to use this route, and its feasibility as an alternative to Suez was adequately proved during those months of tension. Although the harbours in South West Africa are not now equipped to handle voluminous traffic or ships of heavy tonnage, enemy control over them would present a serious menace to the effectiveness of the South Atlantic route.

South West Africa's strategic position is well recognised by military scientists. The American author and military strategist Anthony Harrigan* recently observed that the "neutralist" nations of Africa are

---

* Member of the American Security Council, author of several books including *Red Star Over Africa, Defence Against Total Attack* and *The New Republic*.

eager to destroy the present administration of South West Africa. "No doubt they would like to see installed here a puppet revolutionary regime that would be subservient to the more ambitious powers of northern and central Africa. Removal of the South African authority would create in South West Africa a power vacuum that one of the imperialistic-minded Afro-Asian nations undoubtedly would rush to fill. They would move rapidly to dominate this land which has high strategic significance for the United States and its allies". Testifying before a sub-committee of the United States Congress in March, 1966, General S. L. Marshall, the military writer and strategist, said that he had discussed the South West Africa situation with Admiral Burke, Admiral Radford and General Twining (household names in America defence circles) as well as two former Heads of the American Department of Defence, and they were also in agreement that the decision of the Court (an adverse decision for South Africa was then generally expected) might gravely imperil the longe range strategic interests of the United States. Obviously the top military experts consider South West Africa to be of strategic importance in the cold war.

Thirdly, South West Africa is next in line after South Africa from the Queen Maud Land coast of Antarctica. This proximity may well constitute a major advantage to the West in the coming decades. The importance of the continent of Antarctica is only gradually becoming a factor in world politics and so far international agreements (notoriously fragile items!) have guaranteed its uses for peaceful purposes. But as a scientific base, the continent is already well established and the indicated presence of minerals, particularly petroleum, may bring it further strategic significance. Walvis Bay and Cape Town are the two closest harbours to Queen Maud Land.

Fourthly, Walvis Bay, which belongs to South Africa, is the principal port for South West Africa and ships of nearly 30,000 tons such as the Pretoria Castle, can lie close to shore. Although the port itself is currently only suited for ships drawing 30 feet it could be dredged for a deep water port to serve large naval vessels. As Harrigan pointed out, it could be developed into a naval base for any country that wanted to play a leading role in the South Atlantic. "What Russia has sought to do in the Caribbean," he said, "she could repeat in South West Africa if the South Africans were expelled. Soviet vessels operating out of Walvis Bay could threaten Europe's vital sea communications with Australia and the Orient by way of the Cape route. Thus Communist and neutralist powers are playing for high stakes when they agitate for the end of the South African Administration of South West Africa." Assuming that Portuguese and South African ports would be closed to Communist shipping in the event of hostilities — as they almost certainly would be — the advantages of landing and refuelling facilities in South West Africa become immediately obvious.

Fifthly, in a world facing a population explosion and food shortage, it is of great importance that the sea off the coast of South West Africa is probably one of the best fishing areas (close to the mainland) in the world.

For several years, Russian "trawlers" (one of them a 6,000 ton vessel) have patrolled the rich fishing grounds off South West Africa's thousand-mile coast. Their only open contact with the territory has been an occasional Russian seaman rushed to land for emergency medical treatment. At least some of the Russian vessels are stacked with electronic equipment suitable for tracking Satellites.

The danger of Communist infiltration is real and representatives of outlawed political movements in South West Africa were present at the Tri-Continent Conference in Havana, Cuba, in January, 1966, when the Communist-dominated meeting reiterated its plan to harass and weaken the West by all means including sabotage, infiltration and brush wars.[14]

Certainly a Communist-oriented or neutralist regime in South West Africa would be expected to sympathize with and harbour "freedom-fighter" guerillas from both Portuguese Angola and South Africa. The long un-guarded borders between the territory and these lands

---

14. The real nature of the so-called "nationalist" movements in South West Africa was further illustrated by the statement which a senior *South West African National Union* representative issued in Cairo on May 5, 1966. The statement was carried by the Red Chinese News Agency (Hsintua) on May 12. Not only did the note congratulate Red China with the successful explosion of its nuclear device but it linked China's effort to build a nuclear force with "liberation movements" in the world, terming it "a great contribution to the struggle of all freedom fighters."

would have to be patrolled — a potentially expensive and difficult proposition in the desert, dense bush and sparsely settled terrain through which the frontiers pass.

To really understand what a United Nations demand for South African withdrawal would mean one, therefore, needs to imagine American reaction if the neutralist bloc at the United Nations passed a resolution demanding that the United States get out of Puerto Rico so that a United Nations force of Latin Leftists could occupy the island so essential to United States security.

United Nations occupation of South West Africa would be even more fantastic than seizure of Puerto Rico by a coalition of Latin neutralist nations. The reason is that South West Africa, from the economic standpoint, is as much a part of South Africa as Alaska is a part of the United States.

The parallel (also drawn by Ray Vicker of the Wall Street Journal) is a good one, for both Alaska and South West Africa are almost entirely dependent on trade with and supplies from the "mother" country. The rail network is completely geared to the hauling of freight between South Africa and South West Africa.

Even more important is the electric power situation. The 318,000 square miles of South West Africa would be without electricity were coal supplies from South Africa cut off. And electricity not only provides vital communications, but what is most important, runs the water pumps essential for life in a semi-desert country.

It has been alleged by the Afro-Asian states that South West Africa is coveted by South Africa for its "vast riches and mineral wealth". This is hardly the case for to tap the undeveloped riches of South West Africa requires manpower and funds which not even the United States could furnish. The reason for this is a question of simple economics. The isolated, inhospitable, nature of the terrain where the minerals and metals are located and the ultra-deep mining operations requires such a vast number of skilled workers and so much capital outlay to get the minerals and metals to the surface and then to port that it is simply not worth the trouble or the expense. The mines being operated in South West Africa on a successful scale are few and far between. If the manpower, coal for generating electricity and other essential items for the mines had to be imported or provided by any other country than South Africa, even these mines would be run at a loss. Their *proximity* to industrially-developed South Africa is their passport to profit. Left to their own devices the people of South West Africa would not be in a position at all to tap this potential wealth. For the same reason the Afro-Asian states are not really anxious to "free" South West Africa in order to assist the territory. The entire Afro-Asian bloc is itself an underdeveloped and backward conglomeration of ancient and newly independent states. South West Africa's industrial and mineral riches is not the target — the Communists and Afro-Asians see it merely as a highway to the borders of the Republic of South Africa. Here there is *real* wealth

33

and vast untapped riches which can easily be mined at handsome profits, plus a sophisticated transportation system, cheap power through electricity and several first class harbours.

During the early sixties, South West Africa's annual mineral sales only averaged around R52,000,000 or $75 million. This included such varied products as diamonds (gem and industrial), copper, metallic germanium, lead, manganese, tin and zinc. Oil prospecting concessions (mostly held by American firms) have been granted over much of the northern portion of the territory and there is some hope that the newly-developed Angolan fields extend into South West Africa. Rich phosphate deposits have been uncovered in the tidal waters off its southern coast while the salt beds are also a source of revenue for the territory.

In lesser — but still significant quantities — vanadium, lithium, cadium, silver, arsenic and various kinds of rare earths are found in the territory. Low-grade iron deposits have been discovered in the northwest section of the country, although they have not been exploited so far.

By volume, copper is the most important strategic mineral. The constant presence of "brush wars" since 1945 has brought world use of copper to production capacity and the supply available for consumer use has been restricted in order to make adequate copper available for military preparedness. Caught in the squeeze for copper are the makers of appliances and independent copper fabricators. The Tsumeb mine in South West

Africa — the largest base metals mine in the territory — is expanding production of both copper and lead and two new smelting plants (built at a cost of R18,000,000 or $25 million) have helped raise output. Tsumeb is the largest producer of lead (over 80,000 tons) and zinc in Africa and the biggest lead producer between America and Australia.

But the real significance of the Tsumeb mine lies in its output of germanium. It is the second largest producer of germanium in the world (the other is a mine in Katanga), turning out high quality germanium dioxide concentrates on the spot for shipment overseas. The unique properties of germanium allow it to diffuse heat and to facilitate transfer of AC to DC current. It is essential to the economic production of transistors, those tiny items without which the current Western defence and space programs would collapse. Transistors are vital components of computers and missile technology and germanium is the *sine qua non* of transistors.[15]

The major gap in South West Africa's potential mineral development seems to be in the energy producing elements. Current geological knowledge reveals the absence of coal supplies in the territory and it would be years before oil deposits — if found at all — could be successfully exploited for energy production.

The lack of internal rivers suitable for hydro-electric power production makes the territory almost

---

15. Although it is possible to synthesize chemical materials to do the work of germanium, the synthesis process involves the necessity of starting with a nucleus of the natural mineral.

totally dependent on power supplies imported from South Africa. Coal from the South African fields is railed to steam generating plants in South West Africa for municipal and industrial use. Atomic generators, although theoretically a possibility, would still require imported supplies of fissionable material from South Africa, and the most likely immediate source of supplementary power is the contemplated exploitation of the two border rivers, the Kunene to the north and the Orange on the southern Cape border.

With the political and economic importance of South West Africa in clear perspective, perhaps the prospects for South West Africa will emerge from an examination of its recent history and current situation.

Over the past four score years — the period of European responsibility for the territory — South West Africa has been brought from an area of barbarian chaos to an orderly progressive land with a peaceful population of different nationalities and races and the beginnings of a modern economy. To be sure, it has yet to go a long way before it reaches anything like its full potential. And economists express serious doubts of its ability ever to be self-sufficient. But with proper husbanding of its resources it could provide an abundant life for its kaleidoscope population and perhaps even make a substantial contribution to the progress of man in South Africa.

Although the prospect of an independent "self-governing" South West Africa is a difficult one to consider, it is one which must be contemplated in these dizzy days of independence for islands and postage-stamp sultanates, and in view of the Afro-Asian demand for the territory's *immediate* independence. In the event of *independence,* who would speak for South West Africa? Would a similar situation arise after "independence" as in the case of other black African states who were so anxious for Uhuru that they threatened rebellion against their colonial motherland (some did in fact do this such as Kenya) only to have to resort to political blackmail of the United States and Russia afterwards in order to survive?

Among the "native" groups, the 42,000-strong *Hereros* are the most vocal advocates of independence. Although they are a minority among the Territory's non-White population, they are a closely-knit nation whose traditions re-enforce their belicose demands. For several decades during the latter half of the 19th century, Herero chieftains held a tenuous authority over much of the central part of South West Africa. The descendents of these pastoral nomads, imbued with the spirit of herren-volkism which is their national trait, feel that despite their relative insignificance in numbers *theirs* should be the paramount voice in the councils of an independent South West Africa.

But history and circumstances have conspired to rob them of what they consider their due. As a group, they alone among the diverse peoples of South West Africa, have continued to resist efforts of the Administration to improve their lot. New housing, health and hospital services, and other social amenities, are spurned by the

Hereros who sullenly prefer to await their resurgence to primacy amid largely self-imposed hardships.

They remain one of the most unique peoples in all of Africa. With the exception of one other obscure tribe in Central Africa they are the only people with a matriarchal as well as patriarchal family structure. No one can ever become a Herero through marriage. As one student observed: "one can only be born a Herero". They are a nomadic pastoral nation who believe that "my land is where my cattle graze". For this reason the Herero would love to dominate all of South West Africa and for the same reason their forefathers clashed with the Namas and Ovambos. They violated the most basic rights of African tribes by herding their cattle onto Nama and Ovambo lands. Although no Herero set foot on the same grazing lands for perhaps a century after they had pulled back their cattle they claimed those lands where their grandfathers' cattle had grazed as their own, thereby precipitating some of the most bloody wars with the Namas, Orlams and Ovambo tribes which one could imagine.

Co-operation between the Hereros and the other Bantu nations of South West Africa is impossible simply because their social organization and tribal customs is incompatible. The Herero's way of life urges him to be different. Not all the foreign aid in the world or the unanimous opinion of the United Nations will convince the Herero that it is liberal and democratic to live under a system of one-man-one-vote together with the Ovambos who outnumber them by six to one. This is one of the prime reasons why South Africa's policy of apartheid (separate development of the races) is considered to be the only solution — because it recognises and accepts the deep-rooted differences between people and races and everyones fervent desire to retain his identity. Belatedly, perhaps far too late, even the United Nations which is *the* great champion of the amorphous mass recognise the desire of smaller nations and population groups to safeguard their identity — the birthright of all peoples. This was made abundantly clear at the Seminar on "The Multi-National Society" in Ljubljana, Yugoslavia, organized by the United Nations in June, 1965.

By historical fact, the Hereros' chief competitors for the position of dominance in a potentially independent South West Africa are the *Namas,* a clever and intensely individualistic nation of Hottentot derivation.

Roughly comparable in numerical strength to the Hereros, the Namas were also once masters of the central highlands of South West Africa and thus have an equally valid claim to authority. A "yellow" people who consider themselves superior to the Black (Bantu) peoples of Africa, the Namas could be expected to resist strenuously any efforts by the Hereros to exert dominance in South West Africa.

Herero petitioners at the United Nations (their pockets lined by funds from Ethiopia, Ghana and Algeria) and the activities of a British Minister of religion, Michael Scott (currently also *persona non grata* in New Delhi, India, because of his role in the Naga rebellion for independence) have created the impression that the

Hereros are the *only* people worth any consideration in South West Africa. This woefully inaccurate picture was lent further credence by Allard Lowenstein in his disappointingly one-sided and misleading book *Brutal Mandate*.[16]

In point of numbers, the northern Bantu nations — the Ovambos (239,000) and their cousins the Okavango (27,871) are by far superior to the other non-White groups. The Ovambo scoff at the thought of a South West Africa "dominated" by Hereros. And, indeed, any constitutional government based on universal (or even representative) franchise would certainly find Ovambos in all the key governmental positions.

Historically, their claim is weakened by the fact that they have never ventured far south of "Ovamboland", the northern quarter of the territory, in any great numbers. Even today, the Ovambo and Okavango are largely content to enjoy a facile and unhurried life on the stoneless plains of the Kunene watershed, reaping a leisurely existence from the abundant grazing lands and fertile well-watered banks of that mighty river. Their traditional and emotional roots reach north among the Angola Bantu and east toward the lands of their origin in Central Africa. A reasonably well-organized social structure provides the peoples of these two nations with a firm basis for the development of constitutional government, but delegating to them the responsibility of

16. Widely hailed in the United States and Britain as an "authoritative" work on South West Africa. In her preface the late Eleanor Roosevelt referred to the territory as lying in West Africa!

governing the southern portions of South West Africa would be something like placing Peruvian Incas in authority over Alaskan Eskimos.

It is for this reason and, of course, in recognition of their homogeneous society and their desire for self-determination, that the South African government in March, 1967, offered to the Ovambos self-government within their own state. Not surprisingly the Ovambo who care little for the other nations several hundred miles to the south indicated through their traditional leaders that they welcomed this move and also rejected any suggestion of long range control by the United Nations.

One of the cruelest of the many ironies that afflict South West Africa is the fact that the people with undoubtedly the best *historical* claim to political pre-eminence are certain never to achieve it, namely the Bushmen, aboriginal to this part of Africa and the most ancient race of men on earth. By reason of their scanty numbers and primitive social organization, they are the most gullible candidates for potential exploitation. Certainly the Bushmen were in the territory centuries before the arrival of any of the other groups. But they were persecuted and pursued by each successive wave of non-White invaders until, over a period of several centuries they were forced into the hostile wastes of the Kalahari desert, where they roam in family groups, seeking nothing other than a chance to survive.

It was not until the assumption of control by South Africa that a serious effort was launched to lead the Bushmen to a more settled life. And even today,

41

they are so far below the level of the territory's other inhabitants on the scale of civilization that they would be easy prey for any group seeking to exploit them.[17]

Their very existence creates an acute moral problem for the South African authorities who must decide if they should be "protected" and allowed to pursue their stone-age nomadic lives or to be induced to settle on agricultural plots where they can be "civilized" and initiated into the social and technical skills of the 20th century.

It must, therefore, be apparent to anyone with even a superficial knowledge of the territory that there is no single unified indigenous group of "native" South West Africans to whom the central authority, even over a protracted period of time, could be transferred. The difference between the various groups in customs and culture and in numbers is arid soil for the application of one-man-one-vote.

"South West Africa for the South West Africans" — the simple solution of the sloganeers — thus becomes a mockery of well-intentioned ignorance. And the withdrawal of South Africa from the territory would constitute an abdication of a moral responsibility to its peoples and the abandonment of them to political chaos and civil strife (of the kind that killed the Congo) that would mean a revision to the bloodshed that marked the history of South West Africa in the 18th and 19th centuries.

---

17. Some idea of the Bushmen's code of existence can be gathered from the fact that if a woman should die in labour, her living child is buried with her.

The only group of people who pledge prime allegiance to the territory which they occupied and developed — rather than to a chief or a tribal group — are the Whites. They are the second strongest group (after the Ovambos) in the territory. They, or their fathers and grandfathers, came to South West Africa as soldiers, missionaries or farmers to open up the land and they have succeeded to a remarkable extent in the face of seemingly insurmountable hardships.

Unlike the White men who invaded other virgin lands, the Whites of South West Africa do not bear the burden of guilt imposed by having wrested the land from existing non-White inhabitants. Of course, there were isolated incidents of shady dealings and double-meaning "treaties", but the overwhelming mass of land occupied by White men in South West Africa today was not permanently settled when they arrived.

They dug wells, built the roads, plowed the hard crust of the earth and imposed their will on a grudging environment to create a totally new and potentially fruitful future for themselves and their children. Surely, if their efforts in this remote land are to culminate in "independence", that independence should be one which takes into account their past toils and present loyalty.

Another possibility — one which has been mentioned periodically in academic circles — would be a compromise partition of the territory, its southern portion going to South Africa and its northern portion being launched as an independent nation.

This solution has little support in historical precedent. For although recent examples of partition are almost too numerous to need expounding, most involved the creation of two separate and fully sovereign states; e.g. Rwanda and Burundi, Pakistan and India, Zambia and Malawi.

The very novelty of the South West African dilemma — embodying as it does several peoples of divergent races, cultures and levels of development all inhabiting a territory with moderate potential but poor in past yield — suggests the necessity for a novel solution. Partition would constitute such a solution. But like the other possibilities, it offers serious obstacles.

On social and political grounds, it is arguable as to whether the northern groups of the non-White population are (even in this Age of Uhuru) capable of establishing and maintaining the machinery of sovereign government. There is no cadre of leaders or even a single messianic leader to offer magnetism around which the organisation of statehood could be formed. Internal cohesion in the potentially northern "independent" sector is almost totally lacking outside the tribal allegiance which exists among the individual national groups.

Humanitarian considerations regarding the Bushmen (who reside principally in the northern areas) and the provision for their welfare under an independent government constitute an additional factor.

The concept of partition would undoubtedly be violently opposed by the Communist, African and Asian nations, in that it would involve granting a large measure of the total land area to South Africa. Any North/South partition must necessarily allot the fabulous "Diamond Coast" to the southern sector and this would be objectionable to the advocates of "Africa for the Africans".

But the major and most readily obvious disadvantage to a split is the economic one. The north is principally supported by its mining activities (the Tsumeb complex) with the subsistence agrarian activities of the resident non-Whites, while the southern sector provides mechanized farming and commercial activities as well as an outlet for what surplus produce exists. The northern areas rely heavily on the South for consumer products and for markets for its goods and labour.

Although an amicable interchange of goods and services could conceivably be expected after partition, it goes without saying that the southern portion would look more and more to the Republic for its economic exchanges, where better advantages could be obtained. The north would thus be gradually but effectively frozen out and would have to seek new markets and suppliers, with the long-term expenses involved in the search.

While the southern portion would reap economic benefits from a liaison with South Africa, the northern area would suffer an acute shortage of development capital. Without expenditure on a major scale, the achievement of anything like a balanced economy would be impossible. The projected Kunene scheme to supply vital power and water to the north would almost certainly suffer from atrophy in the event of partition. The Republic of South Africa — already engaged in a

R450,000,000 ($630,000,000) development plan for the Orange River — would be understandably reluctant to participate wholeheartedly in a programme to benefit only an independent north. It seems equally unlikely that the United States could be persuaded to advance capital on such a grand scale (an estimated R49,000,000 or $68 million), and no single nation — not even the ever open-hearted United States could reap sufficient economic, political or propaganda value to justify such a massive investment for a "nation" of perhaps 300,000 people. The only remaining possible source of funds would be a consortium of Iron Curtain countries. But since the Kunene is an international river, whose development would necessarily have to be carried out in conjunction with Angola, help from Communist nations also seems to be ruled out. The Soviet Union has been articulate in its criticisms of Portugal's Africa policy and Lisbon's avowed anti-Communism makes such an alliance completely unlikely.

If independence and partition are eliminated, what other possibility exists? Since South Africa cannot gracefully withdraw from its responsibilities in South West Africa — responsibilities called by the late Prime Minister General J. C. Smuts "a sacred trust of civilization" — what is to be the future of the territory?

The obvious solution would seem to lie in continued and even closer association with the Republic of South Africa.

Under the terms of the Mandate, South West Africa has already been substantially integrated into the Republic's economy. All phases of its *economic development* — its rail and other communications networks, its power supplies (upon which vital water resources depend), and the major proportion of its consumer goods — have been inextricably woven into the fabric of South Africa's own. *Political order* and continuity would be maintained and each of the diverse national groups would be led to self-determination in their homelands or states, according to plans already blue-printed by the Odendaal Commission.

The ultimate status could be a Commonwealth of self-governing states such as in Australia with the powers of the Central Government — in respect of customs, defence, foreign affairs, etc. — vested in the Parliament of the Republic of South Africa or some other supranational body. In all probability the people themselves will elect to enjoy such a constitution.

However, the future of South West Africa also largely depends on the future relationship between Botswana, Rhodesia, Angola and the Republic of South Africa as well as the relationship between South Africa and the autonomous states it is establishing for its own Bantu (Black) population groups. This *vital* aspect is more closely examined in the last chapter.

The Republic is rich enough to finance the large-scale development South West Africa will require to emerge from its long isolation and technical inadequacy. South Africa has the know-how of African conditions and its people have brought their own country from a pastoral and mining economy into the vanguard of industrialized "developed" nations over the past quarter century. Hopefully, they could help to duplicate the feat in South West. Although South West Africa will never be among the major industrial nations of the world because of its lack of local market, domestic capital and ready power, the economic exploitation of its existing potentials could unquestionably be best exercised with the assistance of South Africa.

Most foreign journalists, columnists and editors as well as political scientists who have recently visited South West Africa came away from the territory impressed by the overall development which has taken place in the territory under South Africa's administration, particularly the Odendaal Programme, a R156,000,000 ($218 million) five-year socio-economic project designed to put the territory on the road to internal self-government and economic self-sufficiency. In terms of the United States population and at cost of services in the United States, the programme is worth some $5,240,000,000 or double the entire United States foreign aid programme for one year.[18] This projection is made only to illustrate that South Africa is, relatively, just as sincere and willing as America to carry the burden for the uplifting of backward people in an economically undeveloped territory.

Whatever the moral and emotional arguments for submitting the territory to international or specifically to United Nations supervision, the fact remains that South

18. The United States' population is now twelve times that of South Africa and South West Africa combined and cost of services (cost of bricks, transportation, wages, etc.) conservatively estimated at double that of South West Africa.

Fort Namutoni. Legend has it that seven German soldiers succesfully defended it against an attack by 500 Ovambos in 1904. The fort is now a romantic and popular rest-camp at the Etosha Pan Game Reserve.

INDUSTRIAL DISTRIBUTION OF ECONOMICALLY ACTIVE POPULATION: 1951 AND 1960 [1]

	1951			1960				
			Indigenous inhabitants			Indigenous inhabitants		
Industry division	Whites	Colour-eds	Southern Sector[2]	Whites	Colour-eds	Southern Sector	Northern Sector	Total
A. *Actual figures*								
Agriculture	6,932	2,470	40,511	6,508	2,847	36,260	73,379	118,994
Mining	1,193	52	7,552	1,696	176	9,814	221	11,907
Manufacturing	1,401	570	2,349	1,803	515	4,271	148	6,737
Construction	1,473	687	3,419	2,756	1,417	7,975	221	12,369
Commerce	2,850	207	1,678	5,899	597	3,973	168	10,637
Transport and Electricity ..	2,018	254	2,980	3,107	134	4,164	50	7,455
Services	3,035	1,300	14,288	5,049	2,156	15,426	1,706	24,337
Unspecified and unemployed	316	378	1,404	501	766	6,765	2,803	10,835
Total	19,218	5,918	74,181	27,319	8,608	88,648	78,696	203,271
B. *Percentage distribution*								
Agriculture	36·1	41·7	54·6	23·8	33·1	40·9	93·2	58·5
Mining	6·2	0·9	10·2	6·2	2·0	11·1	0·3	5·9
Manufacturing	7·3	9·6	3·2	6·6	6·0	4·8	0·2	3·3
Construction	7·7	11·6	4·6	10·1	16·5	9·0	0·3	6·1
Commerce	14·8	3·5	2·3	21·6	6·9	4·5	0·2	5·2
Transport and Electricity ..	10·5	4·3	4·0	11·4	1·6	4·7	0·2	3·7
Services	15·8	22·0	19·3	18·5	25·0	17·4	2·2	12·0
Unspecified and unemployed	1·6	6·4	1·9	1·8	8·8	7·6	3·6	5·3
Total	100·0	100·0	100·0	100·0	100·0	100·0	100·0	100·0

[1] Bureau of Statistics.
[2] The 1951 Population Census was confined to the southern sector.

Africa is prepared to invest hundreds of millions in the development of the territory, just as it had sunk millions into it in the past without any hope of returns in the form of cash dividends. Certainly the United Nations — with its own financial burdens — is in no position to invest anything like this amount in one area. It is experiencing difficulties to obtain even its membership fees. Apart from this the far greater majority of the people themselves prefer South Africa's presence and have clearly expressed this desire through their councils and chiefs.

Currently, South West Africa's 74,000 Whites (about 14 per cent. of the total population) carry the bulk of financing the land's domestic budget. The chances of these Whites remaining in any great numbers under United Nations supervision of a non-White-dominated regime seem questionable at best. Where would the money come from under such an arrangement? The most obvious source would be out of the pockets of the American taxpayer.[19]. But, in Africa, cash in hand is no substitute for engineers, doctors, technicians, architects and agriculturalists who know and love the territory and who are dedicated to improve conditions for each and everyone.

Despite the fact that she had been unjustly brought before the International Court of Justice and despite the unfair and unfounded attacks that are being made upon

---

19. Total American foreign aid to all countries in Africa during 1963 was $298 million with the largest single grant going to Algeria ($39 million). During the year, the Republic of South Africa maintained a $16 million *credit* in the United States. South Africa has never asked for or received any foreign aid from the United States.

49

her, South Africa will continue to carry out the "sacred trust" and administer South West Africa to the best advantage of is diverse population.

South Africa's declared programme for South West Africa and the philosophy underlying its stated objectives are set out in broad detail in the last chapter of this book which also contains a detailed analysis of programmes for the economic development of the territory and the re-organization of the internal socio-political structure.

An American newsman may have hit upon the true key to South West Africa's situation when he toured the territory in 1964. One of the standard questions in his interviews among the non-White population was: "Do you know where America is?"

The most erroneous answer he received was from a young Herero shop assistant in Swakopmund who replied: "Isn't it just beyond Windhoek?" Naturally, this is an absurd answer, and yet it contains a latent kernel of truth. For South West Africa is a land just beyond the conscience and consciousness of the Western world. It is one of those places (like Korea, Cyprus and Viet Nam) pregnant with the elements to make it erupt suddenly into tomorrow's headlines.

It is a land where hardship and success have imbued its inhabitants with a loyalty to the land unparalleled in the welfare states of the more developed nations. Here, both the vegetation and the population are scanty. (There are only some half-million souls in an area of 319,000 square miles, compared with three million in 10,000 square miles in the African state. of Rwanda) and success has brought stability and confidence.

It is not difficult to find a man who has killed a leopard with his bare hands and who will walk or ride for twenty miles to see the opening of a new water tower. This same man probably does not know, or care, that the expanse of land he calls his own is part of a territory being discussed in the councils of nations. He relies on South Africa to take care of any foreign threat. What is important to him and his fellow "South Westerners" is that despite all the handicaps, South West Africa has now been tamed and has become a home to him and his children.

South West Africa is a land of grazing cattle, striking landscape, of different races, of fishing and mining towns and practically nothing else — except of course the almost limitless potential recognized by men of vision in South Africa who have taken a sincere and abiding interest in it.

Apart from all its uncertainties, its difficulties and its solitary wastes, it remains a land of rare contrast and beauty where a man of ingenuity, strength and conviction can create for himself a better life.

It is, in the truest sense, a last frontier: If man can survive and prosper in this hostile environment to fulfil its potential, then there are no areas left on earth which cannot be civilized as well.

2

THE NAMELESS LAND

Look at the map of Africa, of Latin America or Asia, North America or Australasia. Every square mile of land is part of a nation state with a name, except this huge slice of Africa which is simply called South West Africa. It shares the distinction with South Africa and the Central African Republic (Capital — Bangui) of being the only country in the world with a name which is a purely geographical designation. This is due as much to its confused history as to its kaleidoscope of races. Yet this nameless land sprawls over an area four times as big as the United Kingdom and twenty times that of Holland. In stark contrast only 525,000 people inhabit this land giving it what is nearly the world's lowest population density at 1.65 persons per square mile. Nigeria, which is about the same size, has a population *sixty* times larger than that of South West Africa.

From the Kunene River in the North where it abuts the Portuguese overseas province of Angola, the territory runs some 900 miles down the coast of the South Atlantic where the Orange River separates it from the Cape Province of the Republic of South Africa. Its average width is 350 miles, but no physical features mark its eastern border. The border consists of two of the longest fences in the world, some 800 miles in all, cutting through the Kalahari desert, dividing it from South Africa and newly independent Botswana — formerly Bechuanaland.[20]

In the extreme north-east, a finger of land points towards the Indian Ocean. This historical anomaly is the Caprivi Strip ("Zipfel" in German) and resulted from a diplomatic effort by Imperial Germany in 1890 to connect its western colony with Tanganyika, its sphere of influence on the east coast of Africa. The Strip touches Angola, Zambia, Rhodesia and Botswana on its eastern thrust and was named after the then German Chancellor Count Leo van Caprivi. When it was acquired the Germans believed the Zambesi River was navigable as far as the Indian Ocean. The point where it touches the Zambesi was later discovered to be about

20. Because the maps of mid 1966 do not indicate the state as *Botswana,* map references elsewhere in this book are still given as Bechuanaland.

sixty miles *above* the awesome Victoria falls. A second geo-political oddity is the presence of a 434 square mile enclave around Walvis Bay which belongs territorially to the Republic of South Africa. Although administered as part of South West Africa for the sake of convenience, Walvis Bay and several islands have been legally part of South Africa's Cape Province since 1878 when it was annexed by Great Britain to keep this important harbour under British control.

The topography of South West Africa may be described as an oblong-shaped highland between two desert-like areas.

Sandwiched on either side by the Namib and Kalahari Deserts the elongated and mountainous plateau forms the backbone of the territory. It also forms the watershed area, draining towards practically all four points of the compass from the broken hill veld just north of the Orange River to the mountainous central part and the sandy plains of Ovamboland, north of the Etosha Pan. Part of the greater plateau of Southern Africa, the central highland rises gradually from some 2,500 feet in the south to about 4,800 feet near Windhoek, the capital, and levels off into river lowlands in the north. It is crossed by various mountain ranges such as the Eros, Hunsberg, Zebra, Auas and Zaris mountains, some of which attain a height of 8,000 feet. The area is also studded by isolated mountains and peaks such as the lonely Brandberg, Chuos, Erongo, the Omatako Peak and the Brukkaros Crater near Berseba.

Often called the Hardeveld (Hard Veld) to distinguish it from the sandy surface of the rest of the country, the central highlands holds the major concentration of industry, farming and ranching of cattle and karakul sheep for which it is eminently suited. It covers roughly fifty per cent. of the territory of South West Africa and offers a diversified landscape of rocky outcrops, sandy valleys hemmed in by mountains, undulating plains and broken terrain. The highest mountain peaks are the Brandberg which rise to 8,556 feet and the Auas Range near Windhoek which reaches a height of 8,150 feet. In the south the Groot Karasberge reaches up to 7,224 feet and in the north, near Grootfontein, the mountains just top 7,000 feet.

West of this huge plateau is the Namib Desert whose constantly shifting sand dunes must surely be the highest in the world, sometimes rising to a thousand feet. The desolate Namib which varies in width from 40 to 80 miles, parallels the Atlantic Ocean. It stretches all the way from the brown coloured Orange River in the South to the mountainous Kaokoveld which borders on the Angolan border in the north, a distance of a 1,000 miles.

The inhospitable surface of the Namib coastal belt formed a major barrier to the country's initial exploitation. Even today, nearly five hundred years after the first explorers went ashore in South West Africa, its only inhabitants are the Nama and the Bushmen nomads who venture into its northern and eastern fringes, the diamond miners near the mouth of the Orange and the citizens of the coastal towns of Lüderitz, Walvis Bay and Swakopmund.

Eight expeditions sent by ship to investigate the land of South West Africa returned empty-handed appalled by the inhospitable coastline, the deathly silence and the waterless desert guarding the interior.

There is something starkly beautiful about this desolate region, particularly when viewed from the air, and when the sun sets it looks like a painted moonscape. On the fringe of the Namib, near Usakos, the rocky outcrop of Kleinspitzkopje stands guard over an area known for its lavish scattering of semi-precious stones.

In startling contrast to the barren shore, the Atlantic waters off South West Africa abound with marine life. The frigid Benguella current flowing north from Antarctica brings great shoals of mackerel, sardines, and numerous other fish which sustain the territory's flourishing industry. Millions of birds feast off this silvery harvest and form the basis of yet another important industry, the collection of guano, nature's most efficient fertilizer.

The desert conditions of the Namib result directly from the conditions which make this marine life so abundant. The air currents above the ocean absorb the moisture which rises from the sea into promising cloud banks against the western sky. But as they drift inland over the desert, the heat of the land expands their capacity to hold moisture and they roll eastwards in unending banks without disgorging their life-giving burdens.

East of the Central Plateau lies the Kalahari belt. It is a wide level sandy surface overgrown with grass and trees but with practically no break in the altitude above

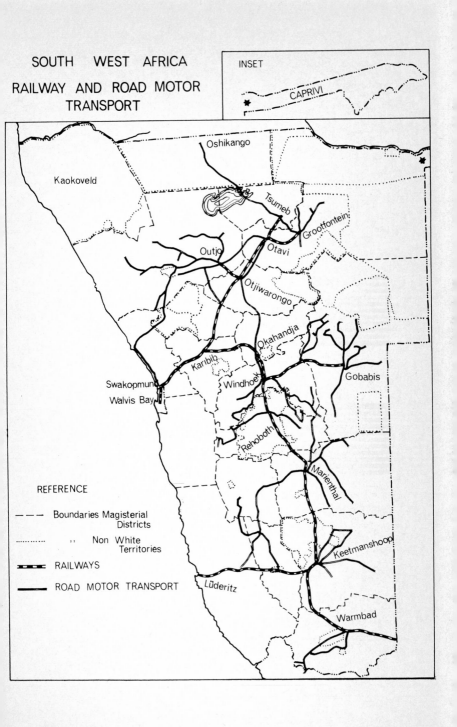

SOUTH WEST AFRICA
RAILWAY AND ROAD MOTOR
TRANSPORT

INSET

CAPRIVI

Oshikango

Kaokoveld

Tsumeb

Grootfontein

Outjo

Otavi

Otjiwarongo

Okahandja

Karibib

Windhoek

Gobabis

Swakopmund

Walvis Bay

Rehoboth

Marienthal

REFERENCE

--- Boundaries Magisterial
Districts

.... ,, Non White
Territories

xxxx RAILWAYS

—— ROAD MOTOR TRANSPORT

Keetmanshoop

Lüderitz

Warmbad

Kolmanskop — an abandoned diamond mining town,
typical of the many ''ghost'' towns of South West Africa.

The aptly-named ''Skeleton Coast'' has claimed
yet another victim; here a police desert patrol
surveys a wreck which will soon disappear
for ever under the sands of the Namib Desert.

Photo: W. Giess, Windhoek.

Aloe in flower near Spitzkoppe
on the edge of the Namib.

Photo: Odo Willscher, Hamburg.

Welwitschia plant —
estimated age 1,500 years.

The 'Kokerboom',
Indigenous to
South West Africa.

Photo: Odo Willscher, Hamburg.

sea level. Unlike the fine sand dunes of the Namib Desert, sand dunes in this part of the country are well consolidated. They sometimes reach a height of 300 feet and form the only break on the monotonous horizon. The Kalahari belt extends along the whole of the Eastern boundary into the northern Okavongo areas. It varies in width from about fifty miles in the south to about 250 miles further north and is home to tens of thousands of wild game. Winds from the Indian Ocean sweep down from the Northeast occasionally, producing spectacular electric storms and flooding great depressed areas or "pans". The waters run off rapidly, but they leave behind them underground pockets that, properly tapped, can sustain life through the long droughts. Since water cannot penetrate more than twenty-five feet of Kalahari sand, the really deep underground sources, a relic of pre-historic times when the area was probably a vast swamp, are not fed by surface rain. Legislation is now being considered to limit the amount of water to be tapped from deep boreholes.

With its vast stretches of sand, the Kalahari benefits from its meagre rainfall to the extent of desert grasses and scrub which cover much of its expanse. Clans of Bushmen, aided by an occasional permanent waterhole, trace a web across it, existing on veldkos (fruits of the veld) and game which they track down with poisoned arrows. Over much of the face of the Kalahari, the grasses are sufficient to sustain large herds of African animals — zebra, wildebeest, giraffe as well as the domestic stocks herded by native tribesmen.

What is popularly referred to as the Kalahari Desert, even on the maps of the distinguished National Geographical Society, is therefore not desert in the strict sense of the word. It does not compare at all with the Namib, Sahara or Gobi Deserts for barrenness, desolation and lack of vegetation.

The Caprivi Zipfel which extends from a point midstream in the mighty Zambesi River (flowing eastwards to the Indian Ocean) to the Okavango River 300 miles in the West, is on average only about twenty miles wide except for its bulge in the far east where it is some 50 miles. Like the Kalahari lying to the south the Caprivi is a similar mountainless level country, but, as in the case of Ovamboland and the northern Okavango region, it is not regarded as part of the Kalahari belt because of its high rainfall and vegetation. Most of the Eastern Caprivi in fact forms a part of the vast Kwando-Okavango swamp complex.

Three distinct areas in the north of South West Africa are the territories known as the Kaokoveld, Ovamboland and the Okavango.

West of the Caprivi Zipfel lies an enormous depression known as the Etosha Pan. This area is dotted with numberless water holes and pans which have no outlet. These shallow pans fill in the sporadic rainy season and become magnets for game in great numbers. By far the largest is the Etosha Pan, itself about 2,300 square miles. Along the edges of the pan one can find wildebeest, springbok, impala, gemsbok, zebra, ostrich and giraffe in great numbers while lion and elephant are also frequently encountered. Even during prolonged droughts the game know that water may be found here by digging below the crusty surface to the underground supplies. With its fine rest camps and improved roads the area may one day become a rival for the world famous Kruger National Park in the Republic of South Africa.

Beyond this pan, which is part of a nationally proclaimed game reserve and the biggest of its kind in the world, the Kalahari belt curves into Ovamboland, a vast stoneless area intersected by numerous shallow watercourses called oshana. Ovamboland is really a continuation of the level country of the Kalahari belt. However, its vast stoneless and grassy plains interspered with woodland and palmgroves, its higher rainfall as well as the high density of the population sets it apart from the sparsely populated and semi-arid Kalahari.

Ovamboland is comparatively a fertile area and the mopani and marula trees whose succulent fruits are so relished by elephants are found here in abundance. Game wardens tell of seeing elephants who became rolling drunk as a result of gorging themselves on fruit of the marula which had fallen in water-filled depressions and so became fermented.

The Kaokoveld lies due north of Walvis Bay and Windhoek, and West of Ovamboland, stretching right up to the mighty Kunene River, the border between Angola and South West Africa.

The Kaokoveld belies its name for unlike the vast stretches of grassy veld in Ovamboland this is a generally mountainous area. Lying parallel to the Atlantic Coast and reaching inland about 125 miles it is a rugged country with high mountains and deep ravines. The mountain ranges of the Otorocha, Baynes and Zebra mountains are fascinating. Although the landscape in the north-west of the country is generally broken (the Kaokoveld being a continuation of the central highland forming the backbone of South West Africa) the true mountainous terrain begins north of Sesfontein (Six Fountains). The northern part is known as the Tjima Highlands.

The dry steppe areas of the Kaokoveld are for the most part covered with grass interspersed with mopani trees while the boabab trees with their huge bulb shaped trunks and even some tropical vegetation occur in the north-western and western regions.

East of Ovamboland and lying parallel to the Angolan border above the Kalahari Desert is the Okavango territory.

The flat Kalahari belt extends into the Okavango but the high rainfall in this area brings to the Okavango territory greenness and fertility. The greater part of the Okavango territory falls within what is known as the northern forest region. Large areas are well wooded and it is only westward towards the oshana region of Ovamboland that the bush becomes more sparse. The basin of the Okavango river is sub-tropical and thickly vegetated. South towards the flats of the Kalahari the vegetation and trees thin out and sand dunes begin to occur.

The face of South West Africa as can be concluded from the foregoing description of its general topography is one of great diversity and this is repeated in its climate, rainfall, soil types and vegetation. Generally the country has a dry, warm climate but while the humidity in the highland areas is very low (mostly around thirty per cent.) in a normal summer month the humidity on the coast, at a town such as Swakopmund, may *average* a minimum of ninety per cent. The rainfall varies from tropical downpours in the Okavango basin two years of drought in the Kalahari and no rain at all in the Namib Desert. There are no less than thirteen major soil types varying from shifting desert sand in the Namib area to rich loam in the Windhoek area of the central highlands. Quite often the various soil types provide surprisingly colourful scenes in areas least expected such as in the Sossus Valley where the dunes are a brick red colour but the valley floor a soft grey.

That the natural vegetation of South West Africa is richly varied can be deduced from the range of climate and rainfall encountered as well as from the wide variety of soil types. More than ninety per cent of South West Africa, however, is ill suited for normal cropping and the marginal areas with relatively good soil restricted for irrigation by lack of permanent surface water and the very low rainfall. In other areas, even if water was available, the soil is of poor quality. For example virtually the entire area east of the line formed by the towns of Rehoboth and Aroab and stretching as far as the Kalahari Desert is a limestone area; there is virtually no soil cover on the limestone except where covered by dune sand. This is known as the "Kalkplato" or limestone plateau.

There are no constant rivers in South West Africa between the Orange on its southern border and the Kunene and Okavango at the extreme North. Because of sandbanks and rapids neither the Orange River nor the Kunene are navigable. Hence the territory is dependent on road, rail and air transport for overland domestic and international links. Although the ports of Lüderitz and Walvis Bay are increasing in importance, a fairly extensive system of railroad carries the bulk of commerce. This is administered as part of the South African Railways system with a managerial headquarters at Windhoek. The open mileage in 1964 was 1,453 which is about eleven per cent of the total route mileage of South African Railways. Diesel-electric traction has been introduced over the whole of the South West African network. (In recent years, public bus services have been instituted in outlying areas and these operate over 4,260 route miles.)

To the uninitiated in rail and road statistics, the total mileage of 1,453 railway track appears insignificant for such a large territory; the ratio of half a mile of railway line per one hundred square miles is only about one tenth of that of South Africa's province of Natal. However, in terms of inhabitants the ratio is by far the best in *all* of Africa. For railroads the ratio works out at almost forty-seven miles per 10,000 persons which compares with Nigeria's 0.8 miles (it has a population of nearly 50,000,000) and 0.4 for Africa's oldest state, Ethiopia.

In respect of roads the figure for South West Africa is 1,076 compared with Nigeria's 17 and Ethiopia's 2.7 miles of road per 10,000 persons. There are about 20,000 miles of usable public roads in the country of which about ten per cent are "main" or national arteries. A road improvement programme aimed at tarring (asphalting) all the main roads is underway and in six years up to 1965 some 700 miles of road were so treated.

Commercial air transport, provided principally by South African Airways, runs regularly between Windhoek and the principal cities of the Republic of South Africa and there are a number of small private airports, notably at Tsumeb. Private planes are used in transport throughout the territory and natural landing fields are abundant, the pans forming excellent hard flat surfaces for small craft landings. There are thirty-five airfields licensed for public use. Several companies own planes as does the Post Office. A new international airport has just been completed near Windhoek and can be used by commercial jets. Trek Airways of Johannesburg operates to Europe once a month via Windhoek (South West Airways operates internal scheduled services) and South African Airways Boeing 707's stop here once a week *en route* to and from Europe. The Portuguese airline T.A.P. provides a scheduled service between Windhoek and Angola while Central African Airways provides regular flights to and from Salisbury in Rhodesia.

For the visitor arriving by ship in Walvis Bay there awaits a tour of South West Africa that should satisfy the most blasé of travellers in Africa. Here he will find a fascinating blend of the old and the new, a country with as many facets as its brilliant diamonds. As Stuart Cloete expressed it: "South West is not a pretty country. It is grand, wonderful, changeable. It has the quality of a 'jolie laide', of a woman whose individual features may not be lovely but whose variety of expression never ceases to enthrall and enchant."[21]

Of the two South West ports, Walvis (Whale) Bay is by far the more important. It is a fine natural harbour and handles over a million tons of cargo a year with this quantity increasing steadily. Imports include building materials, agricultural goods, clothing and other manufactured goods, while exports are mainly karakul pelts, wool, ores, sealskins, frozen meat, guano, canned fish, fish oil and fish meal.

The main wharf has loading installations for large vessels. There are a number of electric cranes, warehouses — some of which are equipped for cold-storage — and a drydock which handles ships of up to 500 tons. Much of the cargo is stacked uncovered along the piers, since the danger of spoilage by rainfall is minimal. Walvis Bay gets less than two inches of rain per annum.

What was once a great whaling port is now the centre of a prosperous fishing industry. During the last three months of each year, millions of pilchards — a sardine-like food fish — swarm into the area. A fleet of over 200 diesel engine boats plies out into the bay to

---

21. *South West Africa* by Alice Mertens: Collins, London 1966, Introduction, Page 7.

The Fish River Canyon
in South West Africa.
The Canyon is reputed
to be the second largest of its kind in the world,
after the Grand Canyon in Arizona.

The German architecture is
evident in this view of the Kaiserstrasse,
Windhoek's principal thoroughfare.

net this silver harvest, daily delivering up to three loads of a hundred tons each to the canneries and fishmeal factories which process the catch. Of a total population of 12,000 people, about a third are engaged in the fishing industry.

In order to protect the pilchard shoals (some as much as a mile long and a hundred yards wide) from over-fishing, the South West Africa Administration limits the yearly catch to 250,000 tons and the season from March to November. Outside territorial waters a sizeable Russian fleet and ships of many other nations operate all the year round. (On occasions Russian ships came into South West African waters and were promptly chased out by a South African destroyer.) Mechanization and efficiency are keynotes of the industry and a can factory supplies producers with containers manufactured on the spot. An oil pipeline carries fish oil from the processing plants to the harbour where it is loaded directly and hygienically into tankers.

Walvis Bay gets its drinking water from the Kuiseb "River", although this appears to be just another dry desert river. At the town of Rooibank — 22 miles inland — large concrete cylinders are sunk into the sandy bed to a depth of forty feet. These cylinders gradually fill by a seepage process from the flowing underground water and is piped to Walvis Bay across the Namib.

The streets of Walvis Bay look tarred, but they are of salt clay rolled firm and, because of the scanty rainfall, require little repair. There are no trees, giving the town

65

a peculiar surface-of-the-moon aura. The fine sand, driven by their fierce south-west wind, creates a house-wife's nightmare for most of the year.

Near Walvis Bay is a rocky island called Bird Rock. Here a wooden platform 300 yards by 600 yards — six times the size of a football field — stands on steel girders embedded in the rock foundation. It was erected decades ago by a single German carpenter, a man named Winter, to collect the guano from thousands of seabirds. It now delivers several thousand tons of guano a year.

In 1828, an American sealing captain, Benjamin Morrell, was working the South Atlantic coast in his schooner *Antarctic* when he sighted the small island of Ichaboe about 25 miles from the present port of Lüderitz. He stared in amazement at the snowy white collection of centuries of guano deposits estimating it to be at least 25 feet deep in places. Later exploitation proved his estimates to be modest in comparison with reality, and up to 75 feet of guano were removed in places. This may sound unbelievable, until you consider that the 20,000,000 seabirds — cormorants, penguins and gannets as well as ordinary gulls — eat twice their weight in fish daily.

In 1866, the Cape government annexed a number of these guano islands and the annual harvesting of this valuable white fertilizer is still carried out by the South African government on Bird Rock and the other off-shore islands named Mercury, Ichaboe, Halifax, Albatross, Sinclair, Roast Beef, Pomona, and Plum Pudding!

The collection and distribution is done by a perma-nent staff stationed on the islands and since the islands are baren a special ship supplies them with food and water. More than two-thirds of the guano used on Southern African farms comes from these islands and their neighbouring coast.

Twenty-six miles up the coast from Walvis Bay lies the town of Swakopmund at the mouth of the Swakop River. Although it flows irregularly water may be obtained by digging in its bed. During their administration, the Germans tried to make the town into a port to rival Walvis Bay. A pier was built to protect shipping but the convenience and superiority of its neighbouring harbour forced its abandonment, hastened by the silting up of facilities. Today, Swakopmund is principally a holiday resort and hotels and boarding houses abound.

As in Walvis Bay, every single tree in Swakopmund was hand-planted. The odd German houses — many of them almost palatial — adorn the dunes of the Namib coast and many South-Westers have vacation homes there, including the Administrator of South West Africa, who moves down from Windhoek together with his staff during the summer months.

Marine sulphur eruptions off Swakopmund occur with some regularity between the months of November and March, causing a pungent odour and killing thousands of fish.

A journey of 80 miles up the Namib coast from Swakopmund lies Cape Cross, a sheltered bay where the first European to touch South West Africa, the Portuguese explorer Diego Caô, landed in 1484 to erect a stone cross.   The area around Cape Cross was once below sea level and enormous quantities of salt — both rock and crystalline — are found here.   Because of its remoteness and the difficulties of transport, no effort was made to exploit these beds until after World War II. A thriving salt bed operation is also carried out at Panther Beacon, not far from Swakopmund, to which it is hauled by heavy truck.

The long stretch of rocky beach at Cape Cross is populated by thousands of seals, which bask in the sun or slip into the icy waters for a playful romp.

Sealing is particularly profitable here and each year a limited portion of the herd (called the karakul sheep of the sea) is killed for the fur trade.   The bulls, which weigh up to half a ton, can be dangerous rascals and have been known to seize a hunter and drag him into the sea.

The hide of the adult seal is covered with coarse hair which makes the pups more valuable as pelts, turned into expensive coats for fashion-minded women the world over.   Many of the skins treated at a sealing station at Cape Cross are exported to the United States.   Aside from their pelts, seals are valuable for their oil and flesh which is processed into meat meal for cattle.

This section of the Namib is extremely desolate and from here north through the Kaokoveld to the border of Angola it has acquired the name *Skeleton Coast.* Strewn with flotsam and pieces of wreckage, the beach has been the nemesis of whatever hapless shipwrecked castaways managed to reach its shores.   North of

Cape Frio, an ill-fated British cargo liner, the "Dunedin Star", ran aground in 1942 and its rusting skeletal remains may still be seen.

In other parts the continually shifting shore line has either covered wrecks or "passed" others with the result that one or two hulks are now lying far inland, ghost ships riding the desert sands.

Despite the almost complete absence of water, naturalists are discovering a whole domain of rare animal and plant life specially adapted to the hostile conditions of the desert. A singular example of this adaptation is the *Welwitschia mirabilis,* a plant first described by Frederich Welwitsch in 1858 although it had been long known to the local tribes who used it for fuel and made stools from its woody stems.

This botanical oddity, which grows to an incredible age, depends on its tap-root which may penetrate to a depth of over sixty feet in its search for moisture. It grows several dull-green leaves — usually torn into numberless shreds by the wind — which manage to reach a length of up to nine feet over the course of a hundred years. Carbon tests have established the age of some plants at 1,500 years but scientists believe that specimens may live as long as two thousand years despite their hostile environment. The Welwitschia belongs to the *Gymnosperm* family and produces both male and female plants. In May each year, the seeds ripen in their cones and are blown away by the wind. Only those moistened by rain are germinated.

This living fossil of the plant family is found in no other part of the world.

In the same region Naras are found, a thorny leafless member of the pumpkin family. This "Wonder of the Waste" has a tap-root up to forty feet deep in a land which has an annual rainfall of less than five inches a year and sometimes sees no rain at all for several years. The Bushmen who roam occasionally in the area use the flesh of the Naras for food and moisture and roast the seeds as a delicacy.

The Desert Tsammas, found on the eastern fringes of the Namib and in the Kalahari, is a type of watermelon which also provides moisture for the Bushmen, who cut a hole in the top, mash up the pulp and drink the resulting liquid. They likewise roast the tsammas seeds and use its rind for containers, pots and even resonators for their musical instruments.

An occasional kokerboom *(aloe dichotoma)* is the only break in the barren landscape. Called the quiver tree ("koker" in Afrikaans), this thick-stemmed tree stands up to twelve feet and branches above the middle. The Bushmen use its hollowed branches for quivers in which they carry their poisoned arrows. It can live without almost any water and is a true desert tree.

Animal life in the desert is equally specialised. Tenebionid beetles which inhabit deserts the world over have developed a waterless existence in the Namib. They build up a water equilibrium in their hard black bodies and draw food from the microscopic organic particles found in the sand structure.

The tenebionids — all 200 species of them — form excellent food for the reptiles. Geckos and the legless, snakelike lizards live on the beetles and their soft-bodied larvae. These in turn give sustenance to the golden mole, a tiny deaf-and-blind nocturnal mammal which burrows in the dunes and surfaces to pounce on its prey when it senses movement above. Existence of the mole only became known to science in 1963.

The chain is continued by the predatory birds, such as owls, and the scavenger animals. Along the Atlantic shore, packs of jackal (and occasionally the rarely seen brown hyena) gather after dusk to feast off the abundant fish life thrown upon the beach by the mighty breakers and the remains of seals left along the shoreline by the sealers.

About 70 miles to the northeast of Cape Cross, the Skeleton Coast slopes upward into the Brandberg ("Scorched Mountain") massive. The black basalt sides of these mountains — some rising as high as 8,550 feet — conceal a unique agglomeration of rock-paintings shrouded in mystery. Remote even by African standards, these paintings are tucked in the walls of shelters and caves accessible only after a harrowing journey up the Tsisab Valley, along a road strewn with huge boulders, and a vigorous hour's hike along the river bed.

In a shelter discovered in 1917 by the German geologist, Dr. Reinhard Maack, stands probably the oldest and certainly the most famous of these paintings. *The White Lady of the Brandberg,* so called because it depicts a procession in which the central figure is a light-skinned princess or goddess, in a frieze some 18 feet long and seven feet high. It is only one of many scenes in the enclosure — some of much more recent date — and is the eleventh layer of painting.

The White Lady was studied intensively during 1947 by the famous French archeologist, the Abbé Henri Breuil. He considered it equally as important as the cave art at Altamira, Spain, and felt it could justifiably be dated as early as Moses or Rameses II.

This painting and most of its later neighbours were done with mineral oxides and retain a remarkable state of preservation, probably because a protective shield of micro-organisms and lime encrusted their surface over the centuries. They depict hunts, burials and family scenes, but the later works differ markedly in crudeness and concept from the White Lady. Certainly, it is the product of no primitive, uncultured people, since its intricacy and sophistication show an elaborate advance in civilization.

The painting shows a hunt in progress with animals, boys and men (some in animal masks). Many people carry bows and staffs or spears, but this is no ordinary hunting expedition. In many ways it bears similarities to the religious procession of the "Second Mystery" of ancient Egypt — the resurrection myth of Isis, Orisis and Horus. There appears to be a variety of races in the procession, calling to mind the frescoes at the Palace of Minos in Knossis, Crete. Other similarities with Egyptian and Cretan art are outstanding.

The White Lady herself stands about $15\frac{3}{4}$ inches and although she is not the tallest figure in the procession, she is certainly the most important. No primitive people would have given such a prominent position to a woman.[22] (A Skeleton Man walking behind her is 19 inches high; no two figures in the procession are exactly the same height.) She wears white tights cinched below the knees and at the waist with beaded (or jewelled) bands and a jerkin reminiscent to those of the girl bullfighters in Crete. Her hair is gathered up in a net of pearls and her breasts are adorned with pearls and ribbons. In her left hand, she carries a slack bow and four arrows, one already fitted, and her right hand holds a large delicate goblet. Close-fitting slippers protect her feet.

Egyptian influence is further suggested by the appearance of a "Crocodile Man", a figure with the head of a crocodile, yellow thighs and black forearms in which he carries a bundle of twigs. In Egypt, the crocodile was considered the "infernal messenger" and was often depicted in black and golden yellow, carrying palm branches. Also the Skeleton Man following the White Lady bears a notched pole. Egyptians used notches to indicate increases in the swelling Nile and Egyptian paintings show Isis carrying a pole with forty-seven notches.

Two theories seek to explain the presence of this painting so far from other indications of past civilization: one holds that it was done by foreigners to South West Africa — possibly Cretans, since there is positive evidence that they were seafarers as long ago as 3400 B.C. and

---

22. The Bushmen recognise no affiliation with anyone other than their near relatives.

that their culture was heavily influenced by their commerce with Egypt. Could they have sailed around the West Coast of Africa as far south as the Skeleton Coast, been shipwrecked and wandered inland over the hostile desert to find themselves in the hardly less hostile mountains where they left their mark on the isolated cave wall? Or could they have wandered into the Brandberg from the northeast, either from far-off Egypt or across from Zimbabwe, that ruined stone citadel in Rhodesia identified by some with the Biblical "Ophir" but otherwise also unexplained?

Some archeologists find neither of these theories satisfactory and maintain that the White Lady is merely a Bushman woman who has smeared her body with white clay. It is, however, hard to trace her delicate features and slim figure in the characteristics of the local native women. So the mystery remains.

In addition to the rock paintings, some of which are obviously the work of Bushmen and only several centuries old, there are a number of interesting rock engravings in South West Africa. The most interesting of these occurs at Twyfelfontein (Fountain of Doubt) less than 80 miles north-west of the Brandberg and 60 from the sea. Although poorly preserved, the cracked and weathered surfaces of the rocks reveal an endless variety of indigenous animals — elephants, giraffes, lions, buck, birds and rhinoceroses — and geometric designs — circles, squares, etc. — etched or engraved with stone chisels by artists who demonstrated amazing sensitivity to shape and design. Over 2,000 separate figures are discernible, many of them humorous and possibly serving some practical purpose such as the clearly defined animal and human footprints which may have served to point late arrivals in the direction of the hunt.

Also near Twyfelfontein is the Burnt Mountain, an inactive volcano whose crust is composed of barren rock. Despite the lack of vegetation, the multi-hued igneous surface presents a spectacular impression.

As if to emphasize the desolate character of the Kaokoveld, a petrified forest[23] lies some 50 miles north of the Burnt Mountain in the Avahuab Valley. This fossilized lumberyard, a national monument, is fenced off from the surrounding farmland. It appears as if some vanished race of titans felled the trees. The great trunks — up to 60 feet in length and ten feet in diameter — lie scattered on the ground in abandon, as if strewn by the wind. Some are broken and splintered, but others lie intact.

Further north, about the same distance inland from the Skeleton Coast, lies the community of "Sesfontein". The small band of Namas living there relies on the "six fountains" to irrigate the fields of corn, pumpkins, wheat and tobacco which sustain their existence. Sesfontein was the site of a colonial German fort, built at the turn of the century, whose crumbling ruins stand as a mute reminder of the first advances of white occupation. The settlement is the last real town on this edge of the territory before the Angolan border, although the outposts of Ohopoho and Kaoko Otavi — about 170 miles still

---

23. Estimated age — 200 *million* years.

further north — are stopping places for the traveller. At Kaoko Otavi a beautiful pool, fed by a permanent spring, supplies water to scores of plains animals and the handful of humans who chance to pass the way. In the 1870's, the Thirstland Trekkers (see Chapter III) stopped and rested here for some weeks before pushing on to Angola.

———————

But if the Namib north of the Walvis Bay offers riches in fish and furs, it is the southern or "Diamond Coast" that is the real treasure house of South West Africa. The beach is divided into Diamond Area No. 1 and Diamond Area No. 2, each of them "forbidden area" (sperrgebiet) to unauthorised persons.

Diamond Area No. 1 is a 60-mile wide strip of desolate coastline which extends about 220 miles from the mouth of the Orange River to a little north of the town of Lüderitz. This is the origin of 20 per cent of the world's gem diamonds and a significant portion of its industrial stones.

Diamonds were discovered here in 1908 by a German railroad supervisor named August Stauch. In the decade afterward, it was possible for a man walking along the beach to reach down and pick up quite a respectable gem and many did. A plethora of small companies were formed and some of these returned as much as 3,800 per cent on invested capital.

During the diamond rush, Lüderitz was a boom town stampeded by fortune-seekers who arrived by sea and overland from the Cape. A small number of ghost towns among the Namib dunes not far from Lüderitz testify to the intensity of the diamond-fever and the resulting disillusion of its sufferers when the task of extracting gemstones from the millions of tons of sand proved too much. There the winds whip the loose boards of crumbling shelters and the sun and salt air rust the remnants of mining equipment and rot the deserted shacks. Only an occasional jackal stares curiously at the scattered cooking utensils and other possessions, abandoned — along with hope — in this desolate place.

Today, the coast is worked by Consolidated Diamond Mines of South West Africa Ltd., commonly called the C.D.M. The mining operations must be carried out on a highly mechanized scale, and giant earthmovers of the C.D.M. must shift over a hundred million pounds of sand and gravel for every pound of diamonds recovered. Huge sand dunes are flattened in the process — the work being done by the world's biggest bulldozers. Each of the six tyres cost R800 or $1,120. For their efforts, however, the company realizes up to R40,000,000 ($56 million) a year from the fabulous fields.

There are some 700 White persons employed here, mostly skilled workers but the bulk of labour needed to extract the stones comes from the Ovambo tribes in the North and provides a healthy economic stimulus for that area. (But, by order of their chiefs, no Ovambo can remain more than two years in the area, minimizing the chance of cultural disorientation.)

At its model town Oranjemund, about three miles inland from the river's mouth, the C.D.M. has created an oasis in the desert. Fresh produce, sold at subsidized prices, comes from the company's own farms up river and social and recreational amenities are provided in abundance for 2,500 White residents and 4,000 non-White employees. Despite its isolation, life here is happy and self-contained with consumer products shipped in through Port Nolloth in the Cape and trucked across the 3,200-foot concrete Oppenheimer Bridge spanning the Orange River.

The C.D.M. exercises stringent security controls over all its employees to prevent smuggling. With the sea on one side and the desert stretching away for miles in the other direction, there is not much chance of getting the gems out except through the company's offices. So every man leaving the restricted area submits to a security check which involves X-raying both his person and his baggage. On the inside, there are well-appointed waiting rooms leading off into the check rooms where radiographers scan departing employees. This discourages anyone who might get fancy ideas about "get rich quick" schemes, although an occasional Ovambo miner decides to test the White man's magic machine by swallowing a pebble or some small metal object. (He is placed in the company hospital where he can be cared for until the object has been evacuated.)

There are two theories about how this coast came to be diamond-covered. Nowhere else in the world are diamonds found loose in sand and gravel as they are here. Conditions necessary to produce natural diamonds include intense heat which rearranges and transforms the carbon atoms into valuable stones and these conditions seem limited to the pipes of volcanoes. There the diamonds, packed in the famous "Blue ground" or Kimberlite, are pushed to the surface very much like toothpaste squeezed from a tube. But although there are patches of blue ground elsewhere in South West Africa with no diamonds, in the Namib there are diamonds but no blue ground.

One group of geologists feels that over the centuries the diamonds have been washing up on the shoreline from some huge volcanic deposit under the sea. Others think they originated somewhere in the interior of Southern Africa from where they were carried by rivers down into the ocean. There they were thrown by waves onto the beach, where they are now found in layers some as much as 70 feet deep. The fact that the bigger stones are found near the mouth of the Orange River seems to support this theory, since — being heavier — they would have settled near the river's mouth rather than be carried away by tides and currents.

In 1962 an American industralist named Sam Collins, started a unique mining venture, the Marine Diamond Corporation, which recovers stones from the diamond rich reefs off the coast. Operating from barges in up to 200 feet of water, the company's suction pipes draw up the surface of the seabed and are beginning to realize 1,000 carats a day from their "vacuuming". In a concession area roughly paralleling that of the C.D.M. and extending out three miles from the low water line, Marine Diamond Corporation is recovering one carat for every ton of gravel processed, compared with one carat for every fifteen tons on the beach. (Test prospecting indicates that there is at least one area where the yield will reach up to 15 carats per ton.) However, this is offset by the high costs of maintaining vessels and crew for long periods and the special equipment required.

Lüderitz, once the port of supply for the diamond coast, has been superceded by Port Nolloth in the Cape Province of South Africa. But although its harbour is a small one, it serves the southern portion of South West Africa and has become the site of a flourishing rock lobster industry. It shelters a fleet of fifty lobstering boats. Of the town's total population of 3,600, fully 2,000 are connected in some way with the catching and processing of these succulent crayfish.

At first glance, Lüderitz is not the likeliest place to expect to find a town. Set among drifting dunes, the town has not a single tree and is wedged on one side by the ocean, on the other by a sea of sand. Every drop of water for its inhabitants must be condensed by electrolosis from sea water at a cost of two dollars per cubic meter. Even the milk is condensed. When available, fresh milk sells at premium.

Despite these disadvantages, Lüderitz is a pleasant little place. Called Angra Pequena by the early Portuguese navigators who were the first to visit its site, it was renamed for Adolf Lüderitz, the German adventurer, who landed there in 1883 to establish the presence of Imperial Germany. Later the area was proclaimed a German protectorate.

Predictably, the canning, freezing of rock lobster and making of fishmeal is the town's major industry. There are six canneries, all of them under strict sanitary control and highly mechanized. Although the catch is limited by quota to conserve the supply, they handle about ten tons annually. Only the tails of the rock lobster are canned or frozen for export; the legs and body are turned into meal used as a protein-rich animal food supplement. The biggest market for rock lobsters is the United States, but British and Continental gourmets also savour the products of this R3.5 million ($5,000,000) a year industry.

The best sites for rock lobster fishing are along the coast north of the port. The fishermen work in 60-foot boats with two or more tenders, all dropping baited nets to the lobster beds. When the smaller boats are full, they unload their catch on the mother vessel and go back for more.

Sometimes the fishermen venture south of the town where, in the midst of the diamond area, they come upon the Bogenfels (Archway Rock). This enormous natural arch rises 180 feet out of the sea, its formation weathered by the south-west wind which whips the coast for seven months out of the year. It must have struck awe indeed into the hearts of the early diamond-seekers.

Of the three pillars in South West Africa's economic structure (mining, agriculture and fishing), lobstering is only a minor — if important — part. Diamond mining is and is likely to remain the most important mining activity and the tax paid on gem sales to the government by the C.D.M. and other producers is no small portion of the territory's revenue. Mining, agriculture and fishing at present account for over 60 per cent. of the gross domestic product.

To appreciate the role of agriculture, one must move inland from the diamond coast to the plateau. The southern portion of the territory from the Orange River to about 70 miles south of Windhoek, the capital and approximate geographic centre of South West Africa, is similar to the adjoining Cape Province. The country is suitable for grazing but the low annual rainfall and recurrent severe droughts make crop growing impossible. This part of the territory has been called Great Namaqualand, because of the roving Namaqua or Hottentot families which inhabit the area. Great numbers of Namaquas (Namas) still live there with their herds of cattle and flocks. In recent years, this area has proved adaptable to the karakul ("Persian lamb") industry.

In the midst of Namaqualand lies the Fish River Canyon. Dipping from the outer edges to an inner plateau, sometimes as much as 2,000 feet down, this sight rivals the Grand Canyon of the Colorado River and testifies to the immense power once wielded by this tributory of the Orange. The Fish River now trickles a sluggish and seasonal flow through its 40-mile canyon bed, but because of its remoteness, it attracts few tourists. However, the hot springs at Ai-Ais, said to have healing powers, is visited by hundreds of campers from all over South Africa.

Except for the Fish River Canyon, the plateau is generally flat and uninteresting. The surface is thinly covered with grass, drought-resistant bushes and shrubs. Going north through Namaqualand, one can notice the increase in rainfall by the gradual change in vegetation. Here and there, camelthorn trees lift their top-heavy umbrella-shaped crowns toward the sky and an occasional quiver tree has taken root. As the land rises, whole forests of mimosa trees spring from the fertile earth, shedding their yellow scented flowers over the ground from the fluffy balls on their thorn-covered branches.

North of Namaqualand the main occupation is the raising of karakul sheep, an industry so profitable that the sheep have been described as the "black diamonds" of South West Africa. The pelts of these Persian lambs are exported to the fur centres of the world where they are fashioned into luxurious coats and accessories.

The name Karakul is derived from Kara-Kul, a village in East Bokhara from which the breed originated. It means "Black Lake" and was applied probably because the curls of the pelts resemble waves on a wind-blown water surface. Since there are no karakul sheep anywhere near Persia, the term "Persian lamb" is less easily explicable. But two explanations would be that the pelts were first introduced into Russia by Persian traders who, as Moslems, could travel through Bokhara where Christian traders were prohibited, or that the breed first became widespread when the Persian Empire encompassed most of Central Asia.

In any event, the shiny black pelts have been long valued by the world's fashion-conscious (there is evidence to suggest their use as early as 1800 B.C.), and the sheep were introduced into Germany around the turn of the 20th century. A Leipzig fur-dealer had the happy idea of introducing the breed into South West Africa, which closely resembled Bokhara in climate and terrain, and the first pure-bred herd of twelve sheep was imported in 1907. The experiment proved so successful that about 300 more were shipped out several years later and the firm basis for a flourishing industry was laid.

By crosses with the local breeds, the territory's karakul herds have been improved until today there are about three million head. From these herds, more than two million lamb pelts, worth about R16 million or $22,400,000 (at roughly R7 of $10 each) are exported annually.

Although mixed ranching of both cattle and karakul is carried on as far north as Windhoek, the southern ranches concentrate almost exclusively on this lucrative product. The size of the average farm is about 25,000 acres supporting anything from a thousand to ten thousand head. Each ewe gives birth to about three lambs over a period of two years. The lambs are killed 24 hours after birth before they lose the curliness of their fur. Wool from the full-grown sheep is sheared for use in carpets.

In addition to the ordinary black karakul, there are brown and grey varieties, called Shiraz and Kamber. The Kamber pelts are in fact not grey at all but rather black and white wool in almost equal parts.

Karakul farmers maintain strict control over their breeds and the pedigree of each lamb is conscientiously registered. Stud stock is provided by government-sponsored experimental stations. A levy on the sale of each pelt provides advertising and promotional funds for the industry's trade association.

Although some ranchers sell their pelts through co-operatives to agents in Windhoek and Cape Town, there are instances of overseas dealers buying direct. Most of the pelts end up in North America, however devious the route.

The southern centre of the karakul district is the town of Keetmanshoop. Standing on a grass-covered plain, the present town of 8,000 grew out of a Rhenish mission station established in 1866. Its modern shops and hotels are attractive and its airport is unusually large for a town of its size. It is the focal point of the district, with roads converging upon it south from the Cape border, west from Lüderitz and north from Windhoek.

Just after leaving Keetmanshoop and some seven miles from the main road, there stands the great forest of kokerboom, the "quiver trees" mentioned earlier. Although these trees are found all over the territory, this must surely be the most intense concentration — over 300 of them in an area about 500 sq. yards.

The next point of interest lies 50 miles north from Keetmanshoop. Here stands the "Mukorob", a Hottentot word meaning the "Finger of God", an eroded rock that has assumed the shape of a pointing finger. It towers 180 feet in the air and near the top contains a number of niches which are used by nesting birds. From a distance it appears as if a strong wind may blow it over at any moment.

An anomoly of this area is the gushing fountains near the town of Stamprietfontein at the western edge of the Kalahari. Here are some forty artesian wells through which millions of gallons of underground water surge upward daily, at great force. The local farmers have placed valves up to 10 inches in diameter over these openings and the resultant crystal streams are used to irrigate hundreds of acres of wheat, corn, alfalfa (lucerne) and other green crops. However, to conserve these precious fountains the use of artesian water is now strictly controlled.

Still further north on the Windhoek road, one comes to the town of Rehoboth. It was settled in 1870 by a group of people of mixed descent who moved north into South West from the Cape (see Chapter III). There in the midst of the finest farming land in the territory, they set up a Republic. Today, some are wealthy farmers with large incomes, but others have preferred to lease their farms to Whites and live in the town.

On a farm near Rehoboth, the advancing German colonial troops first met and fought the Nama people in 1893. The Namas were eventually defeated, but they fought savagely under their leader, Chief Hendrik Witbooi, and cartridge cases still strewn about the battlefield testify to the fierceness of the battle. Overgrown trenches and the graves of both German and Nama warriors are still discernible.

Windhoek, the capital of South West Africa, is an oasis of Continental culture in a distinctly African environment. The German influence is pervasive and may be seen in the bookshop windows, streets (the main thoroughfare is Kaiser Street) and the typical German architecture of some of the houses and shops. Young men are still coming out from Germany to try their luck in South West, and many families save for years to spend vacations in the country their grandparents left decades ago. German is still one of the official languages of South West Africa.

The city's growth over the past two decades has been nothing short of phenomenal. Before World War II, the White population was about 4,000; today it is almost six times that. In addition to being the legislative, judicial and administrative seat, Windhoek is the northern centre of the territory's main cattle and karakul sheep district.

The city is one of the smallest capitals in the world and has no subways, no trains, no skyscrapers and no smog.

At 5,534 feet above sea level, it enjoys a mild sunny climate and the surrounding hills provide a charming panorama. Unlike its name indicates, it is not at all windy. Rain is so infrequent (and the mid-day summer heat so intense) that louvered roofs over the sidewalks may be used in place of awning to allow for shade and ventilation.

There are two versions of how Windhoek got its name, both connected with the Nama people who had a camp on the site for at least thirty years before Whites began settling here. The Namas called it "The Place of Smoke" which was translated by the early Dutch travellers into their own language. Or, alternatively, it was named by Jonker Afrikaner, the Nama Napoleon of South West Africa whose warrior tribesmen terrorized and drove out the Hereros who has lived in the area since the end of the 18th century. Windhoek was his capital also, named — some say — after the Windhoek Mountains in the Cape Colony, near his birthplace.

In any event, a Rhenish mission station was established on the site as early as 1870 and the modern town was founded in 1890 by Captain (later Major) Kurt von Francois, the German officer responsible for the district. Von Francois erected the Alte Feste (Old Fort), garrisoned with about 50 men, as a buffer between the warring Namas and Hereros. It is the oldest building still standing in Windhoek today, looking oddly medieval despite the cacti and palm trees that surround it.

There are three genuine castles in the city, also silent witnesses to its German origin. Although built around the turn of the century, they would look at home on any hillside overlooking the Rhine. Their rough-hewn stone walls, turrets and battlements never witnessed armed conflict, but they served admirably to remind their aristocratic German owners of the land of their birth. Their interiors were decorated with tapestries, paintings, antique furniture and other valuable heirlooms. Today these castles are used as residences.

The old central administration building for South West Africa is the Tintenpalast (Ink Palace) designed by the same architect who planned the castles. It stands on the rise of a hill and dominates the entire town, with its pleasant gardens and small game park of about one square mile. From the rear windows of the building, the occupants can look out on springbok, duiker and giraffes nibbling peacefully among the aloes and thorn-trees. A modern Administration building has been erected nearby and most of the offices have been moved into the new quarters.

Within the city limits are large vineyards, maintained by a Roman Catholic Mission, where excellent table grapes and wines of the Riesling and Burgundy types have been produced for decades. Windhoek's residents can also quench their thirsts with superb beer made in a local brewery. Each bottle features a map of Southern Africa with South West highlighted in red, a piquant reminder that its contents, although favourably comparable to most German beer, are far removed from Europe.

Despite the isolation from the usual centres of the performing arts, Windhoek boasts a remarkable quality and variety of cultural life. Local opera and operetta companies give renditions of major works (frequently translated into Afrikaans or German to accommodate the audiences) and a full symphony orchestra, string quartet, school of ballet and concert choir testify to the talent and interest concentrated here. The large, modern Arts Theatre, well equipped with lighting and stage facilities, provides an impetus for concerts.

The graphic arts also receive attention and a number of painters in the territory give regular exhibitions in Windhoek. The city boasts a splendid new art gallery.

The quality is entirely professional and one artist, Adolph Jentsch, has exhibited at the Venice Biennale. The intense colours of the South West landscape and its myriad races and facial types provide the most frequent subjects.

North-west of Windhoek on the edge of the plateau is the town of Karibib, site of a flourishing marble quarry. In German times, the marble, which is of good quality, was exported to South America and other places. Many of the public buildings in the territory are faced with it. A nearby mining operation produces lithium-bearing ores, although not in significant quantities, and a manganese mine in the vicinity has been worked out.

About halfway between Windhoek and the northern coppermining centre at Tsumeb lies the town of Otjiwarongo, named by the Hereros "place where fat cattle graze". It stands in the centre of a 10,000 square miles area which is one of the finest cattle regions in Southern Africa. The local creamery accounts for about a fifth of South West's annual production of 10 million pounds of butter. Enormous quantities of beef and cheese (cheddar and gouda) also emanate from the town. As might be expected, Otjiwarongo has a fine show ground in addition to its modern slaughtering and cold storage facilities.

Some sixty miles east of the town is the Waterberg Plateau. This geological oddity, with its high northern cliffs is so constructed that rain falling anywhere on the plateau wells up in springs on its southern slopes, watering its luxurious flora. Proclaimed a nature reserve by the Administration, the Waterberg has a rest camp on the summit where tourists may enjoy its unique natural beauty from the site of the old German colonial police station.

At the western edge of the Kalahari where the plateau has levelled out and merged with the plains of Ovamboland, the main towns of the North — Tsumeb, Grootfontein and Otavi — form a triangle. The latter is a "has-been" sort of place, with a total population of about 1,300. In German times, it was the first of the copper outcroppings to be worked and lent its name to the company which went on to exploit the mineral resources of the area. It has recently been given a new lease of life through the establishment of a large meat processing factory.

Africa's largest lead mine is at Tsumeb — about 90,000 refined tons a year. But lead is only one of the strategic minerals taken annually from this peculiar concentration of nature's metallic resources. Copper (some 65,000 tons), zinc, arsenic, silver, cadmium, vanadium and germanium — are all taken from this unique mine.

Indications have been found that copper mining has been carried out at Tsumeb for centuries by an ancient people whose identity has not been established. German colonial occupation spurred large-scale recovery by a German firm, the Otavi Minen and Eisenbahn Gesellschaft, which laid a railroad from Tsumeb to

Swakopmund and began shipping ore around 1907. Intermittent mining was carried out from that date but during World War II, it was impounded by the South African government as enemy property and sold in 1947 to the Tsumeb Corporation Ltd., a joint American, British and South African venture. The company is said to have recovered its R20 million ($28,000,000) investment in the first year of operation processing only the old dumps.

The Tsumeb Corporation operates both lead and copper smelting operations, much of whose output goes directly to the United States. These plus zinc concentrates, are transported by rail to Walvis Bay for export.

The town of Tsumeb, with a little over 7,000 inhabitants, is a pleasant enough place. Except for Oranjemund, it has the only grass golf course in South West. Nearly all the residents are connected in some way with the mining operations or with supplying the miners and their families and about half the population are Ovambo miners who stay in company-provided living quarters during the term of their contracts. Tsumeb, which is the second largest mining town in the territory (Oranjemund is the first), is noted in the region for its variety of flowering trees and shrubs — bougainvillaes, jacarandas, African flamboyants, and poinsettias, and the huge marula and tambuti trees provide ample shade and touches of colour. As at Oranjemund, the mining company provides all the amenities of modern civilization and subsidized food commodities from its own farms.

Grootfontein, the eastern point in the triangle, is named for the perennial springs that supply the town's

4,000 people. The town was founded in 1885 by people emigrating from South Africa.

It is a fast-growing corn and cattle centre and lies at the terminus of the railway line from Windhoek. (Suggestions have been made that the line be extended northeastward to Rhodesia.) The headquarters of SWANLA, the co-operative organization to recruit Ovambo labour for the mines, farms and industries, is located here as the nearest permanent White settlement to Ovamboland. Along its wide, tree-lined streets come hundreds of Ovambo and Okavango young men, riding in trucks, often for the first time in their lives and bound for the White man's land to seek their fortunes. They will return two years later with tales of their travel and enough money to afford to get married.

Near Grootfontein on a farm called "Hoba West" lies the world's largest meteorite, an estimated 66 tons of nickel and iron with traces of cobalt, copper and chrome in a block 9 feet long by 8 feet broad, first examined scientifically in 1929 by Dr. W. J. Luyten, an American astronomer. The quarter of it which lies above the ground is pocked with the blue nitches left by men trying to cut into it. A piece has been donated to the American National Aeronautics and Space Administration to assist in research in the construction of space vehicles.

Beyond the triangle towns is the great game reserve of the Etosha Pan. There are two comfortable rest camps equipped with modern conveniences: Okaukeujo in the south-west and Namutoni at the eastern edge of the pan.

It is believed that the pan was once a great lake, fed by the waters of the Kunene River which flowed south to this point. It is some 80 miles long and 30 wide and, in years of good rainfall, may be completely flooded. Even in the wettest of years, however, most of the water has evaporated by August or September. Fossilized fish have been discovered on its northern border, indicating its former condition.

For decades this area was a hunters' paradise, but the German colonial administration — with remarkable foresight — turned it into a game reserve and the vast numbers of elephant, lion, giraffe, rhinoceros, cheetah, eland and various types of buck that roam the area testify to the wisdom of that policy. Bird life is also found in abundance.

The waterholes over the pan are visited by up to 15,000 head of game daily and "lion parties" staged by the rangers are held twice a week. To ensure that these parties will be visited by lion as well as tourists, the rangers shoot a zebra or wildebeest and chain it to a tree. Park visitors may then drive to the site and watch the feast from the safety of their cars. Some 25,000 tourists visit the Etosha Pan annually to view the lion and gaze in admiration at the great herds gathering at the waterholes and salt lakes.

The Bushmen of the area recount a picturesque legend about the formation of the pan. They tell of a shipwreck, eons ago, from which the unfortunate survivors struggled inland where they were surprised and captured by Bushmen. All the men and children were murdered but the women were taken as slaves into the tribe. One young mother gathered her dead infant into her arms and began weeping. All efforts to comfort her were useless and her tears rolled steadily down into a great pool. There they evaporated under the scorching sun, leaving behind only the salty places and little droplets of moisture which form the pan today.

The Etosha Pan Bushmen, tell another charming tale about the old German fort at Namutoni. Built around 1904 on the principle of an ancient Roman castle, the fort has four towers and rooms to contain an entire garrison.

The fort has been restored and converted to accommodate visitors, with forty guest rooms and a crystal-clear swimming pool to reflect its white battlements and the surrounding palms.

Sometime in January, 1904, it was attacked by surprise by 500 Ovambo warriors. The main portion of the garrison was away on patrol some forty miles distant and there were only seven German soldiers at Namutoni. But these seven fought gallantly against the attacking hordes and managed to hold out two full days. Then, on the following night, their last rounds of ammunition having been fired, they escaped under cover of darkness and managed to reach the main body of the company.

The Bushmen claim that on nights of the full moon, they can make out the apparitions of German troops marching forth from the open doors of the fort and hear faintly the sharp commands and bugle calls accompanying the troops as they disappear silently into the darkness. But if park tourists do not happen to be in the area on the night of the full moon, they can still view the inconspicious stone monument where on a marble plate the names of the seven heroic soldiers are inscribed as a reminder of the few who held out against the many.

East of Tsumeb and Grootfontein lies the Caprivi Strip. To get there the road goes via Runtu and Andara. A stop at South West Africa's two crater "lakes", the "Bottomless" Otjikoto and Guinas Lakes, forms a pleasant break in the journey. Otjikoto is 650 feet by 800 feet and some 400 feet deep while Guinas is even larger. Their crystal green waters swarm with cave fish and cacti, thorn bushes and tropical trees line their banks. Otjikoto is believed to be the crater of an extinct volcano but the water actually comes from Lake Guinas, some twelve miles away, by subterranean passages.[24]

Since water is such a precious commodity in this arid land, it is not surprising to learn that the local Ovambo and Bushmen have revered these, the only two natural lakes in the entire territory, for centuries. According to local legend, anyone swimming in their waters is doomed to die. And although the English explorer Sir Francis Galton swam across Otjikoto in 1851 (to the horror if his native porters who considered it witchcraft), a German soldier helping to dump ammunition into the lake in 1914 was caught in the bindings of

---

24. Some geologists believe that these are not really "lakes" but ancient dolomite sinkhole such as appeared in the Western Transvaal during recent years.

A view of Windhoek,
capital city
of South West Africa.

The **Tintenpalast** (Palace of Ink), former headquarters of the
German Administration of South West Africa which came to an end in 1914.
Today, the **Tintenpalast** forms part of the new complex of administrative
buildings of the South West Africa Legislative Assembly.

The Pondok Mountains, a region of jagged peaks, with Spitzkop in the rear, illustrates the harsh nature of the territory.

the dump and drowned. His body was never recovered.

Going eastward through Okavangoland, the road leads through an even greener landscape and the presence of a higher rainfall is everywhere apparent. It terminates abruptly at Andara, however, and from there eastward into the key-shaped strip, only the most necessary journeys are undertaken and those in only the most rugged vehicles. In fact because of the vast Kwando Marshes there is virtually no road to speak of. The mighty Okavango River forms an additional barrier.

Because of the inaccessibility of the eastern portion of the Strip from South West Africa, the South African government administers the area direct from Pretoria. But "administration" consists almost entirely of medical and social services, education and agricultural assistance since the tribe of the Eastern Caprivi are governed by hereditary chiefs and headmen according to ancient custom. The western arm through which the Okavango River flows from Angola on its way to the marches in Botswana is inhabited by Bushmen. There are said to be less than 300 of these people some who have yet to see their first White man.

Whereas the western arm of the Caprivi is well wooded and sandy the eastern arm lies well within the marshy complex of the Kwando, Linyanti and Zambezi Rivers. Here one will frequently come upon luxuriant marsh and river scenery. The area is well watered. Around the first of the year, thunder clouds roll in and the sudden showers turn the streams into cataracts and swell the Kwando and Zambezi Rivers to flood. The waters overflow their banks and trees and undergrowth are immersed in the life-giving fluid.

As the waters recede the swamps and marshes again become stagnant and their low level is reached some time in July. But in August — the height of the dry season — the waters rise once more. By some still unexplained natural phenomenon, the marshes and pans fill up gradually. The fish-eagles soar over the forests and hippos and crocodiles leave their river homes to venture onto high ground.

In such an area, the Bantu peoples — the Mambakushu, Mafue, Mayeyi, and Masubia — often built their huts on stilts and protect their graneries and other storage houses in a like manner. Villages are laid out on high ground and even the gardens may be planted on ant hills.

East Caprivians numbering about 18,000 are today a friendly easy-going people. With very little effort, they can collect an abundant harvest from the fertile land and still have ample time for walks, chats, and other leisurely pursuits. Their humour is razor-sharp and one of their favourite pastimes is verbal banter.

"If you see a baboon, throw a stone at it," they tell a stranger, who is unaware that no rocks and few baboons are found in the flat countryside.

But life here is not completely idyllic. The stagnant water forms a perfect breeding ground for both the tsetse fly and the malaria mosquito, and both have flourished in the past. A constant battle over the past decades by government health officers has begun to show results and experience gained in Zululand, where the tsetse fly has been completely eradicated, is being put to good use here.

In the malaria battle over 600,000 anti-malaria pills are distributed annually. Indirectly this is also an aid in combating the tsetse fly for as the population grows, more and more trees and bush are cleared and the insidious tsetse — the "scourge of Africa" — is robbed of its breeding ground.

Some of the Caprivians remember hearing, at the knees of their grandfathers, about the arrival of the first White man, the famous "African tourist", David Livingstone. The missionary arrived in the land in June, 1851, after an ox-wagon trip from Cape Town. But few followed him and Caprivians today live much as they have for centuries, except for improved health and the occasional blare of transistor radios.

The Caprivians — passing a peaceful existence in this geographically remote spur of the territory — point up by contrast the major impressions forced on the visitor to South West Africa. They are hemmed in by rivers in a land without water. They are racially homogeneous in a land which is a mosaic of cultural types. They are an untouched cultural pocket in a land where clashing cultures have welded the backdrop of history, and they must guard against floods in a land of thirst.

But like the other peoples of South West Africa, they stand today on the threshold of tomorrow. With the possible exception of the Bushmen, all South Westers originally journeyed thousands of miles to arrive in this sprawling frontier land where Nature has sprinkled abundantly monuments to Her wisdom and grudgingly sown the seeds for future progress. The desolate plains, camelthorn trees and weathered mountains cast a spell over visitors.

Because of the austere conditions which so strongly charasterise the South West African scene, the promise of development latent in the dry atmosphere and seemingly unfertile soil is not immediately evident. Yet people settled here permanently when green fields beckoned them elsewhere, and will continue to do so.

3

THE PEOPLE OF SOUTH WEST AFRICA

South West Africa is a kaleidoscope of racial types. No less than twelve different nations speaking as many languages and several dialects live in this country but of the twelve, six, the *Ovambos, Whites* (European descendents), *Namas, Okavangos, Hereros* and *Damaras* constitute almost 90 per cent of the total population.

The remaining groups including the *Caprivians, Coloureds, Bushmen, Basters* and *Kaokovelders* are exceedingly interesting people but numerically very weak.

The Caprivians total about 16,000 people but the other groups each vary from nine to twelve thousand souls.

Ethnologically the people of South West Africa span the millenias of recorded history. The recently-arrived and highly-developed White man lives here as do the most ancient and primitive race on earth, the Bushmen. Anthropologists generally consider the Bushmen to be no more developed than the Later Stone Age while many of the Whites are newly arrived from Europe.

The *Basters* (Bastard race) are a people of mixed descent with a Caucasian strain and Western way of life. They originally hail from the North West Cape Province. Their language is predominantly Afrikaans. The *Coloureds* have more or less the same racial background as the Basters but, unlike the Basters whose chief occupation is animal husbandry, the Coloureds are found mainly in the towns and cities where they are either employed or have their own business. Whereas the Basters have a Chief and Counsellors administering an area recognised as their exclusive homeland, the Coloureds have neither a distinct homeland nor a Chief and Counsellors. In the Eastern arm of the key-shaped Caprivi Zipfel the black population has no ethnical link at all with the other Bantu-speaking groups of South West Africa but is related to the Lozi and Makololo in Zambia's Barotseland. Similarly the 10,000 Tswanas on the Eastern Frontier are ethnically linked with the Tswana of Botswana.

The *Kaokovelders* consist of three tribes closely related to the Herero as far as origin, language and culture are concerned. They are mainly herdsmen, hardly ever leave the Kaokoveld and are exceedingly conservative in their way of life. History has by-passed them and even in their dress they reveal how little the other cultures have made impression on their traditional way of life.

The *Whites* who number about 80,000 people today, are the second largest group in the territory — outnumbering the Damara and Herero by about two to one. They consist mainly of people of German, South African and British descent but there are also representatives of quite a number of nations of Europe and America. South West Africa today has *three* official languages namely Afrikaans, English and German. Their way of life is strictly Western and they are concentrated in towns and cities and on farms where the principle of individual ownership of land and free enterprise is vigorously applied.

The role of the White man in South West African history, past and immediate past, and his contribution to South West Africa's current stability and prosperity is of overwhelming importance. They not only put an end to a century of strife and violence between the indigenous peoples but as bearers of Western Civilization introduced the rule of law, educational services, welfare and Christianity. They brought the railroad, roads, air transport. In short, they tamed the land. *They turned it into one of the few areas of Africa where tribal warfare is totally absent.* Here the Bantu individual no longer has to fear the coming of the night as in the past when, as will be shown in this chapter, the night brought sudden death, treachery, abduction and wholesale slaughter of tribes by absolute and ruthless Nama and Herero tyrants.

The first White man to arrive in South West Africa was Diego Caô, a Portuguese mariner who landed on what is today known as Skeleton Coast in 1484, eight years before Christopher Columbus set foot ashore in the New World. Like Columbus he was searching for a route to the East Indies. But unlike Columbus, he was taking what was then considered the safer way, around the tip of Africa. Caô and his men put to shore in a small boat and erected a sacred cross of stone at a point about seventy-five miles north of Walvis Bay as the crow flies. This has been known ever since as Cape Cross.

Sailing under the flag of King John II, Caô had left Portugal to explore the African coast. He touched at points along the northern bulge and at the Congo, which he had visited two years previously. The cross he erected bore the arms of King John and identical inscriptions in Latin and Portuguese:

„Since the creation of the world 6684 years have passed and since the birth of Christ 1484 years and so the illustrious King John has ordered this pillar to be erected here by Diego Caô, his knight."

This lonely testimonial to man's adventurous soul was found by the German colonizers four hundred years later. By 1893, it was weathered and crumbling, and Kaiser Wilhelm ordered that it be replaced by an exact granite replica. The original was shipped to Germany by warship and now lies in the Oceanographic Museum in Berlin. Caô is thought to have died nearby although possibly he returned to King John, bearing what must have been an exceedingly pessimistic report — no supplies, no spices, no slaves, and no precious stones (or none that Caô could possibly have seen). This barren land lacked even the most basic of man's necessities: water.

Despite this initial discouragement, a second Portuguese expedition issued forth from the court of King John. In 1487 headed by one of the king's most trusted knights, Bartholomeu Dias, a party of two 50-ton vessels (one carrying supplies) inched down the African coast. He was eventually to round the Cape of Good Hope from the Atlantic into the Indian ocean. But off the coast of South West Africa, he put in at a point which he called Angra Pequena (Narrow Bay). There he also erected a cross made of local limestone on a point over-looking the harbour. (The Dias cross was rediscovered in 1825 by the captain of "H.M.S. Barracouta" on an exploratory voyage. It had been fragmented — probably by treasure seekers digging at its base — and pieces of it may be found in museums as widely scattered as Lisbon and Auckland, New Zealand. The only pieces left in South West Africa are bits unearthed on Dias Point, Lüderitz, in 1953 and taken to the Windhoek Museum.)

More than a century and a half passed before other White men found their way to this desolate land. By that time, Holland had eclipsed Portugal and Spain as the major maritime power and the Dutch East India Company, sending trading parties to the Far East, around the tip of Africa, had established a parmanent supply stop at Cape Town. In 1670, a small exploration vessel was despatched from the Cape with the express purpose of touring the western shores. This vessel, the "Grundel" landed at Angra Pequena.

Seven years later, another ship, the "Bode" set forth from the Cape for the South West coast. The captain's log book shows that parties of Namas lived a perilous existence along the beach, dependent on the catch of an occasional seal for food. At Angra Pequena, his efforts to make friends with the Namas met with resistence and a brief hostile encounter was concluded by his retreat to the boat. This episode ended attempts to explore the country by the Cape Dutch, but the whaling and sealing ships of many nations continued to parallel the shore. American, French and British ships all touched in there; the remarkable discovery of the guano islands by Captain Morrell has already been described. The South West coast even provided a sometime refuge for pirates — what it lacked in comforts and facilities, it made up for in isolation — and legend has it that the notorius Captain Kidd once visited the area.

Meanwhile the Dutch colonists at the Cape were venturing overland farther and farther into the interior. The copper deposits south of the Orange River (then called the Gariep, or Great River) had been discovered and tapped. But in 1760, a farmer and ivory hunter, Jacobus Coetzee, crossed into the Transgariep and wandered northward some 30 miles — the first White man to enter South West Africa overland. Others such as Hendrik Hop and H. J. Wikar followed in 1761 and in August 1779, Captain Robert J. Gordon,[25] the Dutch-born son of Scottish immigrants, reached the Gariep which he believed to be a new discovery. He hoisted the Dutch flag and named it the Orange, in honour of the Royal House of Orange. This name stuck.

The early travellers to South West Africa — traders, hunters and adventurers — brought back fascinating tales of their journeys and of the vast variety and numbers of game to be found there. Their contacts with the local Namas and Bergdamas were sporadic, but what communication there was revealed the existence of a powerful nation of cattle-herding black people to the north. Mineral samples gathered by these explorers proved no trace of gold, but copper content was fairly common.

Three brothers who farmed on the Olifants River in the Western Cape decided to investigate these rumours, and in 1791, the first of the brothers, Willem van Reenen, set off overland with a few men on riding oxen. Along the way, they picked up a small number of Namas who consented to act as guides and the party struggled northward until all the oxen had died in the waterless wastes. Willem's party returned to the Cape without having contacted the cattle-rich Hereros.

A second expedition made by the other two brothers sailed North to Walvis Bay and ventured inland from

---

25. Captain (later Colonel) Gordon was a tragic man. He was in command of the Dutch garrison at Cape Town when the British attacked in 1795. His deeply divided loyalties drove him to a breakdown and, after surrender, he committed suicide.

there. But this journey also failed in its' objective. Nonetheless by the end of the century the first White man (Gideon Visagie) was farming north of the Orange River; trails had been opened throughout the south of this new land; Bushmen, Nama and Dama had been encountered, American whale hunters had set up small settlements at Walvis Bay and Swakopmund, and Angra Pequena, Halifax Island and Walvis Bay had been proclaimed as the property of the Dutch Government, the first authoritative claim to South West African soil. In 1795 the Cape passed into English hands and the British flag was hoisted at several spots along the South West African coast.

After the turn of the nineteenth century, the pace of travel to South West increased considerably for the vast regions north of the Swakop River still appeared on the maps as huge open spaces. In addition to the explorers and traders now came the missionaries. In 1807, the London Missionary Society established an outpost among the Namas at the site of present-day Warmbad, about 15 miles north of the Orange. But the missionaries, two brothers named Albrecht, found work among the Namas a disheartening experience. Their brick houses, carefully tended garden and beautiful piano (the first in South West), which had been brought all the way from Cape Town, were all destroyed by pillaging tribesmen in 1811 and the station had to be abandoned.

Missionaries, however, are a hardy lot, not easily discouraged. Others followed in the wake of the Albrechts, including three gentlemen dispatched in 1825 by the Wesleyan Missionary School who were murdered by their Bushmen guide. They were but drops in the steadily swelling stream of soul-savers who now determined to bring salvation to the natives.

One of these was a Rhenish missionary named Heinrich Schmelen who moved into South West with a party of about 150 of his congregation of Orlams and Namas, seeking relief from a prolonged drought in the Cape. Schmelen settled his band at Bethanie — the present town is on a line between Keetmanshoop and Lüderitz — and built a house there in 1814. It is the oldest existing building in South West.

Up until then no real contact had been made with the Hereros whose actions subsequently led to bitter strife and warfare in South West Africa. However, in 1836 Sir James Alexander accompanied by twelve White farmers visited the mission station at Warmbad and then various other places in the Nama territory and in the vicinity of Walvis Bay. His journey took him over 4,000 miles and well into the year 1837. He met various tribal chiefs including Jonker Afrikaander. He not only recorded for the first time words spoken in Herero but reported extensively on their habits and the enternecine strife among the various tribes.

This remarkable man travelled widely in the surrounding territory, his ox-wagon marking out roads to be followed later by other pioneers. (He mastered the language of the local Namas — the Orlams spoke Dutch — into which he translated the four Gospels.) He reached the Kuiseb River in 1824 and followed its course to Walvis Bay. He came across the Orlams Chief, Jonker Afrikaander, in the neighbourhood of Rehoboth. Afrikaander was to play a significant role in the early history of South West Africa.

In 1840, the London Missionary Society ceded its rights to the Rhenish Missionary Society of Barmen, Germany, which sought the task at Schmelen's prodding. The tide of German missionaries began filtering into the land later to be colonized by Berlin. According to Bismarck's thesis that "the missionary and the trader must precede the soldier", the German clerics were often accompanied by traders who set up general stores alongside the mission stations. Cases of enterprising Germans combining these two functions were frequent, with the proceeds of trade financing the work of conversion. Clothes, brandy and guns were soon being exchanged for cattle, sheep and ostrich feathers.

In some ways, the goals of these two functionaries worked at cross purposes. The missionaries were trying to induce nomadic herdsmen to settle down around agricultural communities to raise them on the scale of civilization. But the traders' aim was to offer more and more attractive goods until at last the infant settlements were reduced through trade to poverty. With their herds depleted by barter, the would-be settlers wandered off into the wilderness where they lived on milk and veld plants until their herds could be rebuilt through natural increase.

But the Rhenish missionaries persisted and over a period of a decade established stations near the headquarters of almost every tribal chief. They set up schools teaching practical subjects like agriculture and sewing in addition to the three R's. They laid out roads, and advised the local native authorities on boundaries and treaty negotiations. However, their services as traders were much more readily accepted than their other efforts, since it was thirty years before the first Herero convert was baptised!

And their peace-making efforts were only a little more successful. These first White men had stumbled into the territory at the time of the greatest period of upheaval in South West history to date.

Midway into the 19th century the Hereros and Namas were continually clashing at friction points across their common border, as raiding parties rustled cattle and plundered villages with great vigour. The story of the rivalry between these two nations is a bloody but fascinating one, in which White men played a disturbingly naive part in their clumsy efforts to secure peace.

When the Dutch were planting the first outposts of civilization at the Cape, there seem to have been only three groups of non-White peoples in South West Africa; the Bushmen, Damara and the Namas.

The Bushmen were then and remain today probably the most primitive of all the world's aboriginal peoples. They belong to the Khoisan peoples (Khoi meaning Hottentot and San for Bushmen) and are generally short in stature with a light yellowish brown skin. In South West Africa the Bushmen consist predominantly of three groups namely the *Khung, Heikum* and *Barakwengo.* Owing to their nomadic way of life the Bushmen have never led a settled existence at any time or place. There is no generally defined area which could be called Bushmanland. Small bands of Bushmen did frequent certain water sources and hunting grounds as is apparent from the many Bushmen place-names. The numerically more powerful Khung lived in the region extending from Eastern Ovamboland through the Omaheke as far as the Botswana border and north-wards into the Okavango area. The Heikum inhabit the region extending from the Etosha pans into the southern portion of Ovamboland. The Barakwengo live along the lower part of the Okavango area and are scattered in small bands, almost as far as the Kwando River in Western Caprivi.

The Bushmen live quiet lives roaming the fringes of the Kalahari and even penetrating deep into its water-less wastes, avoiding wherever possible contact (and hence conflict) with other peoples.

They were unquestionably the first inhabitants of the country. How they arrived and whence they came are mysteries shrouded in the mists of prehistory, but they must surely have been there centuries before the Namas came. They tilled no ground and herded no cattle, con-sidering the wild game to be uniquely their own.

Bushmen paintings are scattered across the whole of Southern Africa, but they were forced first by the invading Namas, then the Bantu and finally by encroach-ing white settlement to retreat into those lands unwanted by others such as semi-desert area of the Kalahari. Rather than defend their preserves against nations so obviously superior, they retreated into no-man's-land.

The soft clicking language and gentle ways of the Bushmen belie an enormous inner strength and adaptability. Their need for mobility vied with the advantages of a complex society, and the Bushmen compromised by organising into family groups of rarely more than twenty. Members of the group not able to contribute to the general welfare were gently but firmly excluded, the orphaned suckling baby was killed and the toothless, useless grandmother was left behind when the family moved to a new hunting ground.

The moral code of the Bushmen is possibly the strictest on earth; and the threat of ostracism is usually sufficient to ensure its observance. Domestic arguments are settled by mutual concession. They have a high regard for private property and, in a land where water is the primary exigency, a Bushman will die of thirst rather than drink from the water cache of another.

Yet despite their arduous life, they are a merry and humorous people. Songs and rhythmic dances render their scanty leisure hours around the evening campfire a time of joy and recreation. And the fertile imaginations of their story-tellers have devised explanations about their origins, their surroudings and the events of the natural and political world around them.

One such myth tells of how God, in creating the world and its people, threw down a huge lump of earth. It splintered on impact into pieces of all sizes. The bigger pieces became the bigger nations of the world while the bits of crumbling dust were turned into Bush-

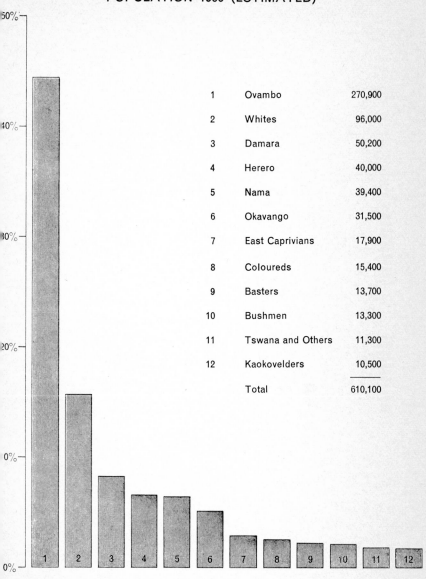

SOUTH WEST AFRICA
POPULATION 1966 (ESTIMATED)

1	Ovambo	270,900
2	Whites	96,000
3	Damara	50,200
4	Herero	40,000
5	Nama	39,400
6	Okavango	31,500
7	East Caprivians	17,900
8	Coloureds	15,400
9	Basters	13,700
10	Bushmen	13,300
11	Tswana and Others	11,300
12	Kaokovelders	10,500
	Total	610,100

Bushman woman.

Coloured, Windhoek.

A Caprivian Chief.

men. But while God gave to the larger peoples herds of cattle and sheep, he compensated the little Bushmen by making them a present of all the animals of the wild. These they have hunted ever since, with their poison-tipped arrows and pointed throwing sticks.

Today there are still about 12,000 Bushmen left in South West Africa. No political organization for the Bushmen has even been tried or has been in existence. There are no bonds between the various bands. Their languages differ from one another. Within the band leadership is determined by hunting prowess, personality and age. The band is usually very small and social life very simple. Material possessions are extremely limited usually confined to a bow and arrow, skin garments and adornments and some utility articles. Their dwellings are hastily constructed of grass or mats.

The majority no longer lead such a strictly nomadic life, sometimes settling for a while at certain points and even accepting work when food and water is scarce, but the old ways die hard.

The *Namas* — also called Namaquas — were members of the great Hottentot family that roamed Southern Africa for centuries before the arrival of the White man. Nama beach-dwellers must have met Caô and Dias on their first excursions to the shores. The Nama belong to the Khoisan race and are also light of colour and short of stature. Together with the Bushman and the Damara they are the oldest inhabitants of South West Africa. They consist of various tribes who settled in the regions of Hoachanas, south of Keetmanshoop, along the Fish River, Warmbad and the upper and lower regions of the Kuiseb River as well as in the vicinity of Sesfontein. The Nama language contains the characteristic clicks of the Khoisan.

Traditionally the Nama are cattle farmers and do not go in for agriculture. Their socio-economic unit is the patrilineal family group which functions within the wider Nama group. The family units usually functioned separately under Chiefs and Councillors who sometimes united against a common enemy.

Today the Nama number about 35,000 souls or nearly seven per cent of the total population of South West Africa. As a result of their later amalgamation with the Orlams who brought with them considerable European influences and the work of missionaries in the eighteenth century, Namas are increasingly selling their labour to White employers but in the more remote areas continue to maintain an economy based solely on animal husbandry.

In addition to the Bushmen and the Namas, there was another group living in South West and who arrived there before the 17th century. These people, the *Damaras* (or Damas) are a short thick-set people, decidedly Negroid in racial characteristics, and are not part of the great Bantu family of Central and Southern Africa, although they show Bantu influences. They were universally despised by their neighbours and were enslaved first by the Namas and later by the immigrating Hereros. Although they spoke the language of their Nama masters, they had some words of their own not used by the Namas, and these words have been connected linguistically with languages in the Southern Sudan from which they may have come. The Namas called them "Cloudaman", which means filthy black people (or dung) and they acquired the name Berg-Damaras (or Mountain Damas) because they retreated periodically to the mountain caves when danger threatened.

Among all the peoples of South West, they alone understood the arts of copper and iron smelting and one of the first tasks set them by the Hereros was the forging of iron speartips.

Prior to the arrival of the Whites the way of life of the Damara did not differ very greatly from that of the nomadic Bushmen. They had no form of agriculture or animal husbandry worth mentioning. As a result of their oppression and enslavement by the Herero and the Nama, the Damara never developed into a larger established community in their own home area.

With the arrival of the Whites and an end to the internecine strife and slavery the Damara were able to develop a new way of life. Today there are about 44,000 Damaras, large numbers of whom have been absorbed now in the economy of the southern part of the country. They became westernised more quickly than the other groups and the Christian religion was readily adopted.

———————

About three centuries ago, there began the first two of three great Bantu migrations into the territory.

The Okavango and their cousins the Ovambo came from Central and East Africa as part of the same migrations that took the Zulu and Xhosa into South Africa. Driving their herds before them, they arrived in the rich land along the Okavango and Kunene Rivers.

The *Okavango,* who now inhabit the extreme northeastern section of South West, settled along the river that bears their name. This mighty stream — which except for the Zambezi, has the most constant flow in Southern Africa — provided them with water for their cattle and crops and an unending supply of fish which they seine in funnel-shaped reed baskets.

The Okavango which today number about 28,000 people actually comprise five individual tribes each inhabiting an area of its own, close to the southern bank of the Okavango. Numerically the Kuangari tribe is the strongest and their language is generally used except in the case of the Mbukushu tribe. The people themselves are established tillers and herdsmen whose mode of living corresponds greatly with that of the Ovambo. They utilize the grazing and veld products on a communal basis and have individual right of occupation over cultivated land although no payment is made for this. The land is allocated by the peoples authority which consists of a hereditary chieftanship for each of the five tribes. The Chief functions in conjunction with counsellors and village headman. Although each tribe's chief is autonomous in his area, they sometimes meet to discuss matters of general interest.

The social organization of the Okavangos is based on the matrilineal system and children belong to the lineal group and clan of their mother. The tendency is to live in family villages in which the family naturally constitutes the most important socio-economic unit.

The *Ovambo* moved further west where they settled the land between the Etosha Pan and the Kunene River extending west to the Kaokoveld. A strong, dark people, they also practised fishing and agriculture. The adequate rainfall in this area provided some of the best farming land in South West Africa.

A well-developed social organization, coupled with this comparative ease in obtaining the necessities of life, resulted in a happy and contented people. Today the Ovambos are far and away the most numerous of all South West's many groups, totalling some 239,000 or just a little under half of all the territory's population.

The Ovambo nation is made up of eight different tribes each with its own residential area. Of the eight the Kuanyama and Ndonga are numerically the most powerful forming about two thirds of the population. The social organization of the Ovambo peoples is fairly similar to that of the Okavango just described with the family forming the most important socio-economic unit. Their political organization is well developed with hereditary chiefs at the head of three tribes. The chiefs are advised by headmen and, where no chiefs are in power, the tribal headman advised by village elders, is the authority. Headmen are elected by the people and the title is not hereditary. The government of each tribe functions as an autonomous authority within the homeland of that people.

The Ovambo live a life corresponding closely to that of the Okavango but while the Okavango obtain their land for cultivation from the tribal chief, the Ovambo has to purchase his right of occupation by payment of cattle to the district headmen who purchased this on his part from the headmen or chief.

Since 1870 the Ovambo peoples have been strongly influenced by the activities of the Finnish Mission, later followed by the Roman Catholic and Anglican Churches. As a result of the educational services provided by the churches and administration of South West Africa, the literacy rate among the Ovambos is among the very highest in Africa, including the Bantu of South Africa.

Because the Ovambos are geographically and politically remote from the rest of the territory and no great danger of a permanently expatriate population exists, as it does in the case of some potential Bantustans of the Republic of South Africa, the South African offer of self-government to Ovamboland was not only a natural outflow of the policy of separate development but endorsed by the Ovambos themselves.

The third great influx of Bantu was that of the *Hereros,* who crossed the Kunene River during the late 17th and early 18th centuries from the Mossamedes Province of Angola. Part of the Herero nation remained behind in the Kaokoveld where the Ovahimba (elected people) and their poor brothers the Ovachimba (piglets of the earth) — still live. The main stream of the nation, continued southward occupying empty territory until they reached outposts of the Nama settlements. They were mistakenly called Damaras (black skinned people) by the early White men from the Nama word for them and the country they occupied — from the Kaokoveld to Bechuanaland and south past Windhoek — became known as Damaraland, a designation it still holds today. After their revolt against the German administration in 1903-1907 the Herero lost most of their land and cattle — in fact they were practically disintegrated. After South Africa occupied the territory in 1915 refugees began returning and new lands were allocated to them.

Ovambo legend has it that the Ovambo and Herero peoples descended from two brothers who encamped at the great omumborombonga tree near Ondongo. From there, they separated, one going West into Kaokoveld with the Hereros and the other staying behind with the Ovambos. The legend may have some foundations since the omumborombongo is sacred to the Hereros. The two nations share many other customs, including their belief in the power of a sacred fire, which, if extinguished, brings disaster.

The origin of the word Herero is shrouded in mystery but a possible explanation lies in the reputed answer of an ancestral chief who, when asked if his wandering brothers would remain in South West Africa or return to Botswana, replied: "Va *herera* okukare" (They have decided to stay). In any case, at least since the middle of the 19th century, they have been commonly called Hereros, or "the people who have decided".

The Hereros regard themselves as the aristrocrats of South West Africa. They are generally tall and slender with a dignified bearing. Their aquiline features suggest a possible Hamitic origin; they came from a "land of fountains" known as Raruu. This place has yet to be possitively identified, but it seems reasonable that it was a marshland west of Lake Tanganyika and that several centuries ago they were part of the Bantu migration southwards from the Great Lakes settling in Angola by the turn of the 16th century.

They speak a beautiful and lyrical Bantu language which has lent itself to the naming of many geographical places in South West. They are a musical people and the traditional songs which survive recount epic tales of their leaders and describe in detail the strength and beauty of their cattle, a trait they share with many of the cattle-orientated Bantu peoples of Africa. In their social structure they maintain both a patrilineal and a matrilineal system. Traditionally this group are nomadic herdsmen and it was because of this that they encroached on the lands of the Nama and so sparked off a long and bitter war. The land of the Herero unlike the Ovambo and Okavango is communally owned.

The Herero have never been united under a central political authority. The present form of government consists of Headmen and Councillors in the various home areas. Today the Herero number about 35,000 people or less than seven per cent of the total population. They are established mostly in the southern section of the country and consist of two sections, the Herero and the

Mbanderu.   Approximately half are employed in the diversified economy in the south of the country while the rest are herdsmen.   The Herero have a religious organization of their own known as *Oruwano*.

After their arrival and settlement in South West, it was perhaps inevitable that his nation of herdsmen would eventually clash with their southern neighbours the Namas, who for centuries had ventured occasionally to the north with their own cattle and sheep.   Sporadic outbreaks of violence were the rule when the White man first arrived in the land, but the major force of the rivalry was not to sweep the country until the middle and latter half of he 19th century.   In this struggle the long-resident Namas (called the Red Nation because of their dull red complexion) found overwhelming support from an unexpected source, the *Orlams.*

The origin of the word *Orlam* is uncertain but it may have been a perversion of the Malay "Orang Lama", meaning *old* (and hence wise) *man*.   In any case the Orlams were five clans of Namas who came back into South West from south of the Orange where they had lived for generations.   In the Cape, their blood lines had mixed with some of the Dutch pioneers and they served the White man on farms and as domestics, speaking his language and adopting his ways.

Towards the end of the 18th century, many of them began drifting north again, variously seeking more freedom or escaping from the police for charges ranging from petty thefts to murder.   One of the clans was headed by a man named Jager Afrikaander, a sort of "Jesse James of the Cape" who had murdered his Dutch master and escaped to the southern bank of the Orange with a goodly amount of stolen cattle. Jonker Afrikaander, the younger son of this wily old character, saw that his fortune lay in following his father's wicked habits. He set out north at the head of a party of like-minded renegades, stealing cattle at every turn which he used to buy guns and shot from the traders. As his power spread, so did his fame.

Realising the futility of trying to stop the Hereros on their own the Nama Chief sought the aid of Jonker Afrikaander and his Orlams — Jonker agreed. In three major battles, he defeated the Hereros and made off with their herds. Many of the Herero fled back to the safety of the Kaokoveld; the others, devastated by the modern fire arms of Afrikaander, decided to come to terms.

The Orlams' chief decided to make his capital at Windhoek and it was there that Sir James Alexander, the British explorer, found him in 1837 amidst a flourishing town of about 1,200 people. Jonker had chosen the site not only because it reminded him of his home in the Cape, but also because of its strategic position; he certainly did not intend to set up a buffer between the Namas and the Hereros, but rather he was motivated by the thought that from Windhoek he could observe the Hereros to the north and chart their cattle movements.

Only 45 miles to his north lay Okahandja, sacred capital of one of the richest Herero tribes and seat of their most important chief, Tjamuaha. As the Hereditary Guardian of the Sacred Ancestral Fire, Tjamuaha was forced to consider the welfare of his people. He realized that they were in no position to engage in open warfare with the Orlams tyrant and through a so-called "treaty" with Afrikaander was virtually reduced to the role of a vassal.

To pacify Jonker, the Herero leader agreed, however reluctantly, to his settlement at Windhoek and to send his son and heir, Maherero to Windhoek to be trained by Jonker in the use of fire-arms, or so he thought. The treatment of this proud young prince in Windhoek was far from kindly, a treatment which the Namas would come to regret. He suffered all manner of verbal and physical indignities, not the least of which was being bound to the wheel of an ox-wagon for several days to teach him that Afrikaander held all the power. But, although his father endured these insults for the sake of his cattle and people, a fierce desire for redress and revenge grew steadily in the breast of young Maherero. Together with this smouldering hatred, Maherero also took away from Windhoek a knowledge of the efficient use of firepower — the source of the Orlams' power.

It was, however, the Namas and the Hereros themselves who began the longest period of strife. First the Nama Chief murdered a Herero leader Kabitjene without Afrikaander lifting a finger to help the Hereros recover their stolen cattle. The Herero Chief Tjamuaha thereupon decided to withdraw from his so-called alliance with Afrikaander and within a few months Katuneko, a Herero Chief, brutally murdered a group of Mbanderu tribesmen, stealing all their cattle. Afrikaander, using this as an excuse, immediately set upon the nearest Herero tribe. A period of terror and confusion set in. He struck to the north and east, frequently assisted by Herero warriors who had joined his motly army. Falling on the unsuspecting Herero encampments, his men rivalled the savagery of Atilla's Huns. They massacred men, women and children, hacking off the limbs of women in their eagerness to obtain their copper ornaments. Following Jonker's example, the other Nama chiefs launched raiding parties and the "Red Nation" practically annihilated the Eastern Hereros (Mbanderus). To make matters worse Herero began attacking Herero, greatly adding to the reign of terror. Even Maherero was pressed into Afrikaander's service for the terrible work and a missionary, the Rev. Hugo Hahn, recorded that the young prince was like "a mouse in the claws of a cat".

But a decade of pillaging had taken its toll from Hereroland and the raids, aggravated by periodic drought, left the countryside all but empty. Those Hereros who had survived Afrikaander's murdering hoards were enslaved by the Namas. Whole areas lay desolate, with nothing moving about but the wind.

The Rhenish missionaries tried to shelter the fleeing Hereros and appealed to the Cape government for assistance in stopping the holocaust, which only succeeded in provoking the wrath of Jonker against them. He had, in the past, frequently acted as their benefactor in their efforts to reach the Hereros and he regarded their ingratitude as traitorous.

124

A conference of missionaries in 1856 reported that: "The Herero race has so far as we know, ceased to exist. There are now only individuals left, without any kind of link between them, who wander about in a state of great misery."

The Nama reign of terror was not to be stopped by outside interference, however. Its momentum died through its very success, abetted by the death of its instigator. With nothing left to plunder south of Ovamboland, Jonker led an expedition to the far north in pursuit of the last fleeing Hereros. The party was gone six months and on it Jonker acquired 20,000 head of cattle and a fatal disease.

In 1861, the Nama Scourge lay down to die unrepentant at Okahandja, barely a hundred yards from where his old enemy Tjamuaha of the Herero also lay grievously ill. Perhaps in the end Jonker realized the extent of his mischief, for he called for his own son, Christiaan, and for Maherero. When they stood before him, he enjoined them to live in peace, ruling over Nama and Herero alike. (It was said that he handed Christiaan his right shoe and to Maherero the left.) He was buried nearby under a camelthorn tree.

When Tjamuaha heard that his seemingly invincible enemy had been vanquished by death, he felt he could himself die with honour. He also sent for the two young heirs and, with equal solemnity, ordered them to live peaceably. But when Christiaan Afrikaander asked for his blessing, the old man refused it. He instructed the young Nama chief to bring him a blanket of fresh lambskins in order to merit a special benediction. When it was produced, he still refused to bless Christiaan, gaining a final sly triumph over the Namas in the waste of so many lambs.

In death — as never in life — the Herero leader inspired his prostrate people. He had promised his sons that "when I am dead, I will free you of the Namas". Legend has it that two incidents lent immediate affirmation to the prophesy. Shortly after he breathed his last a tornado arose near his dwelling and swept across the plain, levelling the Nama huts in its path. "It is our father's spirit," said the Hereros, and hope of relief rose for the first time in their breasts.

At the burial, the emissary sent by Christiaan Afrikaander dismounted to pay final respects to Tjamuaha. As he remounted, his horse bolted, and the unfortunate messenger was thrown and killed instantly, his back snapped.

———

While the Namas were terrorizing the land and the missionaries were establishing settlements among the people, a number of explorers — particularly Alexander, Galton and the Swede Anderson — were tracing lines across the as yet largely unknown map of South West Africa.

The first was Sir James Alexander, an officer of the Royal Horse Guards, who left England in 1836 for an expedition financed by the Royal Geographic Society, and whose travels were discussed earlier in this chapter.

Next came Sir Francis Galton, a cousin of Charles Darwin who landed in Walvis Bay in 1850, bent on reaching Lake Ngami in Bechuanaland from the West. (It had recently been discovered by David Livingstone.) In his journey to the north-east, he was accompanied by the naturalist Charles Anderson. The two eventually arrived in Ovamboland where they found a "charming corn country, yellow and broad as a sea before us."

Galton's expedition was extremely valuable in gathering information about the uncharted wilds of South West Africa. Although he failed to reach his goal, stopping only seven miles short of Lake Ngami, he penetrated the Kalahari east of Gobabis and was the first to see the Etosha Pan and Lake Otjikoto.

In the manner of the day, Galton described the peoples he met on his journeys in terms of racial characteristics. He had only compliments for the Hereros and Ovambos, but the Namas came out rather less well, having as Galton said "the felon face . . . prominent cheek bones, bullet-shaped head, cowering but restless eyes."

His meeting with Jonker Afrikaander was a piece of quixotic staging worthy of inclusion in any account of South West history.

At the time, the Nama leader was in the midst of his tyranny against the Hereros and Galton had hoped to bring some measure of peace to the land. He decided to storm the bastion of the tyrant himself. Got up in a red English hunting costume — complete with boots and cap — and riding an enormous ox, he thundered into the Nama camp right up to the doorway of Jonker's hut. There he imposed upon the astonished Nama leader conditions of order which were to bring about a year-long hiatus in the strife-torn area.

When Galton returned to London, Charles Anderson remained to make his own mark on the explorations of South West. Where Galton had failed, he succeeded in reaching Lake Ngami. He travelled ceaselessly over the country, financing his wanderings from the considerable trading enterprises he established, and was the first White man to see the Okavango River.

Anderson, who was by training a naturalist and Swedish born, also crossed paths with the Orlams, but unlike Galton, he took a direct hand in their dispute with the Herero. When his entire herd of cattle was one day stolen by Orlams Namas he decided on a punitive expedition. In 1864 together with another early South West Africa explorer and big game hunter Frederick Green, he led the Hereros under Maherero into battle against their enemies. The Namas were routed and the star of the Hereros began to rise once more in the North.

The victory was a sweet one for Anderson, who was appointed by the Hereros' "military commander for the period of his natural life or as long as he desires to hold office". But his success was short-lived for in 1866 he set off on an expedition for Ovamboland from which he was never to return. He died a lonely and painful death in the wilds, plagued by fever and deserted by his native bearers. He is considered today to be the greatest of the many explorers on the country.

Herrero women.

Ovambo Women.

Herero woman (Himba tribe) Kaokoveld.

CURRENT AND CAPITAL EXPENDITURE IN RESPECT OF INDIGENOUS GROUPS:[1]
1963/64–1966/67

Particulars	Current expenditure					Capital expenditure	Total expenditure
	1963/64	1964/65	1965/66	1966/67	1963/64–1966/67		
Education and training	903,028	1,049,935	1,133,810	1,333,879	4,420,652	3,192,562	7,613,214
Health	1,820,214	1,834,461	2,881,214	3,393,821	9,929,710	3,242,058	13,171,768
Housing	—	—	—	—	—	6,802,836	6,802,836
Agriculture ..	—	—	—	—	—	839,078	839,078
Water (boreholes, dams, etc.).. ..	—	—	—	—	—	6,107,555	6,107,555
Purchase of land to enlarge homelands	—	—	—	—	—	22,276,462	22,276,462
Roads, bridges, and airports	—	—	—	—	—	9,498,704	9,498,704
Postal and telecommunication services	356,602	484,264	434,775	515,000	1,790,641	83,858	1,874,499
Non-residential buildings	—	—	—	—	—	2,703,785	2,703,785
Miscellaneous ..	369,089	467,695	559,171	1,095,580	2,491,535	3,803,102	6,294,637
Total	3,448,933	3,836,355	5,008,970	6,338,280	18,632,538	58,550,000	77,182,538

[1] Department of Bantu Administration and Development, Bantu Investment Corporation, and South West Africa Administration.

Until Anderson's travels and discoveries the territory between the Orange River and the Kunene and Okavango had no geographical designation. *Anderson was the first man to refer to this territory as South West Africa.* His grave can be visited today a few miles beyond the South West African border in Angola.

The death of Anderson, however, did not leave the Hereros friendless in their struggle against the Namas, for a strong young leader had arisen in their midst. After the death of Tjamuaha his father, Maherero had retreated with a few followers to the Kaiser Wilhelm mountain, east of Okahandja. There they licked their wounds and gathered strength for the coming revenge. As word spread of their refuge, individual Hereros began to straggle into Maherero's camp to seek his protection.

As their numbers increased, Maherero shifted his headquarters to Otjimbinue on the Swakop River to the south-west. He was attacked there by the Orlams under Christiaan in 1863. In the ensuing battle, Maherero emerged victorious and Christiaan Afrikaander was killed. The fleeting Orlams were pursued mercilessly by the jubilant Herero warriors, who killed everyone in sight.

Christiaan was succeeded by his younger brother, Jan Jonker, who determined to recapture his father's position of advantage over the Hereros. He moved his camp first south and then east to Gobabis on the edge of the Kalahari where he formed an alliance with several Nama tribes. Maherero on the other hand received unexpected assistance from a Nama tribe called the Swartboois. The explorer Anderson, enfuriated by the loss of cattle stolen from him by the Orlams, then marched out with Maherero and on June 22, 1864, the Orlams were beaten and routed at a place known as Gam-Aam or "Two Waters".

For the rest of the decade, Maherero and his people were allowed to rebuild their depleted herds and enjoy their pastoral lives in tranquility. But towards the end of the 1860's a great drought forced Maherero to look south again into Namaland for grazing land. He assembled his warriors and set off on what came to be called the Scorpion Campaign. because the starving Hereros were reduced to roasting scorpions to assuage their hunger. Hundreds died along the way and everywhere he turned, Maherero found the Namas as desperate as his own people, for South West Africa was then in the grip of a severe drought. In 1870, at Okahandja the Rhenish missionary, Dr. Hahn brought about reluctant truce between Jan Jonker leader of the Orlams and the Namas and the Herero chieftain, bringing to an end fifty years of treachery, anarchy and genocide.

The Maherero Treaty of Okahandja maintained peace for ten years and also determined the boundaries between Namaland and Hereroland. During this period Maherero sent two letters to the authorities in the Cape requesting advice on how to govern the land better and what to do when the Nama would not leave them in peace. As a result a special commissioner was sent to South West Africa who remained there until 1880 when animosities between the Nama, now dominated by Orlam leaders, and the Herero again flared up into violence.

130

The meeting at Okahandja also saw an agreement of a different kind. Yet another group of immigrants had arrived in South West Africa to seek their living off the harsh land. These were the "Basters", a people of mixed descent whose family names — Van Wyk, Beukes, Campbell — show only too well the pattern of their origin, and they took pride in calling themselves bastards to distinguish them from the surrounding barbarians.

Being the disinherited sons of White pioneers and their Nama women, these families had lived their own lives on the virgin lands at the outer edges of White settlements in the Cape. The Basters were ousted from these lands in 1865 by the Cape government, which was pressed for farms for the growing community of immigrating Whites.

They gathered their women and children into ox-wagons and, carrying their Bibles and driving their animals, trekked across the Orange River in search of new homes. They found them in the ample grazing lands of northern Namaland. The Baster elders, led by Hermanus van Wyk, sought and received permission to settle at Rehoboth from the local Nama chieftain. For this concession they had to pay the Nama chief a horse annually. Here at Rehoboth, they set up a tiny republic governed under the laws of their fathers ("Vaderlike Wet"), and lived in peace amidst the swirling unrest around their idyllic enclave. The Rehoboth area eventually became generally recognised as their "Father-land" and was recognised as such by the South African Government in 1915.

Today they number about 11,000 persons. Animal husbandry is their chief occupation. In the sphere of culture and religion they maintain a western way of life. Their form of Government is still one of a chief and councillors.

During the period of the Cape Government's representative in the Nama and Herero area, the Dorsland Trekkers (Thirstland Pioneers) trekked through the area. After first progressing through the territory known today as Botswana to a point west of the Okavango swamps they turned south via Grootfontein, and, proceeding south of the Etosha pan, entered the Kaokoveld where they remained for some time. From there they crossed the Kunene River into Angola. A small band returned in 1882 and established the shortlived Republic of Uppingtonia between Grootfontein, Otavi and Waterberg.

The representatives of the Cape Government were, however, recalled after the outbreak of hostilities between the Nama and Herero in 1880 and when the Germans took over most of South West Africa as a protectorate in 1884 the Dorsland Trekkers relinquished their republic.

During all this time, South West Africa had been spurned by the empire-building nations of Europe. Suddenly, with all the more choice areas of Africa already gobbled up, they began looking more seriously at the vast tract of sand and sun-drenched plain in South West Africa. The two leading contenders were those whose nationals had already arrived on the scene: England and Germany. For decades, the Rhenish missionaries had been sending pleas to Berlin, begging the King of Prussia to assert dominance over the area and establish order. But not until after the confederation of the German states in 1871 was Germany ready to assume the task of imperial expansion. Chancellor Bismarck proved a reluctant colonizer, however, and the entreaties for formal protection by the German missionaries in South West Africa were to fall on deaf ears for another decade.

Great Britain proved hardly more amenable to exerting formal control over the territory. The first tentative sign of interest came in 1876 with the dispatch of Palgrave to South West Africa. Palgrave's mission was, of course, the result of the two letters from Maherero to the Cape government. His task was to investigate the country, in which he was aided by an official "photographer", and to negotiate documents of protection with the peoples of South West Africa as a prelude to annexation.

The Hereros agreed readily enough and Palgrave managed to secure the permission of the Rehoboth community to the protection arrangements. But the Namas were unwilling to submit themselves to the colonial authority and Palgrave noted in his report to the Cape that, when the time came for annexation, Namaland would have to be invaded. The Cape parliament balked at the idea of having to back annexation of this unruly and supposedly valueless land with military and police authority and the only tangible result of Palgrave's mission was the annexation of Walvis Bay in 1878.

Later Maherero was moved to comment, not without bitterness: "The British flag flew here. It waved this way and that; we attached ourselves to it, and we were waved backwards and forwards with it."

Palgrave was on his third mission to South West Africa in 1880, negotiating with the Namas at Gobabis, when war suddenly flared again with the Hereros.

A new Orlams leader, Hendrik Witbooi, had arisen to challenge Jan Jonker and the Afrikaander tribe in heading the Nama rivalry with the Hereros. His rise to power came in a period of raids, wars, ambushes, attacks and retreats between Namas and Hereros which spelt utter confusion.

Hendrik considered himself divinely inspired and lost no time in joining battle with Maherero. For the better part of the 1880's his warriors harried the shifting border between the two nations. Once again the exposed missionaries and traders sent entreaties to Berlin and Cape Town, begging for imperial protection in the disordered land.

Chancellor Bismarck inquired politely if the British were prepared to extend aid to German nationals in South West Africa. The reply was that Great Britain felt no responsibility for any area other than the Walvis Bay district annexed in 1878. So the German citizens in South West were left to defend themselves as best they could. There was a growing number of them to do so.

The most important of these was Adolf Lüderitz, a Bremen tobacco merchant who had travelled widely in

North and Central America as a young man. Lüderitz was obsessed with the idea of building an African colonial empire for Germany and, as much for patriotic as commercial reasons, he sent an agent (Heinrich Vogelzang) to Angra Pequena in 1883 to purchase land from the resident chieftains. A year later he went out himself to inspect the new "Lüderitzland" for which he by then had secured the protection of the German government. Additional purchases from the Namas, who were only too happy to sell a supposedly worthless strip of beach, gave Lüderitz possession of the coast all the way to the Orange River.

The agitated British authorities at the Cape realized too late the cost of their vacillation and a British naval vessel dispatched to Angra Pequena found, much to its chagrin, the German gunboat "Nautilus" lying in the harbour. Germany had laid claim to the territory and in August, 1884, a German Protectorate was formally declared over the area of Lüderitz Bay.

The role of Adolf Lüderitz in German South West Africa was pivotal — but short. Two years after his arrival at Angra Pequena, he accompanied a prospecting expedition along the Orange River. In October, 1886, he attempted to return to his base in a small canvas boat and was drowned. In his honour, the German government changed the name of his town to Lüderitzbucht (Lüderitz Bay) and erected a small monument to his memory on Shark Island.

At the death of Lüderitz, a German company, the Deutsche Kolonial Gesellschaft für Südwestafrika, took over his holdings. In the tradition of other great chartered imperial firms (the British East India Company in Asia, the Dutch East India Company at the Cape), the company was given a virtually absolute domain over the area. It could maintain its own private army for the preservation of order and prevention of attack, build railroads, grant mineral concessions and otherwise administer affairs in its developing property.

But the financial strain of opening up a land which needed everything and offered nothing in return proved too great, and the German government was compelled to assume responsibility for its newly acquired protectorate.

Soon after the proclamation of the German protectorate of Lüderitz Bay, the Germans also declared the coastal area from the Orange River up to Cape Frio, excluding Walvis Bay, as a protectorate. In October 1884 the German flag was also raised over Namaland. In the following year German agreements with the remaining Namas, the "Rooi Nasie" (the Red Nation) and with the Basters at Rehoboth followed. In October, 1885, the Hereros accepted German protection.

While Germany was extending its sphere of influence to the interior, Britain, in March, 1885, proclaimed a protectorate over Bechuanaland. In the north the Portuguese were already in possession of Angola. The boundaries of the new territory of South West Africa were then laid down in broad outline by agreements with Portugal in 1886 and with Britain in 1890. All of present-day South West Africa was included in this new German colony-cum protectorate but the area around

Walvis Bay which had been incorporated in the Cape Colony in 1884 retained its status quo.

Germany's diplomatic fiat of annexation was followed up by the arrival in South West Africa of Dr. Heinrich Goering (Göring), appointed by Bismarck as a special "Reich Commissioner" to solicit treaties of "protection" with the native peoples. This able civil servant, whose son Herman was to become Field Marshal under the Nazi regime, went first to Maherero and succeeded in negotiating an agreement with him by promises of aid against the Namas.

Negotiations in the southern areas fared less well. The Rehobothers, with their natural affinity to the White civilization in a land of heathen non-White peoples, were readily enlisted. They obtained a charter from the Kaiser guaranteeing them complete sovereignty over internal affairs in their 5,000 square miles territory in return for furnishing fighting men — crack shots all — at the request of the German authorities. But the Nama clans were practically unanimous in their refusal of the German treaties.

In any case, Dr. Göring did not have the men and arms with which to back up his promises of protection. In April 1888, Hendrik Witbooi and his Nama warriors surprised the Hereros. Only their superior defence installations enabled them to repel the attackers. But Maherero was sufficiently disillusioned with German "protection" to revoke the German treaties and to expel its emissary. Dr. Göring withdrew hastily to Walvis Bay, from which he returned to Berlin where he no doubt advised the colonial authorities that means stronger than friendly promises would be required to control South West Africa.

The vanguard of Germany's stronger means arrived in July of the following year. A token force of 21 riflemen, under the command of Captain Kurt von Francois, was instructed to establish order. This task obviously involved the defeat of Hendrik Witbooi.

Von Francois' plan was a simple one. Not having the manpower to confront Witbooi in the open, he established a fort along the Windhoek-Walvis Bay road where he could block the arms flow to the Namas. Leaving a contingent of his men there, he moved on to Windhoek — deserted since the eclipse of the Afrikaander tribe — and constructed the Alte Feste.

As Jonker before him, Von Francois recognized the strategic importance of this site. It lay at the crossroads of the country and from it he could be supplied from Walvis Bay, go north to the Hereros at Okahandja or strike at the Namas to the south. Gradually the German commander was reinforced by fresh recruits from Germany — including his younger brother, who was to be killed in South West in 1904 — and by 1893 he felt strong enough to challenge Witbooi. He sent one final ultimatum to Hendrik demanding that he submit to German protection. The answer was a defiant insult in which the truculent Nama leader declared that those under protection were the slaves of the protectors. "Against whom are we to be protected?" he railed.

In a surprise dawn attack, von Francois' "schutz-truppe" assaulted the Witbooi camp at Hoornkrans near Rehoboth. The women and children, and Witbooi's diary were captured but the wily Nama and his men slipped through the fingers of the Germans and retreated into the mountains. He realized that he was unable to resist such tactics indefinitely and therefore sought an alliance with his old enemies the Hereros.

He sent a letter to Samuel Maherero, who had become head of the Herero nation after his father's death in October 1890. Samuel was a baptised Christian and, hence unable to inherit the position of keeper of the Sacred Ancestral Fire. But he was trying, between his tipples of trader brandy, to fill the shoes of his father and grandfather. He could not see himself coming to terms with the Namas, even against the common threat of rising German power, and he completely rejected the overture. He hoped in fact to enlist German support in his favour.

Von Francois acting as mediator between Witbooi and Samuel Maherero succeeded in concluding a treaty between the two. Thus he brought to an end a century of strife between the Nama and the Herero with neither being able to claim victory. The wars had left the country exhausted, stocks depleted, thousands killed on either side and bitterness in the hearts of everyone. Henceforth an alien element, the Germans, would be calling the tune.

In 1894, after five years in South West Africa von Francois was recalled. He was replaced as military commander (subsequently appointed first Civil Governor), by Major Theodor Leutwein, whose initial philosophy of dealing with the native peoples was hardly more benevolent than his predecessor's. Leutwein soon captured the Nama leader and in July, 1894, forced Hendrik Witbooi to surrender.

One of his first official acts was to force Witbooi into signing the protection treaty. Thereafter Leutwein tried to deal justly with the Nama chief, allowing him to return to his home at Gibeon and to maintain his position within the tribe. In turn Witbooi agreed to furnish aid to the Germans in the event of hostilities.

This promise was tested in 1897 when the eastern branches of the Herero nation, disgruntled by German recognition of Samuel Maherero as chief, joined with the Kalahari Namas in trying to throw off German authority. Witbooi's men accompanied the German forces on a punitive expedition and were rewarded when the defeated Namas were placed under his control. Two major East Herero chiefs, Kahimemua and Nikodemus, were executed and the remnants of the rebels fled across the Kalahari to Bechuanaland.

Insurgency among several of the other Nama clans (particularly the Swartboois at Fransfontein in the North and the Bondelswart Orlams near Warmbad on the Cape border) was effectively suppressed by Leutwein's soldiers.

By the end of the century, German rule over South West Africa had become a fact and the various protectorates were protectorates in name only. Germany had in fact succeeded in establishing a colony. Considering the internecine war in the area and their brief occupation before order was generally established, the impact of German rule was quite impressive. The Herero who had sided with the Germans had emerged as the privileged non-White group. However, revenge for the Nama was not far off and for this the Herero had only their own leader to blame.

At this time Germany was sending more than just soldiers to South West Africa. Since Walvis Bay was firmly under British control, the Germans set out to develop their own port at Swakopmund. A wharf was constructed to handle the steady stream of supplies and settlers arriving from North Sea ports, and a railway line was laid between the town and Windhoek to facilitate passage inland.

Two new mining companies began to exploit the mineral deposits in the north.

The South West Africa Company, a British firm, gained concessions from Berlin for the Otavi copper area, some 3,000 square miles over which it had exclusive rights for mining, railroad building and administration of White affairs. (A railway surveyor for the company founded the modern town of Grootfontein.)

The *Otavi Minen und Eisenbahn Gesellschaft,* a joint British and German concern, brought secondary mineral rights over part of this area from the concessionaires. It began tapping the Tsumeb veins and building railroads to the coast; the Tsumeb-Swakopmund line was put into operation in 1906 and ore began to flow out for export the following year.

Farmers and traders developed thriving settlements at Omaruru, Okahandja, Windhoek and as far north as Grootfontein. Others landed at Lüderitz and, following the trail of the Rhenish missions, moved to Keetmanshoop.

A bemused Samuel Maherero, acting on his own authority and without consulting the tribal elders, sold great tracts of Herero grazing land to the new arrivals. It was not his to sell and he soon had cause to wish it returned. Suddenly, a people who had herded their cattle over the pleasant upland pastures for centuries found themselves evicted. Magistrates, administering a law completely in conflict with the Herero customary code, denied them access to grazing land and watering places which they considered inalienably their own. It was only a matter of time before the smouldering resentment flared into a bonfire.

When the Bondelswarts rising in 1904 drew a major portion of the German troops deep into Namaland, Samuel saw his opportunity. Ordering that "women, children, missionaries, Boers and English" be spared, he sent his warriors to isolated German farms where in the first night 123 farmers and traders were massacred. A general Herero uprising commenced. German troops returned post-haste from the south. In the vanguard was the major part of the Omaruru garrison, under the command of Captain (later Colonel) Victor Franke. By a series of forced marches, he and his men reached the fortress at Okahandja which was under Herero siege. They attacked without delay and succeeded in driving off the aggressors.

Samuel Maherero withdrew to his father's old stronghold on Kaiser Wilhelm mountain. The German forces pursued him there and flushed the Hereros, who fled with all their cattle and possessions to the refugees in the Waterberg mountains. There they were joined by other segments of the nation, driven before the advancing Germans. Gradually, the major portion of the Hereros — some 60,000 of them — were entrenched for a final stand.

There now arrived in South West Africa General Lothar von Trotha, a sort of colonial trouble-shooter for the German Reich, fresh from his ruthless suppression of a rising in German East Africa and brilliant military exploits in the Chinese Boxer Rebellion. Leutwein, who saw that an unconditional defeat of the Hereros would require the annihilation of the entire nation, was recalled to Berlin because of his lenient sympathies and the fate of the Hereros was sealed.

Von Trotha closed in on the Waterberg on August 10, 1904 with about 3,000 troops (many of them newly-arrived reinforcements) and heavy artillery. The light Herero rifles were no match for this tightly disciplined phalanx wielding rapid-firing guns and Hereros were slaughtered in uncountable numbers. After only one day of bitter fighting, they silently abandoned their camp and, trickling all night through a gap in the German lines, fled toward the desert.

With the Germans at their heels, their orderly escape soon turned into headlong flight. The Hereros plunged in blind panic towards Lake Ngami and British asylum in Bechuanaland. Their pursuers followed their trail which cut a wide swath across the desert and was marked by discarded possessions and the bodies of dead and dying Hereros and their cattle. The laggards who escaped quick death at the hands of von Trotha's men were condemned to grovel helplessly in the waterless wastes of the Kalahari. Of the thousands who set out, only some 1,500 managed to reach British territory.

A treacherous act on the part of the Herero thus led to the virtual annihilation of the Herero as a nation.

Samuel Maherero spent the next nineteen years in exile. When he died in Bechuanaland in 1923, the South African government allowed his people to return his body for burial beside his father and mother in the ancient capital at Okahandja. There a stone today reminds the passerby: "The Herero Chiefs Tjamuaha, died 1859, and his son Maherero, died 5 October 1890. Samuel Maherero, born 1856 died 14 March, 1923. Here lie three chieftains at rest. They ruled the country for the good of the Herero people, but now they are dead. They were chiefs indeed."

All that remained for the Germans after the battle of the Waterberg was to mop up the north and clear away isolated pockets of Nama resistance in the South. After seeing the terms of surrender inflicted on the Bondel-swarts, Hendrik Witbooi formally dissolved his treaty with Germany in 1904 and revolted while the *schutzen-truppe* were still chasing the Hereros. It was an abortive effort. Several of the Nama clans refused to

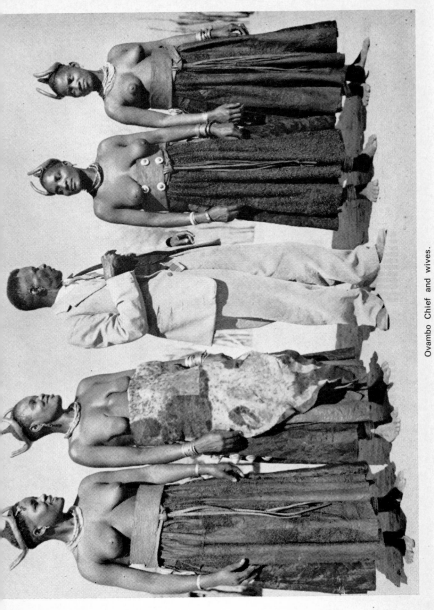

Ovambo Chief and wives.

Nama woman and child.

join him in rebellion and von Trotha had little trouble stamping out the fragmented Nama rebels. In a skirmish near Keetmanshoop on the 29th October, 1905, Witbooi was mortally wounded and died shortly afterwards. He was 80 years old. After several skirmishes in 1906 the Bethanie people and the Bondelswarts were subdued. *The Treaty of Ukamas in 1907 brought an end to the rebellions of the Orlams, Nama and Herero in South West Africa.*

Thus, after twenty years of bloody occupation, about R60 million ($84,000,000) and the lives of thousands of soldiers, Germany could at last turn her attention to the development of the ravaged colony. She was to have only ten years to devote to the task. Her resources were meagre. Of the territory's three major assets — mineral deposits, farmland and a plentiful supply of native labour — only the first remained. The country's farms had been devastated. Half the Namas and their Bergdamaras vassals had fallen in battle and the Hereros, once mighty people some 80,000 strong, were now less than 15,000 starving, cowering stragglers.

A new civil Governor, Friederich von Lindquist, arrived from Germany to repair the damage wrought by von Trotha, and a new era of progress began. Rail lines were laid from Lüderitz to Keetmanshoop. Schools and agricultural experimental stations were founded. Wells were drilled and dams built. Hundreds of settlers arrived from Germany and were established on the central highland areas. Sporadic outbreaks of rinderpest and foot-and-mouth disease caused set-backs but, by and large, agriculture was resumed.

The surviving Namas and Hereros were gathered into camps where they would receive food and medical treatment and then dispatched to work on improvement projects throughout the territory. The Namas were allowed some measure of self-rule, but the Hereros, who by then had a reputation for treachery and bloodletting of some magnitude, were stripped of their lands and forbidden to own even their few remaining cattle.

Mining operations also benefitted from the push toward progress. The copper mining near Tsumeb was begun in earnest and the marble quarry at Karibib was opened up.

But the biggest mining venture of all was about to turn the territory into the goal for fortune-hunters around the world. The railway line across the Namib desert from Lüderitz to Keetmanshoop required constant clearing from the encroaching sands and, in 1908, the foreman of one of these cleaning teams, August Stauch, picked up a "pretty stone" which turned out to be a diamond.

When the news reached Lüderitz, a helter-skelter conflux of prospectors struck out across the dunes. Geological studies confirmed the presence of the gems both in the desert and along the very coast where Adolf Lüderitz had walked unsuspectingly twenty-three years before.

Practically unlimited wealth was now locally available to finance the internal development of the territory. Dr. Theodor Seitz, who came out to become Governor in 1910, presided over the building of a lattice of graded roads and narrow gauge railways. Trade was greatly expanded and in 1912, aided by the diamond profits, exports exceeded imports for the first year during German occupation.

The towns were greatly improved by the erection of permanent government offices, hospitals and churches and a radio transmitter was established at Windhoek, powerful enough to communicate with Berlin. A remarkable period of stability, prosperity and justice followed and the Germans paid far more attention to the welfare of black and white than is generally recognised. Missionaries spread out all over the area and in 1910 the first church in the Okavango was completed.

But Germany was not allowed to enjoy a return on its colonial investments for long. The outbreak of the 1914-18 war in Europe found South West Africa a firmly entrenched island in a sea of British influence. Surrounded as it was by the British territories of Rhodesia and Bechuanaland, and her newly-created sister-nation, the Union of South Africa, it was a prime target for attack. (Portugal was not a participant in World War I, but traffic between South West and Angola was in any case minimal.)

The Germans seem to have deluded themselves that they could quarantine the colony away from their European difficulties. A cable from Berlin requested Governor Seitz to reassure the colonists that South West Africa would not be involved in the hostilities. But, if that was Germany's intent, it chose a peculiar means of bringing it about. Walvis Bay — the only Allied port on the west coast — was seized, and the Germans monitored Allied ships in the South Atlantic, relaying their movements over the Windhoek station.

This was an untenable position for Great Britain and South Africa alike. General Louis Botha, the first Prime Minister of the Union, was instructed by the Allied Command to deal with the German menace and turned his attention to South West Africa as soon as he had mobilized his forces at home.

Germany had a regular colonial garrison of some 2,000 men to which 7,000 reservists could be added. Many of the reservists were former members of the colonial troops who had retired in South West Africa after their terms of service, and they were a hardened corps of battle-seasoned veterans.

From long experience of dealing with unrisings in various parts of the territory, the South West military command could mobilize these units with great speed, sending them in concentrations to points of greatest need over the newly-completed 355 mile railway network.

But in General Botha they found a powerful adversary, one who was hardly a neophyte in the conventions of warfare in Southern Africa. As a teenager, he had fought with the Boer forces that supported the Zulus in the intertribal wars of South Africa. He spoke fluent Zulu as well as Sesutho and Swazi and had absorbed a great knowledge of their lore and customs. During the Anglo-Boer War, he had led the commando forces with such vigour and acumen that he rose to the post of Commandant-General of the Transvaal forces.

Botha launched a three-pronged attack on South West Africa, sending an overland column under the command of General Jan C. Smuts across the Orange River from the Cape and ferrying South African commandos to the Namib ports of Lüderitz and Walvis Bay to attack the Germans from the west.

Although it was somewhat unorthodox for a Prime Minister to assume military command in the field, Botha went himself to Walvis Bay to direct operations. South African public opinion was divided over participation in this "British war" but the General knew his country's interests lay incontrovertibly with the British. He felt that a person of no less authority than himself could "have the full confidence of both sections, English and Dutch", which composed the invasion force.

He therefore accompanied his troops to the northern port which they occupied easily. The Germans had abandoned Swakopmund in such haste that the remains of meals were found uneaten on the tables and it became obvious that the major defence would be made to the east.

They were greatly outnumbered (Botha had fielded some 40,000 troops) and their plan was to delay the South African advance in the hope of an early German victory in Europe. They called every available man into uniform and even called in their treaty with the Rehobothers, who refused to serve on the grounds that their historical homeland was South Africa. The Baster chief, Cornelius van Wyk, slipped a letter through the German lines to Botha on the coast, offering to join the South Africans in their attack. This offer was firmly declined. It was, said Botha, a White man's war but he thanked the Rehobothers for their support and promised that their lands, guaranteed under treaty with the Kaiser, would be respected by the invaders.

With the coastline secured, Botha started inland to meet the Smuts column advancing from the south. His men — 10,000 mounted commandos — in peak condition, set off into the desert and he pushed them night and day across the baking Namib dunes. A final herculean march of forty miles across waterless territory strewn with land mines brought him to the town of Karibib, juncture of the north and eastern rail lines. From there, it was a simple matter to advance on Windhoek.

Again the Germans spurned a stand and Botha found the military and government officials evacuated and the radio station destroyed. With the main body of the German forces retreating to the north, he called a truce conference with the Governor. Dr. Seitz declared that he had no authority to surrender the colony without permission from the Kaiser, which, owing to the communication hiatus, was impossible to obtain. He then proposed a cease-fire along prevailing lines of possession until events in Europe should be resolved. This remarkably audacious suggestion from a man outnumbered seven to one was of course completely unacceptable to Botha.

The commander of the German forces, General von Heydebrack, had been killed accidentally in an action quite unrelated to the South African invasion.

Military responsibility had fallen to Colonel Franke, the hero of the Herero War, and he followed the strategy of his previous enemy, retreating first into the Waterberg mountains and from there to the north-eastern towns.

Botha, now reinforced by his southern contingent, pursued him. Using a modified version of an old Zulu strategy, he sent out two flanking columns to surround Franke's headquarters at Tsumeb, while he himself prepared to meet the Germans face-on.

Even Dr. Seitz realized the hopelessness of their position. All hopes of reaching the German army in Tanganyika under the famous General von Lettow Vorbeck had been dashed by the eastern arm of Botha's attack and further resistance seemed futile. With his permission Colonel Franke arranged to meet Botha and Khorab where on July 9th, 1915, the surrender was signed.

But General Botha was temporarily out of contact with the officers of his flanking columns. It was of course necessary to reach them and, for this purpose, Colonel Franke hurriedly offered the use of his field telephone. This Botha accepted and he conducted his conversations including instructions for the imprisoning of the captives, entirely in Zulu, a language calculated to give the surrendered enemy very little information on which to base any rash desperate plans to elude internment.

In the entire campaign, Botha's forces suffered only 532 casualties, of which 269 were killed. It was a momentous victory lightly won and marked the end of an era for the strife-torn land.

South African military officials assumed the administration of the territory and life returned to a semblance of normal. The German regulars and the colonial government were interned until after the war, when about 6,000 of them were repatriated. But the bulk of the population, including the reservists, were permitted to remain on their farms, where they were to become an integral part of the territory's population.

The release of the non-White peoples from German rule was a cause for exultation among them. South Africa took early steps to gather the scattered remnants of the Hereros and to restore to them the security of land tenure and their rights to own cattle. A special commission of inquiry heard testimony from Hereros, Namas, Rehobothers, and all other sectors of the non-White inhabitants.

The railway line was extended from Prieska in the Cape to Karasburg, the southermost part of the German system, about 75 miles from the South African border. South West Africa now had an overland route to the outside world, and over this route, progress was hoped to flow into the land as never before.

4

THE STRUGGLE FOR SURVIVAL

South West Africa was not easily tamed.

Nature unwillingly conceded the right of survival to man, and then only after a titanic struggle. The desert and the uncompromising regions claimed innumerable lives, as did the tribal wars which raged continually throughout the territory in bygone times.

The wastage of life was halted only when Western civilization, embodying as it does the rule of law, was introduced to the territory. The European pioneers slowly led the warring tribes to a peaceful, useful co-existence by precept and hard work and even forced concessions from nature.

The history of South West Africa will probably be seen in the future as one of a compulsory compliance between extremes. But the emphasis will then have to be placed upon the triumph of Western skills over reluctant nature and of civilization over barbarism. The role of South Africa in this triumph is one to which the people of South West Africa owe an eternal debt.

Those who pioneered civilization in South West Africa were not daunted by the primitiveness and forbidding nature of the country. Many lonely graves bear witness to their courage. Graves of missionaries, farmers and children are still found in the most unexpected places.

In a country where the need for water is of paramount importance, nature proclaims stagnation and drought. Civilizing man did not accept this and rose to the challenge presented by such inhospitable conditions.

South West Africa remained under military government of the Union of South Africa from July 9th, 1915, when the German Forces surrendered to South African troops, until December 31st, 1920.

At the Versailles Peace Conference, the Supreme Council of the Allied Powers formally entrusted to South Africa the administration of the conquered territory. This was subsequently confirmed by the League of Nations. The task was to be undertaken for "the well-being and development of primitive peoples" and would constitute a "sacred trust of civilization". At that time the total population was about 224,000 of whom less than 20,000 or some 11 per cent were Whites.

But the problems presented by this vast and unde-veloped land were enormous. Kaiser Wilhelm's colony was suddenly the responsibility of the Union of South Africa, a country which had itself been a combination of colonial territory and conquered land only ten years before, and immense quantities of capital and human resources were needed to bring it to anything like its full potential.

Analyzing the situation which South Africa faced in this huge territory in the early twenties the noted agro-economist, Professor D. C. Krogh of the University of South Africa, observed as follows: "The history of peace-ful co-existence between the various Native tribes before the administration of the White man and between Whites and non-Whites during the German regime, is among the bloodiest imaginable. Similarly, the course of economic development in South West Africa prior to 1920 is one of the poorest on record. Suffice it to recall that during the four centuries following the Portuguese, who first set foot on the desert coast of South West Africa in the last quarter of the 15th century, several expeditions were sent out by them, the Dutch, British and the Cape Govern-ment to determine the economic possibilities of the territory, but that they all returned with most dis-couraging reports".[26]

When, in 1884, the Germans, to the surprise of all, declared the territory annexed, the British Imperial Government, in welcoming its new neighbour, conceded

26. Krogh, D. C.: "South West Africa: Economic Change and Political Outlook," *Africa,* Johannesburg, May, 1965.

it never thought South West Africa worth acquiring and that it was a most difficult country to develop.

Professor Krogh also pointed out that the thirty years ending with the outbreak of World War I "was characterised by drastic experiments in finding the appropriate formula for the development of South West Africa and its diverse population groups, most of which ended in failure. Professor Bonn, then of Munich University, summed up the period of German control over South West Africa in the following words when addressing the Royal Colonial Institute in 1914: 'We wanted to build up on African soil a new Germany and create daughter states as you have done in Australia and Canada . . . we carried this idea to its bitter end. We tried it in South West Africa and produced a huge native rising causing the loss of much treasure and many lives.' He concluded as follows: 'We succeeded in breaking up native tribes but we have not yet succeeded in creating a new Germany'."

Such then were the conditions in South West Africa when South Africa assumed responsibility of its development.

The major problem was of course the scarcity and, in some places, the total absence of water. But there were others: the lack of skilled manpower in both the White and non-White sections of the population, a totally inadequate communications system (there were only 355 miles of rail track in 1922 — all of it narrow gauge), and the presence of endemic diseases among men and livestock. The total population represented only about one person for every two square miles of territory; the non-Whites were composed of different races and different tribes at totally different stages of development, speaking different languages and living in the shadow of a century of war on each other. Of common loyalty to South West Africa there was no question.

The cropping potential and livestock carrying capacity of the country was limited to relatively small areas. Environmental conditions were harsh; the cost of transport and communications prohibited development; there were no coal or natural oil resources worth exploiting; to crown this dismal picture was the knowledge that deflation and depression resulting from World War I had also left their scars on the new mother country, South Africa. The gross domestic income was then only about R13 million or $18,000,000.

In the southern half of the country, the non-Whites were wandering bands of socially disorganized trouble-seekers. A century of internecine wars and colonial occupation had decimated their numbers and demoralized the survivors.

But a start had to be made somewhere.

The non-Whites were the subject of immediate and extensive improvement projects. Wandering groups of Hereros and Namas were collected and transported to their old homelands where they were given security of land tenure. Under German rule, only 3,900 square miles were set aside solely for non-White occupation. After 1922, some 85,000 square miles were proclaimed for the exclusive use of the various non-White groups including the 5,236-square-mile Rehoboth Gebiet.

The right to own cattle was restored to the Hereros, and the government established order and let it be known that any tendency the Namas and Hereros might feel to slip back into their old ways of marauding and cattle-thieving would not be countenanced.

They were assisted to build peaceful lives by the drilling of wells and construction of dams. Cattle dipping and pasture fencing were instituted to control the spread of stock diseases. By and large, each nation was allowed to resume its own customs of internal government through the traditional chiefs and headmen, but White commissioners were available to these authorities in their dealings with the mandatory government.

The Germans had never made any attempt to impose their colonial authority on the Ovambo and Okavango in the North. Even missionary incursions had been superficial and the tribes retained — along with complete internal autonomy — their ancient tribal customs, the most innocuous of which was polygamy and the most barbarous, ritual murder. A White commissioner was stationed among them to curb the more barbaric of these practices, but a policy of noninterference was otherwise strictly maintained.

To prevent their possible exploitation by Whites and to ensure their exclusive rights to the land, the northern sector of the territory was closed to settlement by Whites, and movement by unauthorised White men was restricted. The southern part, covering large arid and sparsely populated areas, was called the "Police Zone" because movement and habitation by White people was allowed and police protection afforded. The northern part was closed to Whites except by permit and enjoyed almost total internal autonomy. The eastern end of the Caprivi Strip, also reserved for its inhabitants, is governed direct from Pretoria, largely as a matter of practical necessity.

For forty years, there was not a single White policeman in the Kaokoveld-Ovambo-Okavango area, and the two resident White commissioners stationed there possessed the confidence and support of the native chiefs and headman. Order was maintained solely through reliance on tribal laws. In 1961, the Police Zone was extended to include Ovamboland and Okavangoland. This was principally because the territories adjoined the Portuguese Angolan border and also because of infiltration of dissident political elements who threatened to disrupt the system of tribal authority.

One of the difficult tasks which had to be faced in South West Africa was to provide a physical home for each of the different native groups. *Lack of clearly-defined homelands had been one of the reasons for the century of conflict which preceded South African administration.* There was and is no reliable information about the exact extent of the areas inhabited by the various groups prior to the second half of the last century. Claims to specific areas e.g. of the Hereros to Nama land gave rise to continual clashes. The Germans in 1898 and 1903 made provision for establishing such areas. However, on the termination of German rule in 1915 only the Basters of Rehoboth, the Nama of Berseba and the Damara actually had home areas, for the Nama and Herero rebellion in 1904 had scattered tribes all over South West Africa.

The Kaokoveld, Ovamboland, Okavango and the Caprivi strip were not affected by German rule since the peoples in these regions were not involved in the rebellion or previous escapades. In addition these areas were clearly defined by traditional rights and were inhabited exclusively by fairly homogeneous groups. The problem arose with the wide and often extravagant claims for land posted by the Herero, Nama and Orlams and even the Bushmen.

The principle of inalienable homelands for the various peoples was embodied in the *Treaty of Peace* and *South West Africa Act* of 1919 passed by the Union Government. In 1922 a Native Reserves Commission was set up to report on progress in the establishment of the homelands and during the period 1923-1951 the assignment of land on the basis of inalienable homelands proceeded apace and the physical moulding of the territory by demarcation completed for the time being.

It was a legal and orderly process which evoked, at first grudgingly and at a later stage virtually complete support from the traditional leaders of the various nations.

A tragic incident during the early years of the mandate showed South Africa the magnitude of patience and understanding that would be required of it in the wise administration of its unsophisticated charges. The so-called Bondelswarts rebellion of 1922 was the result of blundering among all parties concerned, and its handling became a lesson in how not to approach peoples naive in the workings of a modern bureaucratic government.

The Bondelswarts were Orlams Namas who had settled just north of the Orange River and in the Warmbad vicinity. They had shown themselves under the Germans to be an arrogant and independent people. Indeed it was their uprising in 1904 that had drawn much of the German colonial garrison into the South and given the Hereros an opportunity to revolt.

On the occasion, a hurriedly negotiated punitive peace, signed at Kalkfontein (Karasburg), had preserved their lands. But some of them had sought refuge in South Africa and the refugees included their hereditary leader, Kaptein Jacobus Christian. Ten years later, they had willingly furnished scouting parties for General Smuts' invasion force.

During the winter of 1921, some of these scouts decided to return with their families to their old homes in South West Africa. They failed to secure a permit for their boundary crossing, were stopped shortly after leaving the Cape Province, and then allowed to continue their trek. When "Kaptein" Christian arrived at the Bondelswarts community, he found that during his absence of nearly twenty years a new leader had been chosen and the appointment recognized by the government.

In the ensuing confusion, a local police official decided to investigate the returned wanderers and issued a warrant for the arrest of five of them. When the Bondelswarts refused to hand over the prisoners, the police threatened action. The Bondelswarts took this to be a declaration of war. Subsequent events are jumbled beyond accurate historical reconstruction, but it appears that the Administration in Windhoek — faced with what reports from the scene described as open defiance — called in air support for the police and a number of Bondelswarts were killed.

The use of airplanes provoked vigorous protests in South Africa where public opinion was outraged. The South African Parliament appointed a commission to investigate the whole affair and the local officials were castigated for excessive harshness in dealing with what should have been a minor disagreement. Kaptein Christian was granted amnesty and recognized as the rightful Bondelswarts leader.

But the significance of the Bondelswarts affair lay in the stringent measures instituted by the mandatory government to prevent the repetition of such an incident — measures which have proved remarkably effective. Relations between White civil servants and the non-White peoples have since been characterized by mutual respect and courtesy.

While providing for the welfare of the non-Whites, South Africa had to deal simultaneously with the territory's other problems. The resident White population — better off only in comparison to the abject wretchedness of the non-Whites — was divided against itself. The remaining Germans found themselves squatters in an alien land where they eked out a grudging existence on stubborn farms in a hostile climate.

Because it had no coal or natural oil resources worth exploiting and since it had to export virtually everything it produced (in view of the extremely limited and scattered local market) South West Africa was one of the most difficult areas to develop on the African continent. These were *structural* limitations and difficulties which called for decades of carefully planned development. Lack of capital for improvement and ignorance of scientific agricultural methods, aggravated by recurring drought and persistent cattle disease, kept the land far short of is carrying capacity. Huge tracts of potential farmland — some 40,000 square miles — were unoccupied.

Even the towns were startlingly primitive. The narrow gauge railroad ran right down the main street of Windhoek, where a White population of 2,400 managed to exist without municipal sewage or electric power.

The Union government's first two steps were to improve water supply and communications. There were a necessary prelude to the third and most important step of attracting qualified settlers to develop the territory. Wells were drilled, dams built, railways laid and roads graded.[27] Agricultural experimental stations were opened and stock breeds were strengthened.

---

27. Paving of roads is largely superfluous in South West Africa where, because of low rainfall, gravel surfaces withstand years of wear. Dust is a problem, but chemical treatment overcomes this difficulty. The only significant paving in the territory even today is along the main artery from Keetmanshoop to Windhoek and Otjiwarongo, but an improvement programme is currently under way which will tripple the distance of tarred roads in about five years' time.

The improvements had the desired effect. Immigrants began arriving in the country at an unprecedented rate. A 1921 census showed a White population of over 18,000 (of whom 10,673 were South Africans); this had swelled to 30,000 by 1936. The new settlers were allocated farms from government lands and given subsidized loans for buildings and stock purchases.

But where men laboured to open up the country, nature threw obstructions in their way. In the middle Twenties, a severe drought — unduly harsh even by South West standards — brought hardship to the struggling farmers, and the market price of cattle dropped precipitously as men raced to sell their dwindling herds.

This drought was followed by the Great Depression of the Thirties, whose effects encircled the globe and penetrated to even so remote a place as South West Africa.

A chapter of dissension of those years resulted from the uncertain political status of the territory's White inhabitants. As early as 1921 there were encouraging signs of co-operation between the South African and German sections of the population and the De Wet Commission, appointed by the mandatory, recommended that South African citizenship be conferred on those Germans who had settled permanently in the land.

In response to the De Wet proposals, the second Prime Minister of South Africa, General Smuts, met two representatives of the German government in London during 1923. A plan was divised whereby South Africa would accept the Germans in South West as citizens and protect the use of the German language in the territory.

(Smuts also agreed to a provision absolving the South West African Germans and their children of military service against Germany for a period of thirty years, a clause which relieved them of obligatory service during World War II.)

The London agreement was a tremendous assistance to the effort of unifying the Whites of South West. In all, over 5,500 people were automatically naturalized, and only 300 Germans filed objections to the naturalization procedure.

A beginning of political responsibility was made in 1925 when the South African Parliament conferred a constitution on the territory, establishing a Legislative Assembly for the White community. This 18-member elective body could handle all matters within South West Africa except for defence, the railways, harbours and aviation, customs, police, foreign affairs, and the administration of justice. In these fields, the South African Parliament retained authority.[28] The care of the non-Whites was of course also reserved.

Under the constitution, an Administrator, appointed by South Africa, is the chief executive officer. He acts in consultation with a four-member Executive Committee chosen by the Legislative Assembly.

The customs and immigration laws of South Africa apply to South West, but free movement of trade, capital, and labour is allowed between the two. The

---

28. In 1949, the South African Parliament authorized the election of ten representatives from South West Africa to its own ranks, six to the House and four to the Senate.

absence of customs barriers has contributed substantially to the development of the territory. Since South West Africa has virtually no secondary industry, much of her consumer goods are imported from South Africa and her exports cross the border duty-free. *For all practical purposes a common market such as is ultimately envisaged for Europe, exists between South Africa and South West Africa.*

The terms of the Mandate prohibited financial integration and South West Africa has its own budget and system of taxation. The inhabitants of the non-White areas pay no taxes to the Administration; any grazing fees collected by them are deposited in trust funds which — supplemented by taxes on the Whites — are used for developing the respective non-White home-lands.

The uncertain nature of the territory's future impeded capital investment, however, and the social and economic hardships of the population were further aggravated by the rise of National Socialism in Germany. Nazi agents arrived in South West where they capitalised on the frustration of the younger sections of the German population and founded an ominous array of organizations to promote their ends. These included the Deutscher Südwest Bund, the Kultürvereine, the Deutsche Maedchen, and the Hitler Jugend. Some young firebrands even went to Germany where they inlisted in the army and air force of the Second German Reich.

It gradually became apparent to the South African government that the activities of these organizations were directed pointedly towards the strengthening of Nazism in South West Africa and the return of the territory to Germany.

To check the dangerous aspects of these bodies, the Administrator of South West Africa declared them "political" bodies in 1937 and dissolved them. But the net effect was to drive the Hitler agents underground, and scarcely veiled threats against South Africa continued to be hurled by German aliens in the territory. South Africans living in South West received warnings of how they "would be dealt with" when Germany reoccupied her old colony.

The story of Nazi machinations — the spying, the creation of Nazi cells, the systematic undermining of loyalties by Nazi agents in South West Africa — is part of the history of World War II. A large part of the German population remained loyal, however, and this time there was no need for an invasion by South African forces. A number of subversive Germans were interned and, as a precautionary measure, South African defence forces were assigned to patrol the vital Atlantic coastline throughout the war.

There was evidence of an intricate and detailed plan to evoke a German uprising in South West Africa at the outbreak of war in Europe. It may well be that, without vigilance against the Nazi agents, World War II would have broken out in South West instead of Poland.

The coming of war temporarily suspended the push for development in South West Africa. Works projects went in abeyance as South Africa concentrated all her efforts on the task of defeating the Axis powers. South West Africa itself played little part in this effort.

The formation of the United Nations, with South Africa as a founder member, ushered in the post-war period. All of the old mandates of the defunct League of Nations were transformed into "trusteeships" under the supervision of the United Nations by voluntary action of the mandatory powers. But General Smuts, then Prime Minister, formally applied for incorporation of South West Africa as a fifth province of South Africa.

His case for incorporation was a strong one. The White section of the population — by this time some 38,000 strong — had repeatedly asked for annexation in public and private talks and in the press. The desire was expressed formally in a series of resolutions passed by the South West African Legislative Assembly in 1943.

Between December, 1945 and April, 1946 the non-Whites of South West Africa were also polled on the question of incorporation and voted overwhelmingly in favour of it. About 57,000 of them — Bushmen and vagrant Nama and Damara groups — could not be reached for an opinion. Of the total of 244,370 who voted, 208,850 or 70 per cent. of the adult indigenous population said yes. Interestingly enough, although there were 2,810 Nama votes against incorporation, the Bondelswarts voted in favour of it.

Their enthusiasm ranged from childlike acceptance to a more sophisticated historical appraisal:

"We are like a man who has lived a long time with a good wife. A man who likes his first wife does not get rid of her. It is so with this Government of ours . . . A poor man can speak to this Government just as well as a rich man can."[29]

"When you came to this country you saw the bones of our people who died of famine as well as those of people who died in cattle raids. Now you don't see this because this Government is a good one. We can send one small child to herd our cattle and they are safe."[30]

"The Union Government has given us houses, bulls and ploughs and our cattle have increased because they are always innoculated. We have been fed in times of famine. We were very stupid in the old days. We wish the Union Government to keep this country and to continue to look after us so that we can improve."[31]

"I was under the German Government a long time and under their rule. I was no better than a slaughter sheep. Today I am treated like a human being by our Government. I do not want to hear about any other government."[32]

Of the 33,520 votes against incorporation, 27,350 of them were cast by Hereros.[33] It appeared from the reasons they gave that the Hereros had greatly idealized

29. Ovambo Councillor Shitatala Namangangala.
30. Ombalantu Councillor Dalengelue Aitana.
31. Chieftainess Mingele of the Okavango.
32. Jacobus Topnaar Nama at Sesfontein in the Kaokoveld.
33. A preliminary tally in the Kaokoveld and Otjituo homelands of the Herero showed 2,568 votes in favour of incorporation; these were changed in the final ballot presumably to accord with the majority opinion.

their position in the territory before the coming of the Germans. They seemed to harbour a grievance against South Africa for not handing over the whole territory to them after the German defeat.

When it was pointed out to them that they had no more right to the land than the Namas, Damaras and other peoples who had occupied the country in olden days, they took the attitude that they were the natural leaders of the territory and should be placed in authority over the others.

"We want our land to be returned to us and then want to stay under the protection of the Trusteeship Council," said Fillipus Tjapaka, a self declared spokesmen for the Hereros. The idea that United Nations intervention would bring about a paradise in South West Africa, with them as the masters, remains a part of the Herero "Mystique". In 1963, Joshua Mbulu, a 24-year-old Herero clerk in Windhoek, told a visiting American newspaper reporter: "The United Nations will bring plenty mealies, and we will not have to work any more."[34]

Not unnaturally, the other national groups of South West scorn the idea of Herero ascendancy in a united independent country. The Ovambos find the concept particularly amusing. "We are seven to their one," laughs a young Ovambo near Namutoni, "We will swallow them!" The Namas and Damaras are equally contemptuous, and the Rehobothers have nothing in common with any of the other non-White groups.

So despite this lone island of resistance in the sea of affirmation, General Smuts had resolved to seek an end to

---

34. *The Wall Street Journal*, New York, 1963.

the territory's uncertain future. His resolve was thwarted when the United Nations refused to agree to South African incorporation of the mandated territory. South Africa then declined to place South West Africa under the trusteeship system and its geopolitical status remained undetermined until the verdict of the World Court at the Hague in July, 1966, brought the whole matter into sharp focus.

The fact that it was mandated had discouraged investment by private sources, and the nature of the mandate system was not conducive to massive public expenditure in the territory, since the finances of South West Africa had had to be accounted for to the League of Nations.

Substantial loans from South Africa had financed public expenditure, but by 1937 the territory was R7 million ($10,000,000) in debt to the mandatory and it became apparent that it was getting deeper into debt every year without having anything to show for the mounting obligations.

To meet this precarious situation, South Africa suspended payments of both redemption and interest on loans to South West. These amounts were debited against the territory, but no interest was charged on the arrear interest. By 1945, better times had smiled on South West Africa and payments were resumed.

The uses of modern techniques by South Africa in the development of South West Africa's farming industry and improvements in local diamond mining brought increasing prosperity so that a special development reserve fund could be accumulated for helping it over its lean periods and for stimulating local projects. By the end of March, 1946, this fund had R9 million ($12,600,000) to its credit.

South Africa's financial "nursing" of the mandated land had begun to pay dividends.

Another stimulus to progress was provided by South African commercial banks which, at the request of the government played an important role in financing development even during the depressed years. (According to the record of real output in the territory during the 40-year period ended 1960 the inhabitants were spending more than one third of all those years recovering from one or other economic setback beyond their control.) Two of these banks in particular — the Standard Bank of South Africa Ltd., and Barclays Bank — accepted wide risks in advancing loans of more than 150 per cent of local deposits at one period during the Depression. But by 1946, the financial position of the people of the territory had improved to the point where this ratio had been lowered to an average 32 per cent.

South West Africa was far from self-supporting, however. Its mineral resources were at last being exploited on an economic basis for the purpose of earning foreign exchange, but it still lacked those essentials for developing local industry — easily accessible raw materials, an abundant source of electric power, a skilled labour force, and a ready domestic market. A population of 341,000 (est. 1946) more than 300,000 of whom were non-Whites in various stages of barter economics, did not offer an attractive outlet for consumer goods. The years of *real* economic progress were only experienced after World War II when the money and effort that went into the development of the territory's livestock industry began to bear fruit and mining output increased as a result of high mineral prices. The rapid development of the fishing industry also contributed to the growing welfare of the economy.

All South West Africa's natural limitations and the difficulties of development considered, it is all the more remarkable to find that since 1922 the socio-economic development of the territory has been quite outstanding. Professor D. C. Krogh, who testified on behalf of South Africa before the World Court at the Hague in the protracted South West Africa dispute, pointed out that the severely adverse natural environment of South West Africa and the lack of any internal market put great emphasis on the use of capital, scientific knowledge, and above all, the enterprising qualities of man to produce agricultural surplusses for sophisticated foreign markets. Given limited financial resources on the one hand and the ultra-conservatism of traditional Bantu livestock owner on the other, he said, there could be no optimism about early transformation of traditional African subsistence livestock farming into commercialized production for export. "The only solution was seen to be the further encouragement of enterprising and experienced White farmers to settle in the unoccupied northern and central parts of the territory. The most northern portion of South West Africa with the highest rainfall was densely populated by non-Whites while the southern section is virtually a desert area. It was hoped that by relying on White agricultural enterprise more wage earning opportunities could be created for the unsettled non-White groups for whom there were also set aside certain reserved areas which could be further expanded as and when prospects of their becoming commercialized farmers improved."

What South African administration in South West Africa achieved in this respect is theretore all the more remarkable. There were less than a half-million head of cattle in South West Africa when South Africa assumed the mandate; the 1962 cattle census showed 2,434,000.[35]

Karakul ranching was in its infancy in 1924 with a sheep population then of 50,000. The first consignment only arrived from Germany in the latter half of 1908. There were 12,000 pelts sold in 1924. Today, Karakul is a R16 million ($22,400,000) industry with three million animals and exports of over two million pelts annually. The United States and Canada are the largest importers of Karakul from South West Africa followed by Germany, France and Italy. Since the southern semi-arid portion of South West Africa is only suitable for sheep farming, the large scale expansion of the Karakul

---

35. Meat must surely be among South West Africa's earliest exports. When Napoleon was interned on St. Helena, British ships carried Stock, purchased from the Namas, to the island.

meant a major improvement in the productivity of this otherwise poor area. As Professor Krogh observed: "Thanks mainly to the enterprise, skill and perseverance of the White farmer in some of the worst parts of the territory, South West Africa has come to top the list in terms of the number of livestock per head of population in Africa".

Drought conditions exercise a limiting effect on dairy products, so the output is not constant. On average 7.8 million pounds of butter are produced in South West each year and nearly four hundred thousand pounds of cheese — cheddar and gouda — processed at the territory's factory at Outjo annually. Meat canning plants at Windhoek, Okahandja, and Otavi handle 180,000 carcasses a year, and sausages, meat extract, and bone meal are also manufactured.

In 1922, the first two fish canneries were started at Lüderitz. From this humble beginning, a R24 million ($33,600,000) industry has developed, second only to mining in the territory's economy. The expansion of this industry has been truly spectacular.

A chocolate plant, soap factory, several furniture plants, a metal container factory, and the breweries at Windhoek and Swakopmund are other factors in South West Africa's manufacturing industry. Jute bags are manufactured at Walvis Bay while grain mills and bakeries and mineral water factories are found in all the major towns.

Recent developments in the territory's mineral exploitation include the discovery of billions of tons of low-grade iron ore in the Kaokoveld, new tin mining ventures, and the production of semi-precious stones. The Germans were aware of some of the beautiful semi-precious stones, and a heliodor set in a gold cross was presented by the Deutsche Kolonial Gesellschaft to Kaiser Wilhelm's wife. But their amazing variety and value have only recently been recognized.

The heliodor, a yellow beryl found nowhere else in the world, is only one of a staggering array. Rose beryl, aquamarines, amethysts, rose and translucent quartz, turquoise, topazes and more than seventy hues of tourmalines are collected and set in ornaments and jewelry. The South West African tiger's-eye is particularly lovely, yet it is so common that it can be used for key-rings, good luck pieces and other low-priced items.

The total value of mineral sales during 1965 was just short of R115 million ($161,000,000), an increase of R57 million ($94,000,000) over 1960. The production included diamonds, lead, copper, tin, zinc and germanium, the vital element in the manufacture of transistors.

The per capita income of the territory rose from about R30 ($42) in 1940 to R191.6 ($268) in 1962 — equal to that of several European countries. Over the last twenty years, it has shown an average annual growth of 12.8 per cent, one of the highest in the world.

A question often raised at discussions overseas is the gains which the non-Whites made in the sphere of private income as compared with that of the White man. This aspect has been thoroughly investigated by Professor D. C. Krogh and also Professor Richard Logan, Professor

100,000,000 pounds of sand
have to be removed to obtain
1 pound of diamonds.

Gem diamonds
mined in
South West Africa.

Photo: Odo Willscher, Hamburg.

THE MINING INDUSTRY: 1962–1965 [1]

PARTICULARS	Unit	1962	1963	1964	1965
A. *Sales of principal minerals*[2]					
(i) Quantities: Diamonds	carat	943,187	1,329,649	1,527,211	1,585,287
Refined lead	ton	—	478	46,065	78,245
Lead/copper/zinc concentrates	ton	189,209	167,556	94,035	136,394
Blister copper	ton	793	21,073	31,496	33,235
(ii) Values: Diamonds	R '000	34,221	43,907	60,256	70,311
Refined lead	R '000	—	48	7,109	14,812
Lead/copper/zinc concentrates	R '000	14,057	10,422	7,857	10.198
Blister copper	R '000	302	8,092	13,953	15,034
All other minerals	R '000	4,553	2,612	4,171	4,781
Total value all minerals	R '000	53,133	65,081	93,346	115,136
B. *Expenditure by mining companies*[3]					
Wages	R '000	6,683	7,799	9,724	11,199
Local purchases..	R' 000	13,253	13,285	21,233	24,606
Local road, sea and railway transport.. ..	R '000	1,849	1,941	2,569	6,590
Customs, direct	R '000	96	215	675	391
Machinery purchased	R '000	6,512	6,373	6,049	6,359
Total	R '000	28,393	29,614	40,251	49,143
C. *Diamond export duty and profit tax*[4]	R '000	6,921	7,027	9,650	12,161
D. *Revenue collected in respect of claim fees, grant and mining areas fees, etc...*	R '000	74	105	142	148
E. *Prospecting activities*					
Prospecting licences issued	number	424	416	452	438
Claims held at end of year	number	2,486	7,371	8,068	7,571
Claims registered during year	number	1,346	5,369	2,594	2,748
Claims lapsed/abandoned	number	367	484	1,897	2,229
Number of claims converted into mining areas	number	53	—	—	5
Mining areas registered..	number	12	1	—	3

[1] South West Africa Administration, Mines Division, *Annual Report*.
[2] Sales and production figures during any particular year are not identical but the difference is so small that production figures need not be shown separately in this context.
[3] Due to rounding, the totals are not necessarily equal to the sum of the constituent figures.
[4] Figures refer to financial years commencing on April 1 of the years shown, and are net royalties paid to South West Finance Corporation Limited.

(1R = $1.40)

of Geography at the University of California. In his testimony before a sub-committee of the United States Congress in 1966 Professor Logan gave several examples of the progress made by the non-Whites in terms of housing, living conditions, incomes, etc. "It is obvious," he said, "that the living standards of the natives have risen almost unbelievably in this (the past) decade." Professor Krogh pointed out that while it is true that Whites were holding the more skilled and better paid jobs, this state of affairs belongs to a dynamic setting in South West Africa. He then quoted statistics to prove that the distribution of income (as represented by wages) is less unequal in South West Africa compared with that in other African territories where the ratio of Whites to non-Whites in the total population is far less favourable. (For example, whereas there are six non-Whites in South West Africa for each White person, in Kenya and Uganda the ratio is 94:1 and 598:1 respectively, yet the income differential between White and non-White is 30:1 and 32:1 in these countries compared with 13:1 in South West Africa. The increase in monthly wages of non-Whites during the period 1945 to 1958 is also very impressive. In Industry and Construction it was up 79%; in Railways 48% in Mining 146%; in the Public Service 42% and in Farming 301% giving an average rise of 85%. Professor Logan, moreover, maintains that it is fallacious to compare non-White wages with wages earned by Whites "because of the totally different nature of expenses incurred by the two groups". *Such a comparison is vastly favourable to the non-Whites.* As Professor Logan rightly points out "the housing costs of the native are largely subsidized by the employer and the Municipality; medical treatment is essentially free; transportation costs, admission fees, etc., are greatly reduced; there are no taxes to be paid; and custom dictates that very substantial gifts of clothing and cloth must be made by the employer on a number of occasions".

But progress in economic terms was also accompanied by great strides in human progress. During the forty years *after* 1921, the population more than doubled — from 203,750 to 526,000. The average annual rise under South African administration was 2.1 per cent which is slightly above the world average. By African standards, it compares favourably with increases in Ethiopia (0.8 per cent), Ghana (1.4 per cent), Angola (1.0 per cent) and Liberia (1.4 per cent). In South Africa itself, the rise was 2.4 per cent. In sharp contrast over the forty-year period *preceding* the administration and development of the territory by South Africa, the native population actually decreased.[36]

Great progress was also made in the provision of health and educational services in the territory.

Endemic diseases were the subject of attack by scores of dedicated doctors. The Hereros and Namas were particularly struck by venereal disease. As a result of the Herero dispersal after the defeat of 1904, many of their women turned to prostitution as the only hope of

36. *Odendaal Report,* page 37.

178

survival; the result contributed to a radical drop in the birth-rate until the once-mighty nation numbered a mere 15,000. By 1960, however, there were about 40,000 Hereros in South West Africa.

Full-time government medical officers are stationed in Ovamboland and the Okavango area; their salaries, living expenses, etc., are met from the general revenue of the territory and they disperse free medicine to their patients. Allowances are paid to the qualified missionary medical and nursing staffs and their medicines are also received free. Special clinics for the treatment of venereal disease were established and welfare officers in the non-White homelands assist the district surgeons in bringing the best of modern medicine to the people.

Early efforts to treat the non-Whites encountered resistance. Hospitals set up for central care were shunned by the sick because of their superstitious belief that a dead spirit could injure a living one. The Hereros were particularly rigid in following the custom of never entering a hut where someone had died, leaving it to fall down of neglect and building a new hut a little distance away. Unfortunately, people do die in hospitals, and many of the non-Whites felt that people who went to hospitals ran the danger of having their spirits snatched away by the dead.

Gradually these problems were overcome or partially solved, and the present trend towards improving the general health of the population established.

The problems of education were enormous.

In the *first* place the country had a heterogeneous population consisting of divergent language groups, each of which has a different background, different customs and different ideals. In the *second* place this population was scattered over a huge territory and schooling in some sparsely-populated regions was virtually impossible. *Thirdly* most of the non-White groups had no established tradition of education. As in many parts of Africa the population groups were completely illiterate prior to the advent of Western civilization. Education in the Western sense of the word was simply non-existent.

Organized education services for the whole population of South West Africa were only introduced in 1921 when the Government of South Africa took over the civil administration of the territory. Although under German rule there were already government schools these were for Whites only; the education of the other population groups was undertaken solely by the Church missions. South Africa therefore, had to build up an educational service almost from scratch. In view of the lack of services and the basic problems of differences in language and the rate of 100 per cent illiteracy among the non-Whites, the volume of educational services, painstakingly built up over the past forty years, has been a magnificent achievement. From less than R20,000 ($28,000) in 1916, expenditure on schools soared to R5 ($7,000,000) in 1965.

Initial efforts were hampered by the lack of trained teachers and the large variety of language groups. Missionaries working in the educational field were reaching only about 15 per cent of the possible school population in 1922.

Aside from trying to provide mother-tongue instruction in the European and non-European languages (the latter of which had very little literary development), the administration was faced with the problem of distances which separated the available schools from potential students. Pupils from outlying areas had to be housed with families in the towns or in central dormitories during the school term, and the size of the problem can be judged from the fact that about half the White school-going population was served in this way.

Among Whites, there had been no significant development of educational facilities during the first twenty years of German colonization, since most of the colonists were European-born adults. Children born in the territory were given basic instruction on the farms and sent back to Germany as soon as possible. But by the time South Africa inherited the territory's administration, the need for local educational facilities was acute.

The obvious step was to encourage the existing schools — most of which were founded and run by missionaries — and to provide facilities where no missionary schools had been established. The Finnish missionaries in Ovamboland had set up centres for industrial training and these, along with schools offering the regular syllabus, were subsidized by the government. Teachers' salaries were paid, equipment provided, water and sanitation furnished; the administration assisted with books, stationery and the maintenance of school buildings. But attendance among the non-Whites was hampered by the reluctance of parents to send their children to live in remote boarding schools, and of those who did, dropouts after the first year or two were legion.

Of the missionary institutions, the Augustineum Institute for non-Whites at Okahandja deserves special notice. It was founded in 1864 by Dr. Hugo Hahn after a visit to Germany on which he collected funds for a native teacher-training centre. (Princess Augusta of Lippe was a major contributor.) The Hereros were enthusiastic about the project and two of its first students were Wilhelm and Samuel Maherero. Today, after a century of service by the Rhenish missionaries, the Augustineum provides for teacher training, a regular college entry academic programme and technical training in the industrial arts.

In 1924 only about 15 per cent of the potential school population was receiving instruction. By 1960 the percentage was 56 and by 1970 it is expected to reach 70 per cent, or twice that of Eastern Europe. Currently the percentage is higher than that found in Africa's twenty most populous states excluding South Africa and Rhodesia. In Africa's biggest state, Nigeria, the percentage was only 12; in Africa's oldest state, Ethiopia, it was only 13 and in the brainchild of America's emancipated Negroes, Liberia, it was only 12 per cent.[37] The ratio of 37 pupils to each available teacher also compares favourably with, for example, Kenya (42:1), the Congo (60:1) and Tanzania (48:1) and most other African states.

---

37. Cf: United Nations: Compendium of Social Statistics, 1963 pp. 323-324.

The curriculum for schools of all races is standard, although non-White teachers are in such short supply that their training period and level of performance for admittance to teaching positions in the lower primary grades is somewhat lower than standard.[38] The government sponsors feeding programmes in the non-White schools and tuition is entirely free. Board is also supplied where necessary and the administration provides travelling expenses for pupils who have to attend boarding schools.

There are no universities in South West Africa, but students of all races may enrol in the University of South Africa, the world's largest (19,000 students) and oldest recognised correspondence university. Students also attend other higher educational institutions in South Africa, including several universities, all of which recognize the preparatory work done in the territory.

The greatest single problem which had to be overcome (and is still to be overcome to a far greater degree) is the shortage of water in all but the north and northwestern areas of South West Africa. What water means to South West Africa, its people, its animal life and its future progress has been illustrated in striking manner by many observers. An article in *South African Panorama*[39] pointed out that water is of such paramount

---

38. An unusual boon for non-White teachers comes in the form of a free rail ticket for themselves and their entire families for a vacation at any point in the territory.

39. *Panorama,* Pretoria, September, 1964.

importance that the inhabitants can be said to be over-conscious of that precious commodity. To illustrate and substantiate their contention the editors pointed to the following examples:

Windhoek lights up its water tower at night. The reason for this probably lies deeper than mere pride. Perhaps it gives the local inhabitants a feeling of security to look at the hill on which the magnificent tower stands.

Water towers are not merely water towers in South West Africa. The ever-present consciousness of water has influenced their artistic and tasteful designs. The tower in Windhoek looks like a gigantic grain basket of the Ovambos. At Grootfontein the water tower resembled the popular idea of a flying saucer.

The official opening of a water tower is an event of social importance to the South West African community. People come from afar, often over difficult roads, to attend the ceremony.

Even the windmills look pretty in South West Africa. On the road to the north windmills are painted in a variety of colours.

The first and last question asked in South West Africa of someone undertaking a journey is: "Have you enough water?" In some parts many miles separate the sources of water. A shortage of water might mean death.

As in the case with human beings, animals, insects and plants must also adapt themselves to nature. The *steenbok* never drinks water. The liquid which it gets from plants and bulbs is sufficient for its existence. There

Harvest of pilchards: Walvis Bay.
South West Africa ranks among
the first ten fishing
countries of the world.

EXPORT TRADE[1]: 1963-1966[2]:
(Amounts in R'000)

Product	Total exports				Exports to Republic of South Africa			
	1963	1964	1965	1966	1963	1964	1965	1966
Agricultural products								
Karakul pelts	16,053	13,747	14,027	15,875	—	—	—	—
Livestock	15,357	16,503	17,193	14,115	15,357	16,503	17,193	14,08
Livestock products[3]	3,069	2,626	2,144	2,525	2,320	2,013	1,571	1,81
Other agricultural products[4]	100	90	123	120	100	90	123	12
Sub-total	34,579	32,966	33,487	32,635	17,777	18,606	18,887	16,02
Fishery products								
Fish meal	11,400	13,900	19,700	22,400	2,280	2,780	3,940	4,48
Canned fish	5,800	10,000	13,600	14,000	1,160	2,000	2,720	2,80
Other fishery products	5,300	10,300	11,650	12,500	300	1,120	940	98
Sub-total	22,500	34,200	44,950	48,900	3,740	5,900	7,600	8,26
Mineral products								
Diamonds	43,907	60,256	70,311	85,014	43,907	60,256	70,311	85,01
Blister copper	8,092	13,953	15,034	19,242	—	—	—	—
Refined lead	48	7,109	14,812	12,287	—	1,300	1,900	2,10
Lead/copper/zinc concentrates	10,422	7,857	10,198	7,876	—	—	—	—
Other mineral products	2,612	4,171	4,781	3,339	—	—	—	1,28
Sub-total	65,081	93,346	115,136	127,758	43,907	61,556	72,211	88,40
Total exports	122,160	160,512	193,573	209,293	65,424	86,062	98,698	112,68

[1]Source : *South West Africa Survey*, 1967, p. 103.

[2] Official trade statistics do not differentiate between the Republic and South West Africa. The figures shown ha♦ therefore, to be compiled from various sources, and cannot in all respects be regarded as fully reliable. This appli♦ in particular to *exports to the Republic*, in which case the following qualifications should be noted:
Agricultural products: Fairly accurate for livestock; informed estimates for remaining products.
Fishery products: Very rough approximations.
Mineral products: All diamonds are marketed through the Diamond Producers' Association so that it is somewh♦ arbitrary to allocate exports to Republic. Refined lead: Estimates based on figures obtained from the trade.

[3] Includes dairy products, wool, hides and skins; but excludes canned beef, beef-cuts, and offal, in respect where♦ information is not available.

[4] Teak (dolf) wood only.

(R1 = $1.4)

Cattle in the railway
stockpens at Windhoek —
en route to the South African cattle market.

GROSS DOMESTIC PRODUCT[1]: 1920, 1945, AND 1960–1965[2]

	Year	G.D.P. at factor cost (current prices)				Total		Increase of real G.D.P.[3]
		Agriculture	Fishing	Mining	All other sectors	Actual value	Adjusted to 1958 prices	
		(Rand millions)	(Rand millions)	(Rand millions)	(Rand millions)	(Rand millions)	(Rand millions)	% per annum
A. Amounts	1920	1·7	*	7·6	3·7	13·0	18·5	—
	1945	9·0	*	2·6	8·2	19·8	36·3	2·7
	1960	9·9	3·3	49·3	59·4	121·9	117·8	−1·7[4]
	1961	12·6	3·4	48·5	60·8	125·3	119·4	1·4
	1962	31·6	4·3	47·2	64·2	147·3	139·6	16·9
	1963	34·3	5·2	57·0	66·5	163·0	153·9	10·2
	1964	39·4	6·0	79·4	68·8	193·6	180·4	14·7
	1965	36·0	6·8	99·7	71·4	213·9	191·7	6·3
B. Percentage distribution		%	%	%	%	%		
	1920	13·1	*	58·4	28·5	100·0		
	1945	45·5	*	13·1	41·4	100·0		
	1960	8·1	2·7	40·4	48·7	100·0		
	1961	10·1	2·7	38·7	48·5	100·0		
	1962	21·5	2·9	32·0	43·6	100·0		
	1963	21·0	3·2	35·0	40·8	100·0		
	1964	20·4	3·1	41·0	35·5	100·0		
	1965	16·8	3·2	46·6	33·4	100·0		

[1] 1920 *and* 1945: *Report of the Commission of Enquiry into South West Africa Affairs 1962–1963*, (R.P. No. 12/1964), pp. 319 and 321, Tables CVII and CVIII.
    1960–1965: Unofficial estimates.
[2] Data for 1960–1965 are preliminary unofficial estimates and must be interpreted with due caution.
[3] Comparable rates are: 1920–1965: 5·3% *per annum.*
                 1920–1945: 2·7% ,, ,,
                 1945–1965: 8·7% ,, ,,
                 1961–1965: 12·6% ,, ,,
[4] Change 1959–1960.

(R1 = $1.40)

are insects in South West Africa which crawl as much as a foot under the surface of the earth to suck at a moist grain of sand. Fish lie patiently in the moist sand in river beds waiting until it rains again.

The birds of the north find water in the hollowed-out trunks of dolf-trees. One such hollow tree has been known to contain as much as 100 gallons of water.

Beasts of prey obtain sufficient liquid from the blood of their victims to quench their thirst. Some animals dig holes in dry river beds to obtain water.

The only inhabitant of Sandwich Bay, Mr. Hans von Broen, a Coloured, obtains his drinking and gardening water in a unique way. His house is situated on the beach with its back against the high sand dunes. The Namib desert stretches away from the back door. There is no river or water hole in the immediate vicinity. Mr. von Broen digs holes in one of the dry courses at the mouth of the Kuiseb River and waits until the tide is high. The sea water pushes up under the sand and the fresh water, which is lighter in weight, seeps into the holes and lies on top of the sea water. All that is necessary is to scoop out the delicious fresh water.

The story of South West Africa's progress is, there-fore, in a great part also the story of success in the endless search for water. Since 1920 over R20 million ($28,0000,0)0) has gone into water conservation from public expenditure and thousands of private boreholes, dams and irrigation projects have been completed at an estimated cost of R30 ($42,000,000). Investments in water projects from Tribal Funds and Municipalities bring the total to about R60 million or $84,000,000.

But finding water in the first place is not enough. An ordinary open dam would lose up to 98 per cent of its capacity in a two-year period under South West's blistering sun. Obviously, unusual means have had to be devised to combat an unusual problem.

One of the more resourceful methods is an engineering marvel called the sand storage dam. In this dam, Nature's own materials are turned against her purpose to serve the ends of men and cattle. An ordinary dam retaining wall, usually about three feet high, is constructed across a river bed or drainage path. On those rare occasions when it does rain, the water runs toward the dam, carrying sand and gravel with it. Over months and months both the water and silt build up until a hard layer of sand, level with the top of the wall, stands behind the dam. The top foot of sand, called a blanket, is baked dry through evaporation, but the layer beneath is a reservoir of pure water that may be drawn off through the filtering sand and gravel from a pipe or sluice at the base of the dam. A considerable amount of water — a third of the total capacity — may be retained in one of these dams and, when the silt has reached dam level, another dam may be erected above the first. The dams give every appearance of being dry river beds. Cattle wander across them, men and dogs criss-cross their hard surface and tiny insects burrow in their sheltering sands.

Natural versions of the sand storage dams provide almost the entire supply of fresh water for man and beast in South West Africa. Wild game dig with their paws into river beds for the thirst-quenching liquid beneath. Fish burrow into the damp earth to await the next rains. And the larger species of buck will stand patiently while moisture trickles into the holes they make with their hooves in the dry beds.

Each farm has its borehole or well, some of them as much as one thousand feet deep. The subterranean reservoirs provide water for towns and country, men and animals. Even in the arid Kalahari, the wily Bushmen sniff the air and dig, sensing through some mystical intuition the presence of water.

Storage dams are increasingly the main source of water, however. The Avis and Goreangab dams near Windhoek, the Van Rhyn dam at Keetmanshoop, the Daan Viljoen dam at Gobabis and the Hardap dam near Mariental (the biggest in South West Africa) have all proved the value of permanent reservoirs.

The evaporation problem has been the focus of countless experiments by engineers and inventors. One of the more promising recent solutions is the floating of concrete squares containing plastic bubbles on the surface of open dams. Their light exteriors reflect the harsh rays of the sun and impede the evaporation process by up to 80 per cent.[40]

Can the harsh climate of South West Africa ever be tamed? Civilization and development cannot be halted. It is inherent in life, in man's struggle to better himself

---

40. In South Africa itself, the most recent experiments include spraying the huge Vaaldam, the country's biggest reservoir, with alcohol to retard evaporation. In this way, scientists believe millions of gallons of water can be saved *each* day.

and improve his environment. There will always be the continuous struggle against drought, and the desert.

Patience and foresight led gradually to the rule of law being accepted. Superstition and witchcraft were eliminated by the teaching of Western spiritual and physical codes to the more primitive groups in the territory. Only by ridding the tribes of a cult-ridden past could they be assisted towards a full measure of self-fulfilment.

The economic development of the country in the face of seemingly insurmountable odds has proceeded at an impressive pace and for some years now has brought boom conditions to the territory.

A massive effort on the part of the Government of the Union of South Africa, whose aid *per capita* to the people of South Africa represents the biggest *and* most successful foreign aid programme yet undertaken any-where in the world, has placed in the hands of the indigenous population a most powerful weapon: a good education.

Through painstaking negotiations and years of planning each of the different nations inhabiting South West Africa now has an inalienable right to his own homeland. Friction between tribes has been reduced to a minimum. Communications have been expanded and South Wes Africa's general contribution to the progress of mankind increased.

There remains a long and tedious struggle to ensure that civilization is not now extinguished. This is the task confronting the Administration and the South West

African. There can be no relaxation in that task and indeed the final chapter in this book deals with South Africa's huge and imaginative five-year socio-economic development programme for South West Africa and plans for a realistic political future.

The future of South West Africa points in one direction only — an ever closer association with its prosperous and industrially developed neighbour, South Africa, whose big population (18,000,000 people in 1966) will not only be a ready market for South West African products but can provide the know-how and capital to maintain South West Africa's current rate of growth. A major change now in administration or in the direction of its present socio-political development and the territory will recede into the mire of superstition, bloodshed and stagnation from which it has only recently emerged. Such a change is being urged upon the world at the United Nations at this moment in history by men and organizations who do not have the welfare of South West Africa at heart but who are imbued with ulterior and selfish motives. For this reason the following chapter is of extreme importance for it shows quite clearly that those who speak so loudly on behalf of South West Africa are not only *legally* not entitled to assume that role but have no *moral* right either.

If South Africa's grip is loosened on this harsh land the Namib Desert will do to the development and progress of South West Africa what it did to the former German industries at Sandwich Bay and the ghost-towns in the district of Lüderitz. The winds of poverty, corruption, economic decay and, ultimately, the bloodshed and strife which has overtaken almost every state in Africa who wanted to fly when it should have been learning how to walk, will then also blow in South West Africa. The stifling dust will settle on an organized, thriving society. All that will remain will be giant sanddunes impeding the road forward. But the events in Ghana, Nigeria, the Congo and the Sudan, in Zanzibar and Guinea cast a long shadow which no responsible White or Black man in South West Africa can fail to ignore. Hence the widespread opposition to United Nations control over the territory's future.

5

THE SACRED TRUST

South Africa's struggle to get South West Africa onto its own feet and to promote the general welfare of all its inhabitants has not been confined only to the elements, the deep seated superstitions and basic apathy of the Natives or the economic drawbacks of this vast arid land. It has also had to resist the massive legal effort before the International Court of Justice by the Black African states, acting in concert, to wrest the administration of South West Africa from South Africa's hands.

The African states demanded a change, they demanded, if necessary, United Nations military action to force this change. They ignored the fundamental fact that the basic freedoms from superstition, ignorance, disease, fear and poverty cannot be acquired and maintained by the magic words of "political change" or "independence", particularly not in Africa. Even if they realised that this was true, it did not daunt the prosecution; it knew it was riding a crest of liberalism in world politics which refused to be sidetracked by fundamental issues; it was bent helter skelter for *world government* and *world law* and South West Africa, apart from being a means of striking at White-controlled South Africa, was going to be the test case.

The World Court's decision on July 18, 1966, came as a stunning surprise to the African Black States.

In its judgment the Court found that Liberia and Ethiopia who instituted proceedings against South Africa on behalf of he Black African states had no legal right or interest in South Africa's administration of the territory.

The effect of the decision is to give South Africa a free hand to administer the mandated territory as it sees best. The Court also found, in effect, that only the League of Nations, operating as an entity, previously had such rights. The Court came close to accepting that there is now *no* entity, not even the United Nations, which is entitled to act as a watchdog over South Africa's administration. Legally speaking the mandate relations between the South African Government and the inhabitants of South West Africa could quite possibly no longer be of any international concern.

The losers, and all who sided with them are bitterly displeased with the Court. Had they won, the World Court's ruling would probably have served them as a banner to stamp out apartheid in South West Africa and South Africa. As a practical matter South Africa's victory has spared mankind from more bloodshed. The Court itself will not be spared. Already the African states are demanding its reform to include a majority of non-White members; the Court is now called a "White man's Court"; the judges have been abused and every effort made to belittle the verdict and to comfort the African states in their bitter disappointment.

Their disappointment can well be understood. As Graham Hovey, a senior member of the editorial board of the world renowned *New York Times* wrote on August 29, 1966, in "The Times", this was the year the Africans had expected to come to the General Assembly armed with a World Court ruling against South Africa. "They had hoped the Court might go so far as to hold South Africa in violation of its old League of Nations obligations for extending racial segregation into South West Africa". Here was to have been not only a practical move to break South Africa's 46-year grip on South West Africa but "a meaningful international assault on the Republic's apartheid policy". Here, he wrote, would be the first major collective blow "aimed at ending White minority domination in the remaining sixth of the African continent". It might have hastened the end of Rhodesia's "rebellion" and jarred Portugal into modifying its policies in Angola and Moçambique.

The Peace-palace,
seat of the World Court
in The Hague.

Photo: Bulsing Scheveningen.

The World Court in Session: From left to right Judges Abdel Badawi (Egypt), Jacques van Wyk (South Africa), Andre Gros (France), Luis Nervo (Mexico), Philip Jesup (U.S.A.), Kataro Tanaka (Japan), Sir Gerald Fitzmaurice (United Kingdom), José Bustamente y Rivero (Peru), V. K. Wellington Koo (China and Vice President), Sir Percy Spender (Australia and President), Bohdan Winiarski (Poland), Jean Spiropoulos (Greece), Vladimir Koretsky (Russia), Gaetano Morelli (Italy), Isaac Forster (Senegal), Sir Louis Mbanefo (Nigeria).

All such Black African hopes were dashed in July, 1966, when the Court threw out the case altogether. The lengths to which the Black African States (Liberia and Ehiopia) went to divert any spotlight on the plight of their own people can be gauged by the fact that they urged the United States Government to suppress publication of a book dealing with this subject until the International Court finished with the South West Africa case. The book, entitled *Growth Without Development,* is a study of Liberia undertaken for the Agency for International Development by four economists who report that Liberia is run for their own delectation by a small clique of descendents of freed slaves from America who exploit the indigenous African tribes.

In bringing suit against South Africa at the World Court, Liberia and Ethiopia levelled a great many charges against South African policies and its administration of South West Africa which, they contended, was a gross violation of South Africa's "Sacred Trust".

The case against South Africa was set down in 1960 and in December, 1962, the Court ruled by the narrowest of majorities (8-7) that it could sit in judgment on the suit brought against South Africa. For all practical purposes the case came to a close at its 100th session before the International Court of Justice at the Hague on November 26th, 1965. This is a date which will, in years to come, have as much historical significance to conservative political opinion in the Western World as to the population of South West Africa itself. It marked the first organised attempt to legally impose upon a sovereign independent state a norm of political behaviour which, so it was alleged, is universally applicable. After abandoning initial charges of militarization of the territory, exploitation and oppression of the natives, etc., Liberia and Ethiopia accused South Africa of violating a so-called *international norm of non-discrimination* which, they contended, was set by the *international community* as represented by the United Nations. This norm forbids the differential development of people irrespective whether such discrimination was good or bad. Simply by ignoring this norm South Africa had violated its "Sacred Trust" to the people of South West Africa.

It is true that the case related only to an obscure territory administered by the Republic of South Africa but its implications will be felt far and wide in years to come. Success in this contention would have meant that other countries could approach the International Court for a ruling to the effect that neighbouring territories or other states, far removed from their sphere of influence, should also be governed according to the supposed "international norm" as set by "the international community".

At this moment the "norm" is only one of "non-discrimination" — but it could pave the way for the creation of other "norms" set by the "international community".

This form of internationalism which originated in Moscow, mushroomed at the United Nations and is now seeking the blessing of international law, would most

certainly not benefit the Western world. The undeveloped masses of China, India, Asia and Africa have
numbers on their side and numbers have become the
most powerful historical factor of our age. It is mani-
fested in the slogan "one man one vote" which means
that the votes of 50,000 stone age Bushmen in Africa
equal that of 50,000 graduates from American
universities. If on the other hand the *international community* is represented by a number of like-minded
governments, rather than masses of people, then the
Afro-Asian states could still set the so-called "international
norm" or behaviour for other countries — a prospect
which the democratic minded Western states will no
doubt find extremely dismal.

Communism, which recognises no frontiers and to
whom sacred beliefs such as national sovereignty, free
enterprise, religious freedom and secret elections have no
meaning whatsoever (except where they can exploit it)
would in the end gain most from a world subjected to
the norm envisaged by Liberia and Ethiopia.

Such a norm of "non-discrimination" would not
only prohibit differential development on grounds of
race or colour but also because of political belief. No
state in Africa would therefore be able to take legal
actions against people preaching the Communist ideology
to primitive and, therefore, gullible native masses. To
do so would be to invite court action in terms of the
norm of "non-discrimination".

This may now sound far-fetched but carried to its
logical conclusions the establishment of one international

norm by the so-called "international community" must, *ipso facto,* lead to other norms. Even at this stage a "broad" interpretation of the "norm" proposed to the World Court at The Hague would be sufficient to cover governmental action against the spread of Communism.

The South West Africa case can rightfully be considered to be part of the thin edge of the wedge by which the "one-world-one-government" clique and their schemers in the Secretariat of the United Nations had hoped to divest sovereign governments of their domestic powers. Of course there have been other attempts at the United Nations, aimed at undermining the authority of governments over their own domestic affairs, but never before under the cloak of International Law.

For these and other reasons a study of the origin, development and pro- and counter arguments at the World Court in the South West Africa case is of considerable interest to an array of people: political scientists, students of internaional affairs, students of law, people interested in racial affairs and race relations or the future of multi-racial communities in Africa, etc.

Of particular interest to students of international affairs and the United Nations are those sections relating to the pros and cons of the proposed "international norm" as set by the so-called "international community".

———————

The South West Africa case was the most protracted and far reaching dispute ever to come before the World Court or its League of Nations predecessor the Court of International Justice.

South Africa's written presentation alone was sufficient to fill ten good-sized novels while the verbatim record of the oral proceedings took up twice as much space or some 2,000,000 words.

To obtain the necessary perspective of South Africa's argument calls for a brief flashback into history.

As indicated in Chapter III South Africa's right of administration originated in the act of surrender of the German Forces in 1915. At the Versailles Peace Conference the Supreme Council of the Allied Powers conferred upon South Africa the right to administer the conquered territory formerly known as German South West Africa. The task was to be undertaken for the "well-being and development of primitive peoples" and would constitute a "sacred trust of civilization".

The operative article of the Mandate (article 2) can be summarised as follows: that the Mandatory shall have full power of administration and legislation over the Territory as an integral portion of the Union of South Africa, and may apply the laws of the Union of South Africa to the Territory, subject to local modifications as circumstances may require. The Mandatory shall promote to the utmost the material and moral well-being and the social progress of the inhabitants of the Territory.

The eclipse of the League of Nations is now history. The question of whether the Mandate continued to exist afterwards did not arise immediately. It only became "relevant" when the campaign at the United Nations to wrest control of South West Africa from South Africa began to pick up steam after 1948. South Africa, however, had consistently taken the view that accountability to the League of Nations supervisory organs lapsed upon dissolution of the League of Nations, and that no provision for new supervisory organs was made at any stage. It also maintained accountability to the League organs was intended by the authors of the Mandate System to be an essential part of the Mandate, with the result that when the League of Nations collapsed the provisions relating to accountability became nul and void.

Although South Africa takes up the attitude that, legally speaking, the whole Mandate has lapsed by reason of the dissolution of the League of Nations, the Republic has consistently stated that it will continue to administer the territory "in the spirit of the Mandate", which means that it will voluntarily continue to treat the territory as if all the obligations contained in the "sacred trust of civilization" were still in existence. South Africa, however, adamently denies that the United Nations has any legal powers or functions of supervision with respect to South Africa's administration of the territory.

At the time of the dissolution of the League, and the creation of the United Nations, no agreement, not even implied as to United Nations supervision, was reached. On the contrary, new information leaves no doubt that express attempts to grant the United Nations supervisory powers and functions in respect of Mandates were unsuccessful.

The *first* new point showing the above arises from the fact that on April 18, 1946, China advanced a proposal before the last League of Nations Assembly "recommending that the mandatory powers shall continue to submit annual reports to the United Nations and to submit to inspection by the same until the Trusteeship Council shall have been constituted". The second paragraph of the Chinese draft invited the League Assembly to express the view that "the League's function of supervising Mandated Territories should be transferred to the United Nations in order to avoid a period of interregnum in the supervision of the Mandatory regime". After it had become clear that this proposal would not be acceped, *it was dropped* and a neutral resolution containing no reference to the transfer of supervision was adopted. It is self-evident that no tacit agreement to transfer supervisory functions to the United Nations can be inferred if an express proposal to the same effect had been dropped for lack of sufficient support.

The *second* point showing that no agreement could have been reached arises out of the discussions and decisions at the time of the inception of the United Nations. It appears clearly that the United Nations did not consider itself to be an automatic successor in law to any of the League functions. It was further resolved that the exercise of functions of powers entrusted to the League of Nations by treaties, international conventions or agreements would only be assumed by the United Nations after a request from the parties involved had been made and the General Assembly had acceded to such a request. *Nothing of this nature ever happened in the case of the South West Mandate.* It was well known at that time that all the territories formerly under Mandate would not be placed under the Trusteeship System of the United Nations, and that even in the case of those territories which would be placed under the system, a considerable time might elapse before Trusteeship Agreements would be concluded. Nevertheless the establishment of a Temporary Trusteeship Committee had been rejected as no machinery for the possible transfer of, or assumption by the United Nations of, any functions previously exercised under the Mandate System, had been substituted for the rejected proposal.

In logic the inference is inescapable that the omission was deliberate. The only possibility left by which the United Nations could have obtained supervisory functions would have been by special arrangements with South Africa and no such arrangements were at any time concluded.

The *third* point clearly showing that no tacit agreement granting the United Nations Organisation supervisory functions can be inferred, relates to the practice and attitude of States. Such practice, during the years immediately after the establishment of the United Nations and the dissolution of the League, showed a general understanding that the League's supervisory powers in respect of Mandates had not been transferred to, or assumed by, the United Nations. At the time the United Nations consisted of 57 members, of which 51 had been original members. Of the 51, thirty-one had been members of the League at the time of its dissolution, and 34 had been original members of the League. Had these States or any one of them disagreed with South Africa's contention that the supervisory functions of the League had not been transferred to the United Nations, one would have expected them to have contested it, particularly if they had been parties to an agreement, expressed or implied, concluded the previous year and providing for such a transfer.

In fact, representatives of 41 States addressed the various organs of the United Nations on the question of South West Africa during 1947, but at no stage did *any* of them aver the existence of any such agreement or suggest that the supervisory functions of the League had passed to the United Nations. On the contrary, at least 14 of the 41 States who took part in the debates acknowledged either expressly or by clear implication that, in the absence of a Trusteeship Agreement, the United Nations would have no supervisory power in respect of South West Africa: These were Australia, China, Columbia, Cuba, France, India, Irak, The Netherlands, New Zealand, Pakistan, The Phillipine Republic, the Soviet Union, the United States of America and Uruguay.

During 1948 and 1949, four additional States associated themselves with this view, viz. Canada, Costa Rica, Greece and the United Kingdom.

Also in respect of other Mandated Territories, the practice of States up to 1948 shows a clear understanding that the United Nations would have no supervisory power over the administration of a Mandated Territory not placed under Trusteeship. This understanding appears from the following:

The Trusteeship agreement for the Mandated Territory of Nauru was entered into as late as November, 1947, i.e. more than two years after the Charter had come into force, and the United Kingdom withdrew from the administration of Palestine only as from the 15th May, 1948. Nevertheless no reports were in the interim period submitted to the United Nations in respect of either territory. As far as the United Nations records show, no State ever suggested that such reports should be submitted — either in respect of these territories or in respect of any other Mandated Territories during the period after the dissolution of the League and prior to "new arrangements" being "agreed" upon in regard to them.

The case of Palestine is of particular significance inasmuch as it was investigated and reported upon by a United Nations Special Committee, consisting of representatives of eleven members of the United Nations. It is important to note that this Committee unanimously expressed the clear understanding that the United Nations did not take over the supervisory functions of the League of Nations with respect to Mandates which were not converted into Trusteeship Territories. Five of these eleven members (Australia, Canada, India the Netherlands and Uruguay) at various times during the relevant period expressed the same view regarding the Mandate for South West Africa, as has been noted. The further six were Czechoslovakia, Guatemala, Iran, Peru, Sweden and Yugoslavia.

Also in debates on the Palestine question the same view was expressed. On the 19th March, 1948, before the Security Council, the representative of the United States of America stated: "The record seems to us entirely clear that the United Nations did not take over he League of Nations Mandate system."

At no time up to 1949 was any contradiction voiced by either Liberia or Ethiopia; in fact of all countries only five states of which Cuba was one, voiced a contradiction at all.

The understanding which emerges from the above circumstances and in particular the written and oral statements made on behalf of a large number of States, Members of the United Nations, in a variety of circumstances and situations, and within a relatively short time after the establishment of the United Nations and the dissolution of the League, when the events were still reasonably fresh in memory, effectively refutes any suggestion of agreement, express or implied, as between members of the United Nations or other interested parties to the effect that Mandatories would be subject to United Nations supervision in respect of Mandates not converted into Trusteeship.

Similarly these discussions clearly refute any suggestion that such an obligation arose out of a term to be implied in the Mandate instrument. In this regard it must be noted that 18 of the 24 States who expressed the view during 1947 to 1949 that the United Nations did not succeed to the supervisory functions of the League in respect of Mandates, had been founder members of the League of Nations, and 17 had been members at the time of its dissolution.

Despite all these facts, Ethiopia and Liberia instituted proceedings against South Africa at the International Court charging that South Africa had violated her trust, failed to promote the material and moral well-being of the inhabitants of South West Africa and that South Africa was legally bound to submit to United Nations supervision of its stewardship of the territory. More specifically they asked the Court to find that the Mandate granted to the Union of South Africa was still in existence, that the supervisory functions of the old League of Nations had been taken over by the United Nations; that the South African Government has practised apartheid in the territory; that South Africa has treated the territory in a manner inconsistent with the international status of the territory, and has thereby impeded opportunities for self-determination by the inhabitants of the territory; that South Africa has established military bases within the territory in violation of the Mandate; that South Africa has failed to render to the General Assembly of the United Nations annual reports containing information with regard to the territory and indicating the measures it has taken to carry out its obligations under the Mandate and that South Africa has failed to transmit to the General Assembly of the United Nations petitions from the Territory's inhabitants.

On March 30, 1965, shortly after the hearings opened, Mr. D. P. de Villiers, leader of the ten-man South African legal team, extended an invitation to the Court, or a Committee of the Court, to visit South West Africa for an on-the-spot inspection in order to gain knowledge at first hand, of the realities of the situation. This inspection could include anything in South West Africa to which the Applicants in the case (Liberia and Ethiopia) might wish to invite attention and also anything the Court or its Committee might wish to see.

The proposal for an inspection was made to place at the Court's disposal every means of enlightenment that could contribute to objective evaluation and adjudication of the situation.

South Africa argued that African reality had to be seen in order to be grasped effectively. It was virtually impossible for visitors from outside of the African Continent to view and evaluate well-being and progress in an African territory like South West Africa fairly and in proper perspective unless they had been able also to assess comparable standards in other African territories. Otherwise perspective might quite unconsciously be warped by the introduction of European, American or Asian standards to an African context. Inspection of achievements and standards in Liberia and Ethiopia could assist the Court considerably in evaluating the policies and practices followed in South West Africa. In this way the Court could form a general impression of comparable standards of material and moral well-being and of social progress in the respective countries.

Apart from a visit to Liberia and Ethiopia, South Africa also proposed that the inspection should include one or two other sub-Saharan territories in Africa, at least one of which should formerly have been under mandate or trusteeship. Since it was clear from the record that Liberia and Ethiopia were, in these proceedings, acting as representatives of all independent African States they would have been able to secure, at the Court's request, the invitations for an inspecting group to visit one or two of the territories proposed.

South Africa was amazed at the strenuous objections raised by Mr. Ernest A. Gross, Counsel for Liberia and Ethiopia, against the proposed visit of inspection. He pleaded for an outright rejection of the proposal which he termed "unnecessary, expensive, dilatory, cumbersome and unwarranted".

South Africa reiterated that a visit was proposed so that the Court could see from the bearing of the people and from the way in which they lived whether an alleged suffocating weight of restrictive measures rested upon them. The Court could go to the schools to see whether the children were being educated for slavery and servitude, as was alleged. The Court could establish at first hand, whether it was true to say that the non-Whites were merely employed as menial labourers and that they were not allowed to rise above that level at all.

Far from inferring that the South African administration of South West Africa had been faultless — no government could make that claim — South Africa suggested that the Court would find that there was a real endeavour to promote the well-being and progress of the peoples of South West Africa to the utmost.

The strenuous opposition of Counsel for Liberia and Ethiopia to a visit of inspection, was followed by a dramatic *volte face* which struck at the heart of the Applicants' case against South Africa.

This significant shifting of ground in their attack on South Africa's administration of South West Africa was conveyed to the Court by Mr. Gross on May 19, 1965, in these terms:

"The Applicants (Liberia and Ethiopia) have advised Respondent (South Africa) as well as this honourable Court that all and any averments of fact in Respondent's written pleadings will be and are accepted as true, unless specifically denied. And Applicants have not found it necessary and do not find it necessary to controvert any such averments of fact. Hence, for the purposes of these proceedings, such averments of fact, although made by respondent in a copious and unusually voluminous record, may be treated as if incorporated by reference into the Applicants' pleadings".

The significant change in the Applicants' approach meant that they were forced to abandon the factual basis on which they brought the case against South Africa before the Court.

In view of their difficulties to substantiate their original case on the facts, they amended their submissions and rested their new case, as far as the merits are concerned, on the sole contention that South Africa had acted contrary to an international norm and/or standard of non-discrimination or non-separation. There were, they contended, accepted international standards according to which racial discrimination was "inherently and always incompatible with moral well-being and social progress". The mere fact that South Africa's policies differentiate between population groups was the gist of their new case.

Even a cursory glance at the charges Liberia and Ethiopia originally brought against South Africa shows the extent to which they have shifted their ground.

Reduced to its essentials the charges against South Africa were that it acted in bad faith towards the inhabitants of South West Africa by applying policies designed to oppress, suppress or exploit them. These charges covered a wide field of South Africa's administration of the Territory and amounted to a violation of the fundamental obligations conferred upon it by the original Mandate.

South Africa met these charges in its 3,000 page written presentation to the Court and was anxious to call witnesses in order to conduct a full investigation into the original charges of Liberia and Ethiopia that its policies led to deliberate oppression of the peoples of South West Africa.

A list of 38 expert witnesses was laid before the Court. The calling of witnesses was vigorously opposed by Liberia and Ethiopia. By that time they had already discovered that it was not so easy in the World Court as it was in the United Nations to assert oppression. Difficulty to produce proof to the satisfaction of the Court led to efforts on the part of Liberia and Ethiopia to avoid

Wife of the Bushman
Commissioner attending to a patient.

Education — phenomenal growth.

Young Ovambo girls
undergoing training as nurses.

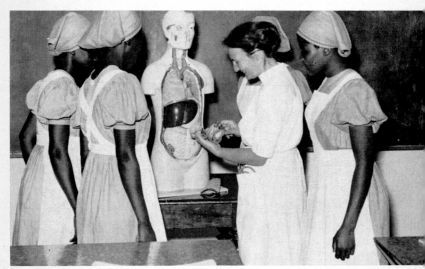

the factual enquiry which they themselves had initiated.

Fourteen expert witnesses were called by South Africa after the Court had upheld South Africa's right to call oral evidence. After Liberia and Ethiopia had dramatically changed their case in regard to deliberate oppression the need for calling more witnesses fell away.

The *volte face* of the Applicants and their problems in substantiating their original charges of oppression and bad faith provided South Africa with the opportunity to prove that the attacks on South Africa were part and parcel of a political campaign aimed at establishing black rule over the whole of Africa, including South West Africa and ultimately the Republic of South Africa.

There was a direct link between this campaign and the case before the Court. Records of the United Nations and resolutions adopted by the Organisation for African Unity proved the point.

Factual evidence was presented in support of this contention. For example the Second Conference of Independent African States, which met at Addis Ababa during June, 1960, discussed Liberia and Ethiopia's intentions to institute proceedings against South Africa on behalf of all the African States, and decided "That a Steering Committee of Four African States, including the delegations of Ethiopia and Liberia, should be established to determine the procedures and tactics incident to the conduct of the Juridical proceedings in this matter". Liberia and Ethiopia were, therefore, only nominal parties to the proceedings. In actual fact they were appearing in a representative capacity. Although they had been indignantly evasive before the Court on this point, there was no practical reason why they should have initiated the proceedings. They had no direct contact and cultural, economic or other ties with South West Africa. Liberia and Ethiopia's acceptance of the body of the factual evidence provided by South Africa made it clear that the standard of progress in South West Africa was as high or higher than in these two countries.

The question then arose why they had brought this case before the Court.

South Africa contended that emotional outbursts and fantastic assertions of alleged facts characterised the conduct of the campaign in the United Nations against South Africa on this matter. The source of this volume of incorrect information was largely a small group of petitioners, principally from South West Africa and England, who played a pivotal part in this campaign. They were keeping the campaign alive with a flood of indefensibly unfounded allegations of suppression and atrocities committed by South Africa in South West Africa. The petitions were described by Liberia and Ethiopia as having been "received from a wide variety of independent sources", in an attempt to enhance their credibility and trustworthiness.

South Africa painstakingly exposed the great majority of petitioners relied on by Liberia and Ethiopia as belonging to a small group of what may be called "professional petitioners", who were united in common purpose to "smash the Whites out of the Government" and to "get South West Africa back no more no less" as some of them expressed their objectives privately. Among them were Mburumba Kerina,[41] J. Kozonquizi and the Rev. Michael Scott.

The objectives of their campaign and the methods employed by them were exposed by the contents of letters of Kerina and others from which it clearly emerged that thir campaign involved incitement and intimidation of the indigenous population of South West Africa, the organization of incidents within the Territory which could be "played up" on international platforms, large scale transmission to the United Nations of petitions, in some cases drafted in New York and sent to the Territory for signature by local associates, the seeking of military intervention by other States, and the creation of organizations which would be given out as enjoying widespread support within the Territory[42]).

In order to influence international opinion, the leaders of the aforesaid campaign adopted a system of flooding the world in general, and the United Nations Organization in particular, with continuous allegations of suppression and atrocities allegedly committed by South Africa. This small group of professional petitioners constantly schemed and devised means to bring the administration of the Territory into discredit, and, as South Africa's review of their allegations showed, were blatantly

---

41. Kerina did not improve his stock when in 1963 he attacked the United States during an "orientation" visit to Red China while praising his Communist hosts for their "progressive" policies.

42. Cf. Molnar: *South West Africa, Fleet, N.Y.*, pp. 120—125.

prepared to distort the facts and present a false picture in their petitions to "flood the United Nations".

Liberia and Ethiopia in their reply, did not see fit to deal with this exposure, have not denied the facts adduced by South Africa, and significantly, placed no further reliance on the allegations of petitioners in their further pleadings.

South Africa went so far as to indicate that it would consider, if Liberia and Ethiopia wished to call the petitioners as witnesses, to offer to pay their transport and other costs so as to allow the Republic's legal representatives the privilege of cross-examining them before the International Court of Justice.

Since the Opposition failed to take up the challenge South Africa had to controvert the baseless allegations of the petitioners in its factual statements. Counsel for Liberia and Ethiopia admitted all South Africa's factual statements and stated specifically in the oral proceedings that *they were not relying on the truth of allegations by petitioner.* This was in marked contrast to their original submission on which they did rely on the allegations of these petitioners, describing them as "a variety of independent sources".

Nevertheless, South Africa contended, these baseless accusations of the coterie of biased professional petitioners were accepted at the United Nations and gave rise to condemnatory resolutions against South Africa.

Invited to give evidence before organs of the United Nations, these petitioners were free to make the wildest possible statements. Their evidence was accepted at its face value. Examples of the fanciful allegations made by petitioners which served to pave the way for United Nations resolutions condemning South Africa's administration of South West Africa were:

— that the indigenous population were herded into cide and racial extermination in the Territory;
— that the indigenous population were herded into concentration camps where they were treated like animals and reduced to slavery;
— that South Africa's policies were rooted in racial hatred and animosity;
— that non-Whites were deprived of their land and confined to desert areas;
— that the education system was designed to prepare non-Whites for an inferior station in life;
— that there was large-scale militarisation of South West Africa and that missile and nuclear centres had been established.

In its pleadings and in uncontroverted evidence by expert witnesses South Africa demonstrated the falsity of every one of these allegations. Even so and even after Liberia and Ethiopia had accepted the evidence produced by South Africa as true, this false information provided by the petitioners was once more accepted unreservedly and acted upon by the United Nations Committee on Colonialism during a recent visit to Africa.

On the other hand information favourable to South Africa's administration of South West Africa was deliberately suppressed. A case in point was the joint communiqué issued by the Chairman and Vice-Chairman of the United Nations Committee on South West Africa, Mr. Carpio and Dr. Martinez de Alva, and the South African Prime Minister and the Minister of Foreign Affairs. The communiqué which had been suppressed as a United Nations document was issued after the visit of Messrs. Carpio and De Alva to South West Africa during 1962. It stated that they had found "no evidence and heard no allegations that there was a threat to international peace and security within South West Africa; that there were signs of militarisation in the Territory; or that the indigenous population was being exterminated".

Untrue and baseless allegations, repeated consistently and systematically, South Africa contended, had unfortunately been accepted by a large number of delegations and by committees and organs of the United Nations. This had influenced these delegations, especially those from the independent African states and their allies, and clearly played a major role in the adoption of resolutions condemning South Africa's policies and actions in the United Nations.

Dealing with various resolutions adopted by United Nations, in respect of South West Africa and South Africa, the latter pointed out that these resolutions were based on the erroneous notion that South Africa's policies were designed to oppress the indigenous population. The Court could, therefore, not safely be guided by these resolutions for any purpose.

In the same way as they abandoned their reliance on the allegations of petitioners after these had been disproved by South Africa, Liberia and Ethiopia refrained from pressing further the original charges in connection with militarisation of the Territory and the establishment of military bases. An American general, General S. L. A. Marshall, appearing as an expert witness on military matters, told the Court that he had seen nothing in South West Africa which he could regard as a military base or fortification. Questioned by Counsel he stated his belief that the Territory was "less militarised and more under-armed than any territory of its size in the world".

Since Liberia and Ethiopia had abandoned their factual case against South Africa which included bad faith and oppression of the inhabitants of South West Africa, the focal point of their attack suddenly became the charge of violation of an international norm and/or standards of non-discrimination and non-separation. They contended that South Africa had to administer South West Africa in accordance with a generally binding rule of international law, possessing the content of the norm of non-discrimination and non-separation. This norm, they further contended, had been created by the over-whelming consensus of the "international community"

South Africa maintained that no such norm and/or standard is in existence.

In his special study of the South West Africa case, Professor Walter Darnell Jacobs[43] the eminent American political scientist wrote: "The South African argument on this point is also worth consideration. What would happen to land reserved for the Indians in the United States if the Court were to decide that such a standard and/or norm existed? What would be the fate of the Lapps in Sweden? Would there then be no differentiation between Moslems and non-Moslems in, say, Pakistan and Indonesia? Would the Lebanese formula for political representation be set aside? Would the Maoris lose their place in Parliament (in New Zealand)? Would a Turk be the recipient of a legal right to become President of Cyprus? Would the disatvantaged minorities in Liberia and Ethiopia have a basis for action against their governments?"[44]

South Africa quoted the evidence of Professor Stephan Possony, Director of the International Studies Programme, Hoover Institute for War and Peace, Stanford University, California, who stated that there were fifty countries in the world in which by law and official practice status, rights, duties and burdens were allotted on the basis of membership of a group, class or race. Of these fifty countries, forty were members of the United Nations and they included both Liberia and Ethiopia.

"From what I have indicated to the Court with relation to the practice all over the world," Professor Possony told the Court, "there is no general observance of such a rule or norm."

---

43. Professor of Government and Politics, University of Maryland, co-author of *Modern Governments* (D. van Norstrand Co., New York), Member of the American Political Science Association and the American Military Institute.
44. *South West Africa in Law and Politics,* American-African Affairs Association. New York, 1966.

Attempts to formulate a concept of effective practice in this regard, Professor Possony stated further, had progressed no further than expressions of general abstract ideas.

Another expert witness, Professor Ernest van den Haag, Member of the Faculty of New York University and of the New School for Social Research, testified that social groups were bound together by a feeling of group solidarity usually based on similar characteristics, sharing of values or common historical experience. Where more than one group found itself within the borders of the same country, the situation could give rise to conflict, especially when one group felt itself or its identity threatened by another.

Cultural differences between groups might be such as to call for legal measures to maintain separation between them, otherwise a technologically weaker group might be overrun by a more advanced group.

Summing up his views, Professor van den Haag said: "The greater the cultural differentiation, the less I would urge any immediate and sudden homogenisation." A similar view was expressed by Charles Manning, Emeritus Professor of International Affairs, London School of Economics and a former assistant to the Secretary General of the League of Nations.

On the basis of the evidence of these expert witnesses South Africa contended that it would be impracticable, if not impossible, to apply the so-called norm of non-discrimination or non-separation under all circumstances and at all times. To do so in countries where there are pluralistic societies composed of different ethnic groups, would be to court disaster. Furthermore, the whole concept of an "organised International Community" as a legal person, capable of possessing legal rights and interests, is in conflict with the most basic principles of International Law. Liberia and Ethiopia were totally unable to define the composition or the legal powers and functions of their so-called "Organised International Community", and could not even suggest what the position would be if two or more organised international communities were to exist side by side at the same time. What, for example, will happen if a new International Organisation were to be created of the same nature as, and in competition with, the United Nations, say by China, Indonesia and India? Which of the two organisations would be able to claim the legal rights alledgedly vested in the so-called "Organised International Community?" The complete confusion and lack of clarity contained in Liberia and Ethiopia's attempt to create a legal person in the form of an "Organised International Community" is merely a further indication that the alleged intent of the authors of the Mandate System to impliedly introduce this concept into the Mandate documents, is in truth a mere afterthought on the part of the propounders of the argument.

It is unthinkable that the authors of the Covenant of the United Nations would have granted legal rights or interests to such an entity, which cannot be defined, or that the Mandatories would have consented to this.

As a last resort, Liberia and Ethiopia abandoned their attempts to define the norm and contended that the norm, although undefined, exists, and that its applicability to the case before the Court depends, not on its definition and application of such definition to facts established to the Court's satisfaction, but purely on the basis that the norm has been declared applicable by the Organized International Community.

Insofar as such declaration involves a factual inquiry, they said that the Organized International Community has spoken the last words about the facts. In short, the Organized International Community is, in the argument as presented by Liberia and Ethiopia in their oral rejoiner, legislator, witness, judge, jury and executioner.

According to Liberia and Ethiopia, there is now a kind of legislative power on the part of organs of the so-called Organized International Community to bind states that do not agree with the so-called consensus or collective judgement or collective will.

This represents a collectivist approach in the Organized International Community, something in the nature of legislation by which a collective will of combined assentives, can bind states who do not agree with that collective will.

The effect of their contention is to put South Africa, who did not place South West Africa under trusteeship (and they admit that there is no obligation on South Africa to do so), in the position where the Organized International Community can order it to do so. And not only the supervisory bodies of the United Nations — such as the Trusteeship Council — but also other bodies said to represent the Organized International Community in some way or other, such as the International Labour Organization, now have this power.

Their basic case is one of attempting to impart quasilegislative functions to the United Nations' organs (and also to the Court) and to establish the proposition that international legal obligations may be imposed on a state without its consent.

They admitted that for the purposes of conventional law, it is necessary to rely on the consent of the parties sought to be bound. Now they rely on custom and they attempt to circumvent their difficulty by saying that in regard to the generation of an international customary law, consent is not necessary, and they take it to the extreme of saying that a custom may develop, and exist despite objection thereto during its period of emergence. That, South Africa contended, is the crucial issue between the parties.

Liberia and Ethiopia, South Africa argued, asked the Court to apply revolutionary principles of law with far-reaching implications and do that merely on the basis of the asserted desirability to do so.

How far-reaching the implications were, was illustrated by examples cited in South Africa's argument. It was pointed out that if all the nations, with the exception of say, the United Kingdom and the U.S.S.R., were to agree that it is necessary to have international control over the production of nuclear weapons, or space travel, could that collective will now be imposed as a matter of law upon the United Kingdom and the U.S.S.R.?

If the major portion of the world (Red China having been admitted to the United Nations in the meantime) were to turn Communist and, say only England were to hold out, could the Communist part of the world then impose its will on England by this preponderant majority? The answer would be "yes" if Liberia and Ethiopia were right. It could simply be said that the collective will of the Communist community directs that, because it is a matter of common concern, the whole world should become Communist and that there has been established, as a matter of law, a norm of non-capitalism.

There are many more subjects on which a world majority could come to agreement, e.g., international regulation of world population density, and the abolition of all immigration control, equal distribution of material assets, international control of all information media and educational facilities, etc.

The effect of what Liberia and Ethiopia contend for is the very negation of the existing world order and it runs counter to the carefully devised checks and balances which have been built into the bodies of the International Community such as the veto right in the Security Council.

South Africa pointed out that Ethiopia and Liberia had repeatedly emphasised that invocation of the norm did not require proof of any improper intent on the part of South Africa. The case of Ethiopia and Liberia did not depend upon any bad results flowing from differential allotment of rights and duties. Differential allotment would be illegal, they said, even if it were intended for the benefit of the inhabitants of the Territory. As a result, both motive and results were excluded as criteria. There could be no question of a charge of unfair discrimination or of discrimination against persons or groups.

Application of a norm under these circumstances, South Africa argued, would not be compatible with the well-being and progress of all the inhabitants of the Territory, in particular the non-White inhabitants.

The facts were that there were a number of separate groups living largely in different regions in South West Africa. These groups differed widely amongst themselves and maintained different institutions. They were in different stages of development. They regarded themselves as different from one another in important aspects and wished to maintain their separate identities.

Certain types of contact between these groups would lead to friction as had happened in the past. Any attempt to force these groups into a single political entity would result in chaos and anarchy. Should a simple majority concept be applied over the whole of South West Africa, minority groups would be deprived of their right to self-determination.

South Africa stated that South Africa's policies in South West Africa were not based on "racist perspectives" but on sociological realities and depended upon whether an individual identified himself with a group and was accepted by that group. Liberia and Ethiopia had distorted the evidence in order to suggest that differential rights were only allocated on the basis of White versus non-White. Seen in its right perspective the evidence

222

was abundantly clear: the interests of each group were protected in its own area and against all other groups.

Conscious of their separate identity, the various population groups (of which there were nine) wished to be treated as separate groups. In the political field the large majority of the non-White peoples supported their traditional authorities which, in fact, exercised meaningful powers of decision-making. The report of the Odendaal Commission on South West Africa[45] provided the further extension of these powers by recommending, for instance, increase of direct representation in the existing authorities on the basis of a universal franchise.

South Africa pointed out that the League of Nations Mandate not only required a mandatory power to differentiate in the interests of the indigenous peoples, but also made it *obligatory* in some instances.

Finally, on the question of the alleged norm, South Africa contended that the United Nations in passing judgement on South Africa's administration in South West Africa did not purport to have applied standards or a norm with the contents suggested by the Applicants. On the contrary, these organs of the United Nations condemned South Africa's policies on an entirely different basis — that of being tainted with improper motives and as being oppressive. Their findings were to a large extent based on incorrect facts and assumptions or on deliberate misrepresentations. They formed part of a cam-

---

45. See Chapter VI.

paign based on political and particularly emotional grounds, rather than upon objective grounds concerned with the well-being and progress of the peoples of South West Africa.

Returning to the important matter of the admissions made by Liberia and Ethiopia, South Africa said it was obviously not an easy matter for them to have made these admissions. Appearing in a representative capacity, representing the collectivity of African states, the facts they admitted ran directly counter to what had been alleged over the years against South Africa and its policies at the United Nations by that very group of nations and their allies.

The abandonment of Liberia and Ethiopia's charge and the acknowledgement of the facts presented by South Africa constituted at the same time acknowledgement of the incorrectness of the factual basis upon which South Africa's policies had been condemned at the United Nations over the years.

On the question of the international status of South West Africa, South Africa contended that Liberia and Ethiopia had produced no proof to substantiate their allegations that South Africa had acted in a manner designed to change the status of South West Africa unilaterally or to incorporate the Territory.

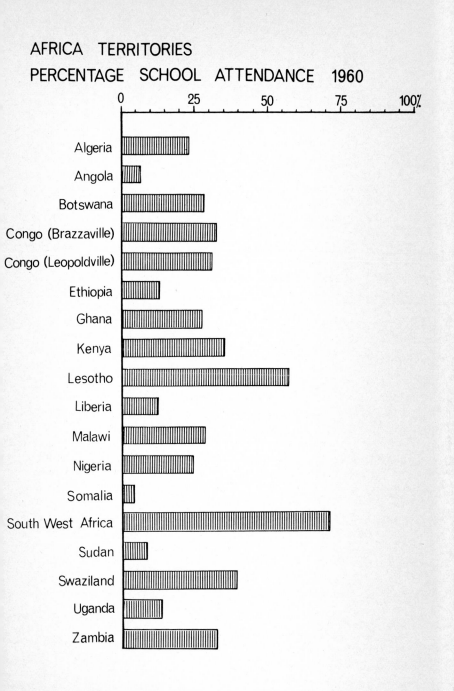

AFRICA TERRITORIES
PERCENTAGE SCHOOL ATTENDANCE 1960

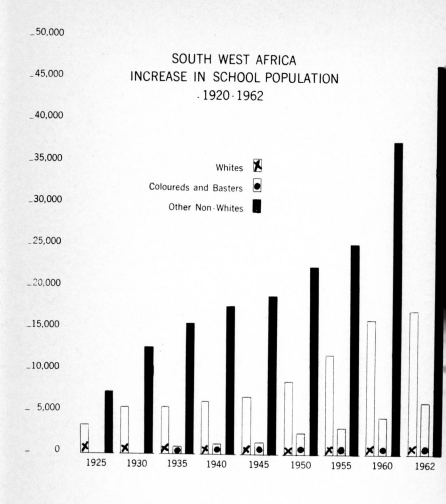

SOUTH WEST AFRICA
INCREASE IN SCHOOL POPULATION
- 1920 - 1962

As pointed out earlier, the Court's rejection of Liberia and Ethiopia's attempt to play the role of policeman resulted in abuse being heaped on the Court and its members. "A slap in the face of world opinion" a spokesman for the African states said. "A technicality" the United States termed it. On the positive side many responsible newspapers in the West applauded the decision calling it a "return to the rule of law".

The tragedy of it all is that the various arguments before the Court over the years went unreported in the world press — a gross disservice to world peace and the rule of law if there ever was.

The South West Africa case can *still serve* a useful purpose in promoting improved international understanding. By a study of the proceedings and the documented evidence interested states and individuals can ascertain for themselves the soundness not only of South Africa's rejection of the suggested supervisory powers of the United Nations but the true nature and content of its policies in South West Africa compared with the motives and methods of its detractors. The evidence which South Africa led in defence of its policy of differential development of distinctly different peoples was truly impressive. As the Editor of *R.S.A. World* (Johannesbugr) pointed out in his lucid and comprehensive analysis of the case: "The accusers had no answer to such evidence, and vigorously opposed South Africa's invitation to the Court that it should visit Africa and see for itself. Of all the world army of critics, not one appeared in the witness box at The Hague to substantiate his accusations. If ever there

W.—15

had been a chance to prove their case, it was then — but none came forward. For the first time apartheid had been removed from the forums of emotion and placed on trial before a bench of judges. The evidence against it was found wanting, and the charge that the policy was arbitrary, unreasonable, unjust and detrimental to human dignity was abandoned. The charge that it was oppressive either in effect or intention was abandoned. The charges were withdrawn by the complainants themselves — and no verdict of the Court could have been more eloquent than that. The Hague case stripped the accusations made against apartheid of all their substance."

6

THE DESERT WILL BLOOM

In guiding the development of South West Africa, South Africa never lost sight of the difficult problems facing the territory such as the scarcity of water, the low agricultural potential, the backwardness of the mass of native peoples, the lack of revenue producing industries, illiteracy and disease among various tribes and the problems of suitable employment. There were of course other problems, as outlined in Chapter IV.

In all the years, however, the uncertain international status of South West Africa which culminated and, hopefully, ended with the judgement of the World Court at The Hague in July, 1966 was never looked upon by South Africa as a reason for postponing or shirking its duty viz. to develop South West Africa to the utmost for the welfare of all its people.

In the years up to 1948 South Africa itself was struggling to remain on an even keel as it emerged from an agricultural society into an industrial state. As with other countries, World Wars I and II, the Great Depression of the early thirties, and a disastrous drought at the same time, adversely affected the orderly growth of South Africa. After 1948, when South Africa began a massive programme of national re-construction to uplift its own millions of illiterate and backward Bantu and to train them for the administration of their own affairs in their own states, trained manpower and funds was naturally at a premium.

In view of the foregoing it is all the more laudable therefore that South Africa did not neglect the planned and orderly development of South West Africa and its peoples. A great number of commissions of inquiry were instituted and their recommendations, with few exceptions, generally accepted. There was for example a Commission on the Economic and Financial Relations between the Union of South Africa and South West Africa in 1935 followed by a similar one in 1951. During 1945-1948 a Commission looked into the Native Labour situation. In 1948 a Commission prepared a long-tern agricultural policy for South West Africa. Education of the non-White population was examined in 1958; the availability and supply of coal to the territory in 1961, medical services in 1962, etc.

The application of the recommendations of these and other commissions of enquiry, massive per capita aid from South Africa, plus the tremendous efforts on the part of the people gradually brought to South West Africa a flourishing economy, a high rate of literacy among its non-White peoples, a sound financial position, a well organised administration, exemplary co-operation between White and non-White and political stability of an order not found elsewhere in Africa barring the Republic of South Africa, Rhodesia and the Portuguese provinces of Angola and Mocambique.

Thus by 1962 South West Africa was poised for a socio-economic take-off and political reconstruction which would form the basis for the country's development in years to come.

At this stage the whole future of South West Africa was at stake before the International Court of Justice at the Hague, yet South Africa did not hold back in continuing its efforts to assist and guide South Africa towards a sound political future and a viable economy.

In September 1962, South Africa appointed a commission of experts to plot an orderly programme for *hastening* the overall development of South West Africa. This commission was headed by the chief executive officer of the Transvaal province, Mr. Frans H. Odendaal, and included technical specialists in financial, economic, ethnographical, and agricultural affairs. *It became known as the Odendaal Commission and its findings and recommendations could well mean to South West Africa what the Marshall Plan meant to Europe.*

It was charged with two principle tasks: Recommending ways for "promoting the material and moral welfare and the social progress of the inhabitants" of South West Africa, "more particularly its non-White inhabitants". It was also asked to submit plans for "the accelerated development of the various non-White groups" and to suggest the best form for their participation "in the administration and management of their own interests", i.e. their political future.

After a series of trips to South West Africa where it consulted all sections of the population and investigated prevailing conditions and possibilties for improvement, the Odendaal commission synthesized its conclusions. They were made public by the late South African Prime Minister, Dr. H. F. Verwoerd, in January 1964, and is to-day considered to form the basis for future planning on the territory's development.

The report turned out to be both imaginative, generous and realistic.

It envisages the *political* reorganization of South West Africa into consolidated homelands for each non-White national group and calls for a total commitment by South Africa of over R156,000,000 ($218,400,000) in a comprehensive five-year development plan. To appreciate the cost of this programme to South Africa it should be noted that the annual American foreign aid programme is about R3 billion whereas South African aid to South West Africa,, projected on the United States population of 196 million people, and calculated in terms of cost of labour and equipment in America, works out at some R5 billion for the five years or R1 billion per annum. The Commission also proposed a second five year plan calling for an expenditure of R91,000,000 ($127,400,000) on the part of South Africa bringing the total for the ten years of development planned for South West Africa to R247,000,000 ($345,800,000). No estimate of expenditure was made for the third five year development programme envisaged by the commission.

The non-Whites of South West have reached the stage where a greater measure of responsibility should be placed on them for their own development, said the commission. The members were unanimous in their conclusion that only two courses were open for achieving this end: the amalgamation of the heterogeneous population into one central authority or the creation of independent geographical units wherein each of the twelve distinct groups could achieve autonomy in the exercise of their own residential, political and cultural rights.

Under the former course, friction appeared the only logical result. Strong antagonisms, engendered by the legacy of historical feuds and differences in traditions, language, religion and levels of social, political, and economic development, made the creation of a central authority tantamount to inviting the type of clashes and chaos that have resulted from such a policy in other

African territories, for example, the Sudan, Nigeria and Burundi.

The commission therefore, recommended the second course and set forth guidelines for the creation of spheres of political influence for each group in his own homeland or state, for example for the Ovambos in Ovamboland.

It needs to be emphasized that the Commission did not lightly arrive at the aforementioned conclusion and that its recommendations were not the product of a few months' deliberation with inhabitants of the territory. On the contrary. Their conclusions and recommendations are backed by years of observation of the political and socio-economic problems facing multi-racial and multi-national countries in Africa and elsewhere.

The moral and practical basis for the policy of separate development which the Commission recommended for South West Africa's peoples formed a most important part of South Africa's argument before the World Court at the Hague. The reason for this is quite evident: few countries would object to South Africa's efforts to improve the socio-economic status of the people of South West Africa but many are dead set against a policy of separate political rights for the different groups and question South Africa's honourable intentions. This aspect has generated tremendous heat and emotion at the United Nations and among the Black states of Africa. Apart therefore from rebutting in Court the charges made by Liberia and Ethiopia against the basic philosophy and implementation of this policy, the South African team also considered it a good opportunity to *explain* the determining considertations of separate development for the benefit of those other states who also questions the wisdom of separate development.

Before proceeding to outline the Odendaal Commissions proposals, the moral and practical basis of separate development for South West Africa's people therefore requires some elaboration. No better and authoritative argument can be advanced than the line of reasoning South Africa's advocates adopted before the judges of the World Court.

The basic conflict between the parties before the World Court in regard to the policies which should be applied in South West Africa was crystalized into this one fundamental question: should there be a differentiation between the various ethnic groups in the Territory or should the government of the Territory be based on the concept of one fully integrated, multi-racial society, in which the principle of "One-man-one-vote" applies? There was no suggestion in any of the pleadings filed by either side that any other or intermediate policy were to be considered by the Court as a possible solution for the problems presented by the existence of at least nine major different ethnic groups in South West Africa. This aspect of the case, therefore, involved a straight fight between the policy of differentiation as applied by South Africa in South West Africa and a policy of complete integration, as advocated by Ethiopia and Liberia.

South Africa pointed out to the Court that it was not true, as it has often been represented, that in its moral outlook and idealistic objectives the policy of differentia-

The Ruacana Falls on the Kunene River which forms part of the northern boundary between South West Africa and Angola. A multi-million rand hydro-electric project which will benefit both Ovamboland and Southern Angola is to be built at these falls.

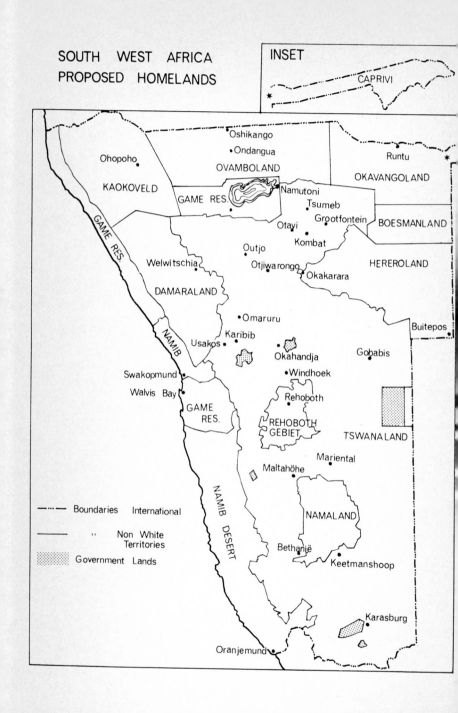

SOUTH   WEST   AFRICA
PROPOSED   HOMELANDS

INSET

CAPRIVI

Oshikango
• Ondangua
OVAMBOLAND
Ohopoho •
Runtu •
KAOKOVELD
OKAVANGOLAND
GAME RES.
Namutoni
• Tsumeb
Grootfontein
BOESMANLAND
Otavi •
Kombat
• Outjo
HEREROLAND
Welwitschia •
Otjiwarongo •
• Okakarara
DAMARALAND
• Omaruru
Buitepos •
Karibib •
Usakos •
Okahandja
Gobabis •
Swakopmund •
• Windhoek
Walvis Bay •
Rehoboth
GAME
RES.
REHOBOTH
GEBIET
TSWANALAND
Mariental •
• Maltahöhe
NAMALAND
NAMIB DESERT
Bethanië •
• Keetmanshoop

---- Boundaries   International
——   ''   Non White
                  Territories
▒▒▒ Government Lands

Karasburg •

Oranjemund •

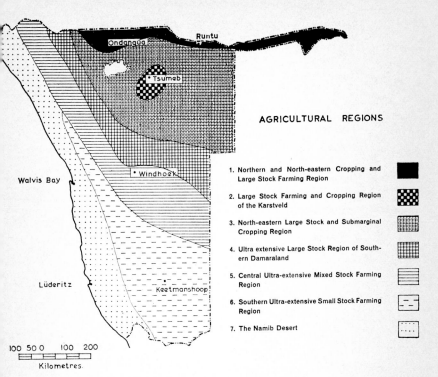

AGRICULTURAL REGIONS

Runtu

Ondangua

• Tsumeb

Walvis Bay

• Windhoek

Lüderitz

• Keetmanshoop

1. Northern and North-eastern Cropping and Large Stock Farming Region ▮

2. Large Stock Farming and Cropping Region of the Karstveld

3. North-eastern Large Stock and Submarginal Cropping Region

4. Ultra extensive Large Stock Region of Southern Damaraland

5. Central Ultra-extensive Mixed Stock Farming Region

6. Southern Ultra-extensive Small Stock Farming Region

7. The Namib Desert

100 50 0   100   200
Kilometres.

Region	Dry-land Cropping	Irrigation	Stock Farming [1]	Timber
1	Normal to marginal; soil fertility low to moderate	Good	Large stock, extensive	Extensively exploitable
2	Marginal; soil fertility moderate	None	Large stock, extensive	Some exploitation possible
3	Submarginal; soil fertility low	None	Large stock, extensive	Extensively exploitable
4	None	Extremely limited	Large stock, ultra-extensive	Negligible
5	None	Extremely limited	Large stock, and small stock, ultra-extensive	None
6	None	Limited	Small stock, ultra-extensive to marginal	None
7	None	Extremely limited	Marginal small stock farming in better parts	None

[1] The following limit values are applied in describing the potential intensiveness of pastoral land-use in Southern Africa (*vide* Wellington, J.H. "A Tentative Land Classification of Southern Africa", *The South African Geographical Journal*, Vol. XXXV, (1953), p. 17):

Intensive: One large stock unit to 2 Ha. or less.   *Semi-intensive:* One large stock unit to 2-4 Ha.
Extensive: One large stock unit to 4-8 Ha.   *Ultra-extensive:* One large stock unit to 8 Ha. or more.
One large stock unit equals 1 cattle unit or 5 sheep or goat units.

SOUTH WEST AFRICA ADMINISTRATION: FINANCES: 1960/61–1965/66 [1]

(In R '000)

	1960/61	1961/62	1962/63	1963/64	1964/65	1965/6
A. Revenue						
1. Ordinary: Customs and excise	5,947	5,350	5,762	6,407	7,641	8,46
Posts, telegraphs and telephone services	1,708	1,793	1,902	2,101	2,535	2,89
Diamond export duty and profits tax	5,243	5,936	5,456	7,027	9,650	12,14
Income tax	13,525	11,774	15,378	14,196	21,801	35,15
Other ordinary revenue	5,432	5,370	5,861	7,187	7,332	10,21
2. Extraordinary revenue..	1,231	1,253	1,762	2,716	5,057	2,93
Total revenue ..	33,086	31,476	36,121	39,634	54,016	71,81
B. Expenditure						
Revenue Services[2]	15,233	20,303	22,070	24,313	26,851	28,73
Territorial Development and Reserve Fund..	21,200	20,752	19,381	20,163	20,930	23,03
Loan Account ..	—	—	—	—	15,826	18,15
Total ..	36,433	41,055	41,451	44,476	63,607	69,92
C. Balance on Territorial Development and Reserve Fund						
(As at March 31)	40,841	35,619	27,938	17,075	16,687	18,772

[1] Controller and Auditor-General, Pretoria: *Annual Report on the Appropriation Accounts and Miscellaneou Accounts of the South West Africa Administration.*
[2] Excluding appropriation to Territorial Development and Revenue Fund.

(1R = $1.40)

tion runs counter to modern conceptions of human rights, dignities and freedoms; on the contrary, these very conceptions underlie the policy, and its objectives are to achieve an end obviating all domination of some groups by others. But the South African Government stresses the distinction between, on the one hand, the said conceptions themselves as matters of general principle or idealistic objective, and, on the other hand, the methods designed to realize them in practice in given situations.

It is in the latter respect, not the former, that the contentions of the parties to the case diverge.

The problems which resulted in the proceedings before the Court arised essentially from the need to adapt to changes of circumstances and ideas which have occurred since the Second World War. South Africa believed that the crucial issue in these proceedings related to the question whether adaptations of policies (in the light of changed circumstances) would consist of ignoring the actually existing diversity and differences among the various population groups, abandoning differentiation and attempting to create an integrated population in which a majority vote is to decide the future destiny of all concerned, *or* of continuing to recognise such diversity and differences and to provide for the separate development of the peoples concerned towards eventual self-determination by each of them — accompanied by such mutual co-operation as they themselves may decide upon. South Africa has made it clear that it is in general agreement with the propositions that it would be sound policy to increase progressively the rights of suffrage of the

Native peoples of South West Africa, that Native participation in government and administration should be encouraged.

The differences between the parties before the Court in these respects related more to matters of emphasis and tempo than of principle. South Africa's attitude was and remains that it would be calamitous to lower the standards of government and administration by a too precipitate advance in either of the mentioned spheres, while its opponents, on the other hand, seem to adopt the attitude either that there is no substantial risk of such lowering, or else that high standards of government and administration are luxuries which should not stand in the way of Native advancement or aspirations in these spheres.

In regard to the only alternative policy suggested, viz. the institution of universal adult suffrage within the framework of a single territorial unit, as propagated by Ethiopia and Liberia and now the United Nations, South Africa stated that it was difficult to conceive of a policy more calculated and more apt to endanger the present well-being and social progress of the inhabitants of the Territory.

Only a due regard for the disposition to group separation has converted life in the Territory from one of continual friction and bloodshed, as in comparatively recent historical times, to one of harmonious development towards peaceful and friendly co-existence. To advance the cause of harmonious relations and to avoid the threat of grievous social disorder, the responsible administration of the Territory demands that the existence of real, substantial and enduring differences between the population groups, and the influences those differences exercise on inter-group relations, should be recognized in the formulation of a policy best calculated to promote to the utmost the well-being and progress of all the inhabitants.

Anyone attempting to choose, on merit, a policy best calculated to promote the welfare of the inhabitants of South West Africa, can do so only after placing in the scales all the respective advantages and disadvantages of each of the only two alternatives mentioned above.

South Africa has analysed in detail the advantages of separate development as compared with attempted integration as a possible policy for South West Africa. It argues that:

(i)   Separate development is not a policy of domination, but the very antithesis thereof. It contemplates evolutionary termination of guardianship in a manner calculated to lead to peaceful co-existence. Attempted integration on the other hand, must in the circumstances prevailing in South West Africa, inevitably lead, at least, to domination of some groups by others. Separate development seeks to avoid a situation where the exercise of self-determination by some of the inhabitants would involve the denial of self-determination to others.

(ii)   Separate development woud not involve, as attempted integration would, the abdication of the sacred trust regarding the least developed groups.

(iii)   Separate development seeks to prevent a situation in which the more developed groups, which are at present responsible for the economic progress and high standards of administration and prosperity in the Territory, may be swamped and possibly forced out of the Territory by less advanced groups with entirely different values and outlook;

(iv) Separate development avoids the deleterious results of ignoring ethnic differences, loyalties and reactions which manifest themeslves strongly when one people feels its existence or basic interests threatened by another. Such results, in other parts of the world, have often included tension, unrest, hostilities and bloodshed and, in some cases, the imposition of ruthless dictatorial rule in order to suppress the tensions in question.

(v) Separate development renders possible constructive co-operation between White and non-White groups, on a basis of equality, to their mutual benefit, in contrast with the fate which has befallen White and non-White minorities in other countries handed over to Native rule — to the detriment of all.

(vi) Separate development leaves to the free will of the groups concerned, the ultimate decision whether, and in what form and to what extent, they will link up or co-operate with others, *inter se,* politically, economically, and otherwise — as opposed to forcing upon them a pre-determined system whether unitary or federal, which some may feel to constitute a threat to their existence, interests or identity.

South Africa pointed out that United Nations organs have not attempted to formulate any universally applicable principle of preservation of "territorial integrity" or development of "territorial consciousness", as alleged by Ethiopia and Liberia. In fact, in some cases Trust Territories were eventually, with the approval of the United Nations, separated into different components or amalgamated with neighbouring territories; as instances South Africa cited the Trust Territory of Ruanda-Urundi, which was divided into two separate states (Rwanda and Burundi); British Cameroons, the northern part of which joined Nigeria and the southern part of which entered into a political association with the Republic of Cameroun and British Togoland, which was integrated with Ghana.

On the other hand the enforced integration of different ethnic groups into a single unit has often resulted in bloodshed, disorder and chaos, more especially where conditions in regard to ethnic diversity are analagous to those in South West Africa.

From indisputable facts, the comments of qualified observers in respect of territories such as Algeria, Congo, Ghana, Kenya, Nigeria, Sudan, Tanganyika and many others, it can be deduced that there are peoples and groups (nations and embryo nations) which are for all practible purposes not assimilable, the one by the other, because of unwillingness to assimilate. The same psycological, emotional or cultural attributes which prevent assimilation, frequently result in a situation in which the groups concerned cannot govern one country jointly in a manner which is fair and acceptable to both or all of them — the underlying reason being not that one is superior and the other(s) inferior, but simply that the differences between them are too great[46].

Thus, within the separated territory of Rwanda itself, the differences and antagonisms between the Hutu and the Tutsi were too severe to be contained within one state; efforts at integration resulted in the virtual extermination or expulsion of the Tutsi. Nevertheless, Ethiopia and Liberia refer with approval to the Trusteeship Council policy for that territory, apparantly unaware that the results of that policy can be measured in terms of thousands of deaths and hundreds of thousands of refugees.[47]

Even in the United States of America where it would seem from the outside that possible integration between White and Negro is favoured by circumstances to a much greater extent than in most other countries, extremely serious difficulties are encountered in all spheres of the application of a policy of compulsory integration, and in the questions whether such policy will in fact lead to eventual harmonious relations, and if so, over what period of time and at what cost seem to remain as open as ever. Moreover, the problems attendant upon the presence of widely different groups, in appreciable numbers, in one integrated political entity have been recognised by many States throughout the world in the formulation of government policy, by devising their immigration laws in such a way as to preserve their national homogeneity and to prevent the immigration of unassimilable elements. In this connection one can mention the

46. Cyprus and India and Pakistan are good examples.
47. Source: United Nations High Commissioner for Refugees, New York.

immigration policies of Great Britain, the U.S., Australia, Canada and New Zealand.

In Liberia itself White men may not become citizens of the country.

South Africa has specifically stated that it contemplates an evolutionary growth of the traditional institutions of the various groups in a manner which would permit each to develop towards complete self-determination, and that it would proceed as fast as is practicable with the development of the political institutions of the Natives, towards attainment of the ultimate aims and ideals of the sacred trust.

In recognition of this objective, the Odendaal Commission had recommended a large measure of self-government for all but one of the Native population groups, covering the greater part of the field of legislation as well as general and judicial administration. These recommendations had included inter alia the institution of a Legislative Council for each Native group in its own homeland with wide powers of legislation, the institution of an Executive Committee, the introduction of rights of franchise, the takeover by the homeland authority, in the fields of general administration and civil service, of the functions of the Department of Bantu Administration and Development.

The South African Government has indicated that it accepts the Odendaal Report in broad principle, and have endorsed the view that it should be the aim, as far as practicable, to develop for each population group, its own Homeland in which it can attain self-determination and self-realization. The Government also accepts that for this purpose, considerable additional portions of the Territory including areas owned by White persons, should be made available to certain non-White groups.

The task of achieving the objectives of the Mandate in the circumstances existing in South West Africa is difficult. A fair and just solution in the political sphere for everybody concerned is obviously the matter of overriding importance. Educational and economic policy, especially in a Territory with such a diversity of population groups as South West Africa, cannot be determined in vacuo, but must necessarily be in accord with the policy found to be desirable in regard to the political future of the various peoples — the determinative factor being whether the objective is an integrated community, within the framework of a single territorial unit, or differentiated development of the various groups towards self-determination for each. The same considerations also apply to policy pertaining to rights of residence and freedom of movement.

The overriding importance of sound political development may also be illustrated with reference to the events in other territories in Africa. No educational or economic policy can compensate, e.g., the unfortunate people of Rwanda for the utter chaos and misery which have resulted from the breakdown of the political system decided upon for that Territory. South Africa's programme is therefore designed specifically to avoid such conflicts while providing for true self determination.

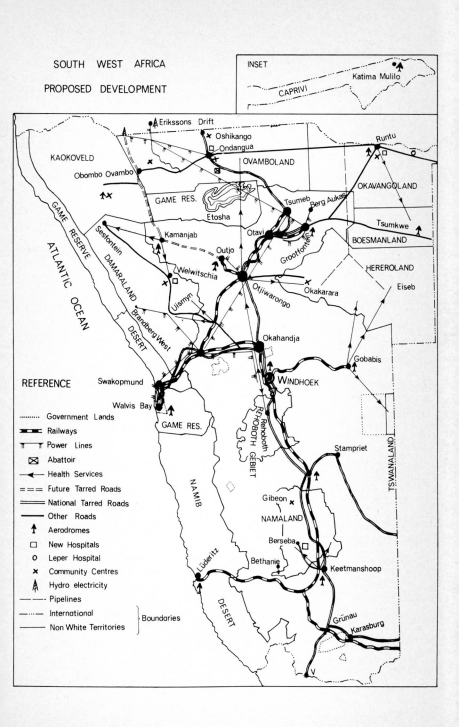

On the stoneless plains of Ovamboland, the Austrian sized territory in the North of South West Africa, which was offered self

Having dealt in detail with the motives for the policy of separate development, it now remains only to examine in equal detail how the Odendaal Commission proposes to deal with this matter in practice, and what it has suggested should be done to advance the general well being of the population and to improve the economic status of the territory of South West Africa.

The Commission's proposals for the establishment of a separate homeland for each of the different population groups are taken first.

The areas reserved for exclusive non-White use would be extended by about fifty per cent, from their present 83,000 square miles to 121,000 square miles. With one exception, the homelands show an increase in size over the existing areas reserved for non-White national groups. The exception is the *Kaokoveld* which loses some 3,100 square miles of useless Skeleton Coast. This leaves the people of the Kaokoveld with a per capita area of about 1,337.5 acres.

The *Ovambo* and *Okavango* homelands on the northern border would be expanded by 21,620 square miles and 16,200 square miles respectively. Because of the racial affinity between the two nations, a merger of their lands seems a logical possibility.

The *Damara* people — those former serfs and vassals of the other non-Whites — would be allotted an area of about 19,000 square miles, compared with their present homeland of only 1,722 square miles. This unprecedented expansion, including the addition of 7,336 square miles of present White farmland, would give them about 267 acres per person. The 158 White farms to be added would be purchased by the Administration from their current owners in the Outjo and Karibib districts for about R17 million ($23,800,000) including allowances for improvements and "verdrietgeld" (grief money).

Some R8 million ($11,000,000) has already been spent for this purpose, and the farmers are being permitted to remain on the land until it is needed for the Damara homeland expansion. A similar project was instituted in Kenya where White farmland was purchased by the government for the use of Kikuyu and other landless Black farmers as a prelude to independence, except that in the end the White farmers on average received only about a third of what they were promised or legally entitled to.

The *Herero* homeland in the East is also of enormous size. The present Waterberg East, Otjituo, Epukiro and Eastern areas — about 14,500 square miles — would be expanded to some 22,800 square miles by the addition of government lands and White farms around Buitepos on the Botswana border. The western section of the proposed Hereroland is supplied with surface water in some areas and the subsurface rock formation makes permanent wells accessible at 500 to 600 feet. About half the land is on the fringes of the Kalahari desert, where seasonal grazing is abundant.

In the southern part of the territory, the *Namas* would inhabit a greatly expanded area between Keetmanshoop and Mariental. Their present residential lands around Berseba, Tses, Gibeon and Soromas would form the nucleus of a new Namaland. A total area of 8,380 square miles, including 165 White farms and a portion of the government's experimental farm Itzawisis, would give the Namas a little over 153 acres of prime land per person. Their current Bondels, Warmbad, and Nauhof lands — tiny enclaves in the dry south and near the Namib edge — would be compensated by the Administration on a unit-for-unit basis to the Bondels Namas and a two-for-one basis for the Warmbad and Neuhof Namas. These areas would become government lands. (Warmbad and Bondelswarts are now largely uneconomic because of trampling and over grazing).

In three cases, groups not now having land reserved for their exclusive use would get such land under the Odendaal proposals. Two thousand immigrant *Tswanas,* now living on the Herero lands of Aminuis and Epukiro, would be given a strip of 600 square miles along the Botswana border. In this way, their occasional journeys to visit relatives in their old homes would be considerably shortened and facilitated.

The *Bushmen,* a little less than 12,000 strong (est. 1960), would get two areas, the western arm of the Caprivi Strip and 7,000 square miles between Okavangoland and Hereroland. The overwhelming majority of the Bushmen already inhabit this area, but the establishment of a homeland for their exclusive use would ensure their rights and primacy in Bushmanland against encroachment from their more competitive Bantu neighbour.

The 12,700 *Coloured* people (of mixed descent) in South West Africa, mainly immigrants from the Cape Province over the past two decades, are engaged primarily in industries in town and in agriculture just north of the Orange River. Their rights in the territory would be safeguarded by the Odendaal proposals. For the rural Coloureds, an irrigated settlement of 227,240 acres would be established along the bank of the Orange currently being farmed by them. The Coloured in the towns would have guaranteed property rights and local town management. The commission recommended a R4 million ($5,600,000) expenditure on housing and community centres for the Coloureds.

The two remaining groups, the *Rehobothers* and the *Whites,* would inhabit substantially the areas where they now reside. About 9,000 of the 11,000 Rehobothers live in their treaty lands, the Rehoboth Gebiet. These will be expanded by the addition of twelve White farms to 5,400 square miles or 304 acres per person.

The 73,500 Whites are the second largest racial group in South West Africa. Three quarters of them are concentrated in the towns where they have developed industries and commercial activities. The remaining quarter will continue to farm in the southern sector, except where resettled (as noted above) to make room for the expanded non-White areas.

The Whites of the territory will continue to govern themselves through the Legislative Assembly. But the Odendaal Commission recommended that a number of its present responsibilities be transferred direct to the

South African government. These were of two types: those that could benefit from the superior technical facilities of South African departments (e.g. postal and telegraphic services, mines, commerce, social welfare and water affairs) and those that concerned the welfare and future of the non-White groups. The commission pointed out that in the latter case the interests of the Whites in South West Africa could logically come in conflict with those of the non-Whites, for whose interests the South African government is directly responsible.

Each of the non-White groups in the territory, with the exception of Bushmen, was considered ready for a greater measure of self-government — participation "in the administration and management of their own interests" and the commission outlined a modified version of the current internal autonomy, introducing a measure of democracy in the Western sense into their traditional governing hierarchy.

For the seven homelands of the Ovambo, Okavango, Kaokovelders, Damara, Hereros, East Caprivians, and Namas, the plan included a domestic Legislative Council composed of existing chiefs and headmen and of elected members, whose decisions would be carried out by an Executive Committee. It is, therefore, to all intents and purposes similar to the form of government successfully introduced in the Transkei, the Xhosa homeland in South Africa.

In view of the fact that the Ovambos have now elected to accept South Africa's offer of self-government in their own state and since they also represent nearly half of all people in South West Africa, the system for Ovamboland — even though typical of the other six — calls for closer examination. An Ovambo electorate would be enfranchized of all male and female Ovambo over the age of 18. Ovambo citizenship would be conferred on the nation, encompassing both those Ovambo residing in the homeland and those working on contract outside it.

A statutory Legislative Council will consist of the currently functioning hereditary authorities (three chiefs and 32 headmen) and elected members based on proportional representation from the seven tribes of the Ovambo nation. A seven-member Executive Committee (the three chiefs or their representatives, and four members elected by the Council) would carry out the decisions of the Legislative Council.

A rapid and orderly transfer of functions currently performed by the South African government to the Legislative Council was recommended. The only functions specifically reserved from transfer were matters of external defence, foreign affairs, internal security and border control, posts and telegraphs, water affairs, power generation, and transport — that is, largely those also reserved from the territory's Whites. However, is it inherent in the policy of separate development that these powers must also ultimately pass to the Ovambos if they so choose.

Exclusive ownership of the land inside the boundaries of Ovamboland would be vested in the Legislative

Council, which would hold it in trust for the Ovambo people[48].

In line with its assumption of control over the administration of justice, the Legislative Council would be empowered to establish lower courts and a superior court for the disposition of domestic conflicts. Appeal from the superior court would, however, be allowed direct to the Supreme Court of South Africa.

Ovamboland would, in short, almost immediately become a largely self-governing state with powers equalling that of the provincial councils of South Africa but with no ceiling to its ultimate political power.

This general pattern for the seven homelands was not recommended for four groups.

The *Bushmen* are in no way ready to assume self-government, the commission said. They should be placed under the guidance and protection of a commissioner, who should map their development with the advice of an expert committee consisting of an ethnologist, social worker, medical doctor, botanist, and agriculturist.

For the limited number of *Tswanas,* the commission advised the institution of a local authority, under the jurisdiction of the White magistrate at Gobabis, the nearest town to Tswanaland.

---

48. The concept of private property is foreign to the social tradition of the Southern African Bantu peoples. Although individual ownership is in theory permitted under the laws governing South West Africa, the situation does not arise in practice. With few exceptions all land is considered to be communal property of the tribe and the right to farm a specific area is purchased from the tribal authority. The working of this system was described in Chapter III.

The *Rehobothers* will continue to govern themselves as at present. But the commission advised that their autonomy be formalized in a constitution to be worked out between them and the South African government.

The *Coloureds* are scattered over the entire southern area with major concentrations in Windhoek, Luderitz, and Walvis Bay. The already functioning Coloured Council should, said the commission, be expanded by additional elective members and the urban Coloureds governed by locally chosen Township Authorities.

Neither the South African Government nor the Blue Ribbon Odendaal Commission have indicated the precise geo-political structure that would ultimately exist in South West Africa once the various states have been established and once they have become completely autonomous. The fact is that there are so many imponderables in the future that such an indication would in any case only be of academic interest at the moment. Take the case of Ovamboland.

According to the South African Government's announcement of March, 1967, Ovamboland is to be put on the road towards statehood and self-rule. In doing so South Africa has of course cut the ground from under the United Nations to the extent of offering eventual independence to nearly half the population of the disputed territory — which the United Nations can hardly oppose in the face of Ovambo acceptance of the offer.

Ovamboland may of course elect to remain a self-governing state under the protection of the military might and economic power of South Africa. Rhodesia enjoyed such a status vis-a-vis Britain for some 40 years and were it not for Britain's naive experiment to set up a Central African Federation on the basis of partnership between Black and White (which soon disintegrated when Malawi and Zambia decided to have things their own way — precisely as South Africans predicted they would do) Rhodesia would probably still be enjoying this status. After all, she was then having the better of two worlds: military protection from Britain, economic and technical assistance, preferential tariffs for her exports to the rest of the Commonwealth, etc. For all practical purposes however, she was a self-governing state — even to the extent of being represented at the meetings of the Commonwealth Prime Ministers in London.

As a similar appendage of South Africa Ovamboland would stand to gain a lot. Technical and financial assistance, the advantage of a common market with South Africa in which ninety per cent of her produce would have a guaranteed outlet, a share in revenue from customs, etc., would be hers. At the same time she would enjoy a political status which would enable her leaders to talk on equal footing with the authorities of the Republic. Given *immediate* independence, as per United Nations formula (the date set by the Afro-Asians is 1968) she would not only have to take over the reins of the entire territory but would have to find more than R100,000,000 ($140 million) to complete just the basic projects which South Africa have launched for the next three to five years in Ovamboland — not to speak of the rest of the territory. The United Nations simply cannot raise this amount of money in aid of a nation of only 240,000 people. There are a number of independent African states, among them Zambia, Malawi, Lesotho and Botswana who discovered *after* independence that the aid which their countries required was no longer so readily available as during the hey-day of *Uhuru* when America and Russia were vying with each other in the size of their hand-outs.

On the other hand Ovamboland may one day elect to become a sovereign independent state (assuming that the United Nations does not get its way) in which case a new element will be introduced in the future of the territory — but not as new and radical as most people are led to believe.

The fact is that in Southern Africa there are socio-political and geo-political changes taking place which would accommodate the "problem" of an independent Ovamboland without undue strain on the fabric of the area. These new currents need to be understood for it will decidedly influence the future status of all non-White homelands in South West Africa for decades to come. (The reader is referred to *The Third Africa,* Nasionale Pers, Cape Town, 1967, for a detailed analysis and exposition of this new development.)

What is taking place in Southern Africa with its 45,000,000 people is the birth of a strong regionalism in which racial affairs are taking a back seat. Consider the following: Two Black states, Botswana and Lesotho, became independent during 1966 and a third one, Swaziland, is due for independence in 1969. For the first time, therefore, Black and White states are rubbing shoulders in Africa. Yet between these three Black states and White controlled South Africa there now exists an advanced Common Market — as it exists between South West Africa and South Africa. Rhodesia, because of Britain's economic and political war on her own kith and kin for leaving the fold of the Empire on their own free will, has moved appreciably closer in orbit to South Africa and politically the two states are now almost inseparable. Rhodesia's relationship with the Portuguese territories of Angola and Mocambique, remained, as always, cordial. The relationship between South Africa and the Portuguese territories is in the same mould. In addition, Malawi, and even Zambia, have indicated publicly that they intend to co-operate closely with South Africa — even at the risk of antagonizing the Organization of African unity in Addis Ababa.

Several important public events which took place during the period 1964-1967 highlight this new relationship between the states of Southern Africa.

First of all was the proposal by the late Dr. H. F. Verwoerd, Prime Minister of South Africa, for the establishment of a Common Market for Southern Africa which would include all the aforementioned countries. (The year before he had also invited Botswana, Lesotho and Swaziland to join with South Africa in a Commonwealth of Southern African states in which South Africa would lead the three countries to meaningful independence.) This was followed, in 1966, by the first ever meeting in South Africa between a South African Prime Minister and the Head of Government of a Black state, namely Lesotho. In January, 1967, Lesotho's Prime Minister Leabua Jonathan again visited South Africa for a working discussion with South Africa's new Prime Minister, Mr. John Vorster. The joint statements issued after both these historic occasions stressed that differences in political philosophy were no longer a bar to fruitful co-operation and emphasised the close interdependence of the two countries.

In March, 1967, a delegation of three senior Cabinet Ministers from *Malawi* visited South Africa to sign a new trade pact. As in the case of Prime Minister Jonathan's visit they were accorded full V.I.P. treatment. Shortly afterwards the same delegation also signed a trade agreement with Mocambique. Two years earlier Rhodesia had also signed a new favourable trade pact with South Africa.

Meanwhile the leaders of Botswana, Lesotho, Swaziland and Malawi made it clear that they did not intend to join the Afro-Asian crusade for the "liberation" of South Africa, Rhodesia or Angola but, instead, looked forward to fruitful co-operation in many spheres. The exchange of diplomatic representatives was forecast and by their forthright opposition to Communism and Pan-Africanism these states removed, almost with one stroke, the remaining obstacles to full co-operation with the White controlled states of the southern tier.

Trade, scientific and government delegations from the Black states of Botswana, Malawi, Swaziland and

Lesotho began visiting South Africa. A South African firm won the government contract for building the new capital of Malawi — a Black state bordering on militant Tanzania.

At the Organization of African Unity the Black states of the south, not including Zambia, publicly refused to go along with the rest of the African states in their attacks on South Africa. However, Zambia stepped up its trade with South Africa and by the beginning of 1967 South Africa became the principal scource of Zambian imports.

Between the Portuguese territory of Mocambique, Rhodesia and Malawi a new cordial relationship became evident. Representatives of South Africa and the aforementioned states met to discuss plans for a hydro-electric network which would link the whole of southern Africa. South African engineers were appointed to investigate the economic possibilities of Lesothos Oxbow hydro-electric project and a top South African industrialist, Dr. Anton Rupert, was appointed economic adviser to the Lesotho government. South Africa and Angola agreed to jointly sponsor the hydro-electric exploitation of the Kunene River. South African companies and funds participated in major projects in all the countries in southern Africa.

The early sixties also marked the first time Black African states had shown that they recognised the permanent nature of the white nation in South Africa and, in particular, the status of a white Government in Africa. Further visits from Heads of State of other African countries such as Botswana and the Malagasy Republic were forecast.

Dr. Verwoerd's vision of a Southern African Common Market was no longer just a vision. Even the most critical of South African newspapers, the Johannesburg *Rand Daily Mail* conceded after the signing of the trade pact between Malawi and South Africa that it had become, instead, a distinct possibility.

In short, Southern Africa is experiencing economic and diplomatic influences which is slowly but surely drawing the various countries in this region in ever closer embrace. A strong economic regionalism is already apparent. Increasing contact between Black and White states are lowering the flame of Black nationalism and there is a blurring of old animosities.

Regional co-operation in various fields is growing apace — in the search for and stockpiling of oil, the use and conservation of water, the exploitation of international rivers, improving communications, in the supply of power to the whole southern tier, in the boosting of two-way trade, the eradication of stock diseases, etc.

South Africa dominates this complex of White and Black nations to the same extent, if not greater, than the United States enjoys pre-eminence in North America. Yet South Africa has persistently worked for economic co-operation only as a means of assuring political stability in the area and to help the newly independent states to build up their domestic economies. Every Black state with whom South Africa has had dealings emphasised the complete lack of South African "pressure", politically or otherwise.

Clearly a new political and economic relationship is being fashioned in southern Africa which will set this area completely apart from the rest of Africa. *Destined possibly to be the most significant historical and political development in sub-Saharan Africa since the colonial disengagement, this trend will make it possible for small and numerically weak African states, such as Lesotho, Swaziland, and others to enjoy untramelled political independence even when not economically viable.*

What is possible for undeveloped landlocked Lesotho is therefore also possible for Ovamboland.

Even if the Ovambos one day elect sovereign independence, the chances are great that they would also join this consortium of southern African states. Surrounded by states who are already virtually committed to this new deal in southern Africa and without frontiers with any other state, landlocked Ovamboland would probably adopt an attitude no different to that of Botswana or Lesotho.

South African leaders have a vision of a *Community of Southern African States,* some big, some small, some economically viable, some not, but all joined in a Commonwealth or consortium of southern African states with political independence and economic interdependence as the keystone for their relationship. At the summit matters of common concern, trade agreements and diplomatic affairs, will be discussed on the basis of absolute equality between states. *In such a geo-political arrangement it is possible even for some of the smaller states envisaged in South West Africa, (Namaland, Damaraland, etc.) to enjoy political independence.*

The balkanization of southern Africa into sovereign states for each of its different nations is probably inevitable and Botswana, Lesotho, Swaziland and the state of the Transkei (homeland of South Africa's 3,500,000 Xhosas) is proof of this development. Because of the deep rooted differences between the various non-white nations in South West Africa, the economic factors, the long range implications of the Odendaal Commission's plan for inalienable homelands for each of the different groups, the *chances* are good that this balkanisation will repeat itself in South West Africa. However, to state categorically, at this stage, that Ovamboland or any of the other states or homelands would become hostile sovereign units in the body of southern Africa, or that they would become either sovereign countries in close association with this consortium of southern African states or remain semi-independent as part of a greater South Africa, is a matter of pure conjecture.

To fulfil the second part of its task (plans for "the accelerated development" of the territory and particularly its non-Whites), the Odendaal commission considered the economy of South West Africa and found it to consist of two phases. This "dual" economy comprises the *exchange sector* and the *subsistance sector.*

The *exchange sector,* developed almost exclusively by Whites with White capital and management and non-White labour, includes the mining activities, the rapidly expanding fishing industry, commercial activity in the towns and the scientifically managed farms. About 60

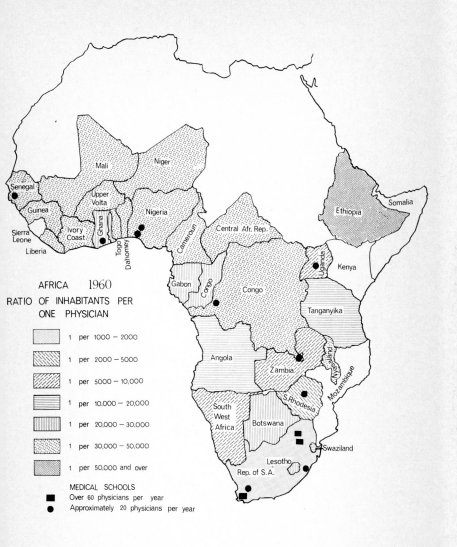

AFRICA 1960
RATIO OF INHABITANTS PER
ONE PHYSICIAN

1 per 1000 – 2000
1 per 2000 – 5000
1 per 5000 – 10,000
1 per 10,000 – 20,000
1 per 20,000 – 30,000
1 per 30,000 – 50,000
1 per 50,000 and over

MEDICAL SCHOOLS
■ Over 60 physicians per year
● Approximately 20 physicians per year

Senegal
Guinea
Sierra Leone
Liberia
Ivory Coast
Ghana
Togo
Dahomey
Mali
Upper Volta
Niger
Nigeria
Cameroun
Central Afr. Rep.
Gabon
Congo
Congo
Angola
South West Africa
Botswana
Zambia
S. Rhodesia
Nyasaland
Mozambique
Lesotho
Rep. of S.A.
Swaziland
Uganda
Kenya
Tanganyika
Ethiopia
Somalia

HOURLY WAGES OF ADULT WAGE EARNERS IN SELECTED OCCUPATIONS[1]: OCTOBER, 1965[2],[3]

Industry	Occupation[4]	South West Africa[5] Various areas Prevailing rates (cents)	Cameroon — Prevailing rates (cents)	Central African Republic Bangui Average earnings (cents)	Congo, Dem. Rep. of Kinshasa Average earnings (cents)	Ethiopia Addis Ababa Average rates October 1964 (cents)	Kenya Nairobi Average earnings (cents)	Nigeria Lagos Prevailing rates (cents)	Tanzania Dar-es-Salaam Prevailing rates (cents)
Food manufacturing industries	3. Bakers (ovenmen)	40	13·2–14·1	11·1	11·3	3·7	13·0	7·5	25·6
Manufacture of textiles	7. Labourers, unskilled	20	5·8–6·9	4·3	9·0	4·0	6·5	—	7·7
Manufacture of furniture	9. Cabinet makers	40	22·1–26·5	13·7	15·5	25·6	36·0	8·2	12·8
	10. Upholsterers	40		17·3	14·3	25·0	26·0	—	12·8
Printing and publishing	15. Bookbind. mach. sew (males)	50	12·9	17·3	14·1	17·0		—	12·8
	16. Labourers, unskilled	20		10·1	11·7	3·4	9·0	—	7·7
Repair of motor vehicles	25. Garage mechanics (general duties)			31·6	18·6	7·1	47·5	11·6	18·0
Construction	26. Bricklayers	60	32·2	15·8	11·5	25·0	33·0	12·5	12·8
	29. Carpenters	35	23·3	12·4	11·5	21·3	31·0	12·5	15·4
	30. Painters	50	23·3	13·7	10·0	14·2	21·5	12·5	12·8
	33. Labourers, unskilled	35	10·4	7·6	8·7	3·4	9·0	9·6	10·3
Transport	40. Truck drivers (under 2 tons)	32	19·6	34·5	15·2	17·9	23·5	11·6	—
Municipal services	41. Labourers, unskilled (public parks and gardens)	20	11·8	6·6	10·0	4·5	9·0	9·6	7·7

[1] South West Africa: Departmental information.
Ethiopia: International Labour Office, Bulletin of Labour Statistics, 1965, 2nd quarter, p. 87.
Others: International Labour Office, Bulletin of Labour Statistics, 1966, 2nd quarter, pp. 86–91.

[2] Wages paid in other countries have been converted to cents (South African currency). 100 cents = R1 = £0·5 = 10 shillings = 3·52 Ethiopian dollars = 347·68 CFA francs = 231 Congolese francs (Congo, Democratic Republic of) it should be noted that whereas the South West Africa data refer exclusively to members of the indigenous groups, the figures given for other countries do not distinguish between Asiatic, European and indigenous Africans. Furthermore, it must be borne in mind that it is extremely difficult to avoid variations from country to country in respect of the definition of any particular occupation.

[3] Payments for overtime and other premiums, as well as earnings in kind are excluded. No information concerning the cash value of earnings in kind is available in respect of the countries shown with the exception of South West Africa. In that Territory, the monthly value of earnings in kind is generally put at about R10 (i.e. approximately 5 cents per hour) but actual figures for many employers are well above that level,

[4] Numbers are those shown in the original I.L.O. source (vide footnote 1, supra).

[5] Data refer to December, 1966.

percent of the territory's gross domestic product comes from its mining, fishing, and farming activity. Secondary industry, although increasing, is limited and consumer goods must still largely be imported.

The other economic sector (the subsistance sector) is that operating in the non-White areas. The non-Whites consume what they produce and have traditionally no experience in entrepreneurial activities. Their productive contribution to the economy (apart from providing labour) is extremely small, probably less than five per cent.

The two sectors merge in farming and livestock producing activities and in the contribution of non-White labour to White enterprises. But whereas the experience of non-Whites in the White economy has served to provide an initiation and apprenticeship in the intricacies of a capital economy, the continued development of South West Africa still depends on the capital and technical skill of the Whites.

The commission insisted, however, that the further disorientation of non-Whites by attracting them away from their homes and families to White centres of employment, should be avoided at all costs as conducive to unhealthy social conditions. The alternative is the provision of capital resources and technical consultants in the non-White areas to assist them in developing productive activities. In this, they must be given protection against more effective competition from the White group.

Some sections of the population have entered White employment, supplemented their subsistance economy with cash wages, and made good use of community services. Due to longer contact with the modern economy, the southern non-White peoples have developed at a faster pace than the Ovambo, Okavangos, and Kaokovelders. But the northern peoples have also benefited in turn by the progress in the South.

Plans to stimulate both economic sectors and to bring the subsistence sector more in line with the general economy were drawn up by the Odendaal Commission.

It set as a first priority the provision of constant water supplies and sources of power for rural, municipal, and industrial use of a total cost of R70 million or $98,000,000. Since South West Africa has no known coal supplies for power production, and artesian wells and other subterranean water sources are inadequate for extensive irrigation, the logical step seemed the tapping of the Kunene River on the Angola border.

A power line will be constructed from Matala in Angola, where the Portuguese have a hydroelectric generator, to Ovamboland and the mining areas at Tsumeb and Grootfontein. The purchased power would also pump water from a dam to be erected at Erikssons Drift on the Kunene. A hundred megawatt power plant at the Ruacana Falls will be built in co-operation with Portugal at a cost of R28 million or $39,000,000. Power lines from the Ruacana Falls project will lead south as far as Windhoek and Walvis Bay. The entire Kunene project will cost R49 million or $68,600,000.

A R23 million ($32,200,000) water supply project was recommended to include storage dams on the Naute River south of Keetmanshoop, on the Swakop River (for

Windhoek), the Fish River (Namaland), and the Omaruru River (Damaraland). Two dams in Hereroland would be situated at Omatako-Waterberg and Omatako-Otjituo.

Irrigation projects are included for both the Coloured agricultural area on the Orange River and the Ovambo-Okavango areas of the North. A network of canals and pipelines in Ovamboland will cost R4 million and be linked with the Kunene power project from which it would get its pumping impetus.

The Commission paid special interest to Ovamboland.

Ovamboland is the most densely populated of all the home areas. The 239,500 Ovambos make up 45.5 per cent of South West Africa's population. The density of the northern area is a little less than three people per square mile, with slightly more than one per square mile in the South[49].

The Ovambos are concentrated along the Kunene basin in the region of the "oshanas" (shallow water-courses) where seasonal flooding provides abundant moisture for cultivating. The main crop is "omahangu", a small grain millet pounded by the women into cereal flour which forms the staple of the Ovambo diet. To remove the roots from the sodden soil, the omahangu is planted on artificial mounds about 18 inches high. (The

---

49. The population density for the country as a whole in 1960 was 1.65 persons per square mile, compared with 50.5 per square mile for the United States of America.

W.-17A

Ovambo version of the Lord's Prayer translates "our daily bread" as "omahangu".)

Cattle ranching is coupled with crop production but endemic lung disease and recent outbreaks of foot-and-mouth disease have hampered the export of livestock to the southern sector and served generally to retard economic development.

Since the Ovambos measure wealth in terms of number of head rather than quality, livestock diseases have proved a stubborn problem. A man with two cows, no matter how sickly, is considered richer than a man with a healthy cow. Administration efforts to reduce cattle disease by shooting infected animals have thus met with great resistance, which was only recently beginning to be overcome[50].

Despite this and the ravages of foot and mouth disease the cattle population has risen to about two and one-half million head (up from less than half a mllion at the beginning of the mandate). Almost a million head are owned by the Bantu peoples of the northern districts.

The Odendaal Commission felt, on the basis of its research, that Ovamboland and Okavangoland could develop a sound agricultural economy. The annual rainfall averages 21 inches although in the period from 1941 to 1961 it varied widely, from $11\frac{1}{2}$ inches to 40 inches a year, and during periods of prolonged drought, grain

---

50. Veterinary technicians are active all over South West Africa, fighting livestock disease with preventative vaccinations and quarantines. The latter method features fencing and check points where animal hooves, automobile tires, and even human shoe soles are decontaminated.

had to be brought in from the southern sector to avert famine conditions. The irrigation canals being constructed for Ovamboland would eliminate this unpredictability. Water would be drawn from the Kunene River for this purpose.

Great possibilities exist for the cultivation of new cash crops in the North of South West Africa, particularly jute, cotton, tobacco, and the Okavango groundnut, a large and meaty nut which could develop into a "cocktail" delicacy. The processing and packaging of this nut could be done in the area, providing the basis for a profitable industry.

Another fascinating possibility lies in the exploitation of the fruits of the marula and boabab trees. Both trees bear heavy yields of fruit rich in ascorbic acid (vitamin C). The marula fruit has a content roughly equal to that of the orange and the boabab fruit has four times the ascorbic acid content found in oranges. In addition to its fruit, the prolific marula also produce a delicious seed of high caloric value.

The local Bantu are familiar with another property of the marula. In the spring when the ripened marula fruit has dropped into the rain-filled pans, elephants drinking from their quiescent waters sometimes become "intoxicated" and lumber about drunkenly for days. This marula brew has no such potent result on men or the smaller animals, and the immense quantities in which it is consumed by elephants probably accounts for its invigorating effect on them.

To facilitate the growth of the livestock industry, the commission recommended the establishment of a producers co-operative in Ovamboland, under the authority of the Legislative Council. A series of quarantine farms would provide controlled slaughtering and marketing conditions. Chilled meat and live animals could be shipped in sealed trucks to processing plants at Otavi and Okahandja. An accelerated assault on stock diseases would be instituted by government veterinary experts.

In March, 1967, the South African government announced that it intends spending an additional R30,0000,00 ($42 million) on the overall development of Ovamboland as part of the process of establishing statehood for the Ovambos.

In the general interest of the territory, the Odendaal Report recommended major expenditures on improving communications. The long-term road building programme of the South West African administration had achieved major results by 1961. In addition to the 20,000 miles of public roads, some 17,000 miles of roads provided access to farms in the rural districts. But there still exists a need for graded roads in some non-White areas and the commission allotted more than R8 million ($11,200,000) for this project.

It also recommended an airport improvement programme to cost R3 million. The vast distances and sparse population of South West Africa make travelling

a time-consuming operation, and contribute to the importance of air travel in linking the various parts of the territory. The creation of an airport of international status at
Windhoek and the expansion of existing airfields was recommended. Secondary airfields would be improved and
five new fields should be created, one of these — for
obvious reasons — at Ruacana Falls. The international
airport at Windhoek is now completed and being used
by the Boeing 707 intercontinental jets of South African
Airways on scheduled flights to and from Europe.

The Commission set high goals for education, rightly noting that trained manpower will be essential to rapid
development in other spheres. A R3.5 million programme for education was recommended. The present school
attendance, 46 per cent of the potential non-White school
population, is less than ideal but practically unheard of
by African standards.[51] It is five times that of Ethiopia.

Schools for primary instruction must be provided in
the expanded homelands, said the commission, so that 60
per cent of all non-White children between the ages of
five and fourteen would be in school by 1970. The curriculum must be planned so that primary education will
be prepared for secondary or vocational training at high
schools, also to be established in the various home areas.
Dormitories will have to be provided to house students
attending these secondary schools.

To meet the increased demand for teachers, a teacher
training college would be established in Ovamboland

---

51. The ratio for Whites in 1962 was 99.66 per cent. and for
Basters and Coloureds 90.36 per cent.

(which would serve Okavangoland as well) and special adult training centres set up. In addition to vocational training and the academic courses designed to meet university requirements, the Odendaal Commission recommended the provision of commercial and clerical courses.

Psychologists have determined that primary instruction in an alien tongue hampers the learning ability of young children. The commission accepted the burden of providing mother-tongue education but only where the number of users justify the need. Even so, nine languages — Nama, Herero, Tswana, Bushman, Kuanyama, Kuangari, Ndonga, Mbukushu, and Lozi (Sikololo) — were deemed necessary for the purpose of primary instruction. The European languages of English and Afrikaans are also, of course, included as second languages in the schools.

The 2.1 per cent annual total population increase over the forty years of the mandate shows both a healthy genetic potential and an environment favourable for survival. But the commission set forth a R1.5 million programme for improving health and medical services among the non-Whites.

At present, South West Africa has one medical doctor for every 5,500 of its population. The comparable figure for South Africa is one in 1,800 but for Liberia it is one in 40,000 and for Ghana one in 25,000. In the thirty countries of the Central African belt with a combined population of 116 million, the figure is one in 20,000.

Per capita expenditure on health services in South West Africa came to R7.86 in 1967, against R1.04 for Ghana, R0.19 for Nigeria, and R0.76 in the Sudan. In 1961 the per capita figure for the non-Whites of South West Africa was R3.80.

To overcome the problem of transport in the sparsely populated outlying districts, the commission suggested the introduction of special "flying doctor" services and a medical radio communication network to link technicians in outlying clinics with qualified doctors[52]. The road improvements in the home areas would naturally benefit medical services and facilitate mobile clinics and ambulance services.

The newly completed R1.60 million government hospital at Oshakati in Ovamboland has 444 beds and features a pathology laboratory, X-ray facilities, operating rooms, an independent power plant, and a dispensary and outpatient clinic. A separate ward for tuberculosis patients has 176 beds.

In a land where witch doctors have only recently been replaced by scientific medicine ("black magic" is still occasionally encountered), the urgent need for doctors will be met in two ways. In the immediate future, registered physicians will be recruited from South Africa and elsewhere by improving salaries and conditions of service. But the long-term plan will concentrate parti-

---

52. This system has been operating in Australia's vast "outback," the arid interior, for many years.

cularly on providing scholarships and other benefits to allow non-White students to study medicine in South African universities.

In drawing up its five-year plan for developing South West Africa, the commission found it necessary to provide for an estimated deficit in the Administrator's budget of about R40 million (of $56,000,000) which South Africa will carry.

———————

A second five-year plan, forwarded by the Odendaal Commission, recommended a second irrigation-power dam on the Kunene at Ondorusu (R14 million), a pumping station on the Okavango River with a pipeline for water supply to Hereroland (R7.5 million), a dam and irrigation scheme near Rehoboth (R4.0 million) and an irrigation-power project on the Okavango at Runtu (R1.2 million). The total expenditure for the second plan is R30 million ($42,000,000) with a projected supplement to the territory's budgets of R61 million or $75,400,000. South Africa would thus be investing R91 million ($127,400,000) in South West Africa over the second five-year period.

The Commission also suggested a third five-year development programme which would include ten additional dams, the construction of high voltage electricity transmission lines, a link-up with the mammoth R450 million ($630,000,000) Orange River power and water project, the development of iron and steel production in the Kaokoveld near Ongaba and the use of water from the Zambesi and Linyanti Rivers for irrigation in the Eastern Caprivi.

Most of the recommendations of an economic nature have already been applied and are either completed or, at the time of publication, well on the way to being implemented.

All of this reads a little like a Twentieth Century "White Man's Burden", but it differs radically from the Nineteenth Century version, where the White man in Central and East Africa offered "civilization" and salvation to the native in exchange for economic slavery and political exploitation.

The Odendaal Commission was careful to stress that the underdeveloped communities must be led to selfdetermination. Inherent in their appraisal of this task was the fact that South West Africa is a poor land and that the financial burden of developing it must be shouldered by South Africa as a "sacred trust" rather than in the hope of any profit on the investment in the foreseeable future. Even the potential revenue source of its highly profitable mining industry is offset by the tremendous obstacles posed by operating procedures. Oppressive taxation of the mining industry would discourage private capital investment and ultimately hinder the advancement of the territory as a whole.

It could be argued that over the South African-built railroads moved land-hungry settlers from the already developed Cape Province and consumer goods to the markets of South West Africa. But the settlers came prepared to make great sacrifices of energy and personal comfort in the task of pioneering a hard and raw land, and the market potential for South Africa's goods was insignificant in terms of her market potential in other countries, whereas the cattle and dairy products of South West found their *only* ready and stable market in South Africa.

A case could be made for the fact that the non-White peoples of South West Africa have been given an unequal share of the proceeds derived from the territory's recent boom. Indeed, they are nowhere near so advanced on the ladder of economic and political sophistication as the Bantu peoples living in South Africa itself. But the progress they have made is remarkable in the light of the fact that South Africa inherited a land where — by estimate of Governor Leutwein — two thirds of the non-White population had been exterminated and the rest were reduced to starving vagabondage. The colonial legacy was one of deep distrust for the White man and little preparation for a useful role in the modern world.

A total of some 83,000 square miles was reserved for the exclusive use of the non-Whites. This included the lands on which the mandatory found settled communities of non-Whites and the treaty lands recognized as theirs under the German colonial regime. To the landless Herero people, the mandatory gave some 14,500 square miles of territory, supplemented by a later allocation of 3,860 square miles. White settlement was only permitted in the vast fallow tracts of no-man's land.

Over the years South Africa has channeled a considerable investment into the territory. Between its assumption of the mandate in 1920 and the period of the commission's investigation in 1963, some R165 million ($231,000,000) was poured into the territory with no provision for interest or recovery. This did not include capital outlays on the railways (modernizing the track, purchase of freight and passenger cars, etc.) of more than R140 million ($196,000,000) and an accumulated operating loss of the railroads and scheduled air service of over R40 million or $56,000,000.

In all, South Africa has contributed financial aid to South West Africa of R300 ($420) *per capita* — surely the most valuable foreign aid program ever given on a *per capita* basis by the people of one country to the people of another.

In place of the Odendaal Commission's well reasoned, well planned and realistically conceived programme to provide for harmonious co-existence between people who are at least as anxious to retain their birthright as the South Vietnamese or South Koreans, the Afro-Asian States are pressing for the same unitary system which is at this moment shaking the very foundations of Nigeria, the Sudan and a number of other African states.

W.–18

If the United Nations succeeds and the Bushmen, the Basters, the Tswanas, the Caprivians and other minorities are plowed under by the majority in an independent one-man-one-vote state in South West Africa, who will fight for their right to existence? The Afro-Asians? The United States? Scandinavia? Will the liberal press condone such cultural genocide in the name of democracy? Will the new proponents of political morality, the Churches, march in Trafalgar Square and petition the United Nations as they have done in the past? Or will their protests be confined, as it is at the moment, to situations where White people are suspected of not knuckling down to demands of Black majority, no matter the nature of those demands?

One does not have to be a cynic to realise that these questions will be answered by a deafening silence on the part of those named above. No, they will expect and continue to urge, in the name of "majority rule" and "moral responsibility", that the minorities of South West Africa accept what they, in similar circumstances, will fight to prevent.

The constitution for Cyprus was also once hailed as an example of a non-racial, one-man-one-vote, in-surance but when the Turkish minority was in danger of being plowed under (as they still are) the same deafening silence could be heard all over the world. When half a million Indians were thrown out of Burma a few years ago not a single parade of Churchmen was seen in London, not a single day set aside at the United Nations for this tragedy in the homeland of Secretary General U

270

Thant. The fact is that if the several non-White minority groups in South West Africa are decimated in an independent state governed by only Black men, the world would take no more notice of it than it did of the tens of thousands massacred in Rwana, Burundi, the Sudan and other Black African States.

In place of a realistic and imaginative economic programme which would eventually benefit the various groups in South West Africa as much as the individuals in those groups, the Afro-Asian plan for the territory would bring the corruption, decay and economic canabalism which have become the hallmark of all but a handfull of states in their own world.[53]

By going along with this Afro-Asian madness to "liberate" South West Africa and to re-build it into a one-man-one-vote Utopia many nations of the West, or at least their governments, are creating a Frankenstein which if allowed to survive will one day turn upon them. It will demand in the name of "mankind" or perhaps for the sake of "unity" that the majority also rule the world. Then there would no longer be need for the liberal press to castigate South Africa or for churches to concern themselves with the political affairs of South West Africa. The Oriental majority would certainly see to that.

---

53. This is a view shared by at least two highly respected observers who recently visited the territory, namely Professor Thomas Molnar *(South West Africa,* Fleet, N.Y. 1966, and author of *Africa, A Political Travelogue)* and Dr. Hans Jenny of Germany (Südwest Afrika, Kohlhammer, Berlin, 1966, and author of *Afrika Ist Nicht Nur Schwarz).*

In their fear of being considered "different" those western nations such as the Scandinavian countries who have joined the Afro-Asian ventetta against South Africa may congratulate themselves that they are in the main current of "world opinion" but this does not absolve them from the responsibility of periodically considering whether this current is not heading for the precipice. In that period of consideration the words of John Bartholomew Gough (1817-1886) could serve to check their impulse to join the masses in their shattering ride onto the rocks below the waterfall.

"The chosen heroes of the earth have been in a minority. There is not a social, political or religious privilege that you enjoy today that was not bought for you by the blood and tears and patient suffering of the minority."

Since "world opinion" has failed to shift the point of view held by the small minority of whites at the foot of the African continent in respect of South West Africa, that point of view is surely worth examining.[54] In order to do so one has to be informed. Perhaps this book will then serve a useful purpose far beyond the borders of South Africa.

---

54. Cf. Röpke, Wilhelm: "South Africa, An Attempt at a Positive Appraisal," *Schweizer Monatshefte,* 1964; Manning, Charles; "In Defence of Apartheid," *Foreign Affairs Quarterly,* New York, 1965; Rhoodie, N.J.; *Apartheid and Partnership,* Academica, Pretoria, 1967.

BIBLIOGRAPHY

ADMINISTRATION OF SOUTH WEST AFRICA: White paper on the activities of the various branches of the Administration of South West Africa for the financial year 1961-1962.

ADMINISTRATION OF SOUTH WEST AFRICA: White paper on the activities of the various branches for the financial year 1962-1963.

ASSOCIATION OF ADULT EDUCATION, PRETORIA: *Lantern,* Journal of Adult Education, Pretoria, Vol. 7, No. 1, 1957.

BRUWER, J. P. van S.: *South West Africa — The Disputed Land,* Nasionale Boekhandel, 1966.

CALVERT, A. F.: *South West Africa during German Occupation,* London, 1915.

DEPARTMENT OF FOREIGN AFFAIRS, REPUBLIC OF SOUTH AFRICA: *South West Africa Survey, 1967,* Government Printer, Pretoria, 1967.

DEPARTMENT OF INFORMATION, PRETORIA: *Ethiopia and Liberia Versus South Africa.* Official Account of Proceedings on South West Africa before the International Court of Justice, at The Hague, 1960-1966.

ESTIMATES, South West Africa Territory, Year ending 31st March, 1964, Government Printer.

FACULTY OF LAW, UNIVERSITY OF SOUTH AFRICA: *Codicillus,* October, 1966 (Special Edition on the South West Africa Case).

FOOD AND AGRICULTURE ORGANIZATION OF THE UNITED NATIONS: Report on the possibilities of African rural development in relation to economic and social growth. F.A.O. African Survey, Rome, 1962.

FRANKEL, S. H.: *The economic Impact on Under-Developed Societies* — Essay on International Investment and Social Change, Oxford University Press, 1953.

GOVERNMENT PRINTER, PRETORIA: *Report of the Commission of Enquiry into South West Africa* (The Odendaal Report) No. 12 of 1964.

GINIEWSKI, PAUL: *Livre Noir, Livre Blanc — Dosier du Sud-ouest africain,* Berger-Levrault, Paris, 1966.

HAHN, VEDDER, FOURIE: *The Native Tribes of South West Africa,* Cape Town, 1928.

HAILEY, LORD: *An African Survey,* A study of Problems Arising in African South of the Sahara, Oxford University Press, London, 1956.

HINTRAGER, OSKAR: *Südwestafrika in der Deutschen Zeit,* Oldenbourg Verlag, Munchen, 1955.

JENNY, HANS: *Südwest Africa,* Kohlhammer Verlag, Stuttgart und Berlin, 1966.

KROGH, D. C.: "The National Income and Expenditure of South West Africa (1920-1950)", *The South African Journal of Economics,* Vol. 28, No. 1, 1960.

LEAGUE OF NATIONS: The mandates system, origin, principles, application, Geneva, 1945.

LEVINSON, OLGA: *The Ageless Land,* Tafelberg Publishers, Cape Town, 1961.

MANNING, CHARLES: "In Defence of Apartheid", *Foreign Affairs Quarterly,* New York, 1965.

MOLNAR THOMAS: *Africa A Political Travelogue,* Fleet, New York, 1964.

MOLNAR, THOMAS: *South West Africa,* Fleet, 1966.

NEW SOUTH WEST AFRICA LABOUR ASSOCIATION (PTY.) LTD., GROOTFONTEIN, SOUTH WEST AFRICA: *Annual Report for Financial year ended 30th June, 1962.*

OLIVER, M. J.: Inboorlingbeleid en -Administrasie in die Mandaatgebied van Suidwes-Afrika, Unpublished D. Phil. thesis, Stellenbosch, July, 1961.

REPORT OF THE COMMISSION OF INQUIRY INTO NON-EUROPEAN EDUCATION IN SOUTH WEST AFRICA, Government Printer, November, 1958.

REPORT OF THE COMMISSION OF INQUIRY INTO THE FINANCIAL RELATIONS BETWEEN THE UNION AND SOUTH WEST AFRICA, 1951. U.G. 26, 1952, Government Printer.

REPORT OF SOUTH WEST AFRICA COMMISSION. Government Printer. Pretoria, U.G. No. 26, 1936.

RÖPKE, WILHELM: "South Africa, An Attempt at a Positive Appraisal", *Schweizer Monatshefte,* Zürich, 1964.

RHOODIE, E. M.: *The Paper Curtain,* Voortrekkerpers, Johannesburg, 1967.

RHOODIE, E. M.: *The Third Africa,* Nasionale Pers, Cape Town, 1967.

RHOODIE, N. J.: *Apartheid and Partnership,* Academica, Pretoria, 1967.

SCHAPERA, I.: *The Koisan Peoples of South Africa,* London, 1930.

STEWART, ALEXANDER: *South West Africa, The Sacred Trust.* Da Gama, Johannesburg, 1963.

VAN RENSBURG. H. M. J.: *Die Internasionale Status van Suidwes-Afrika,* Leiden, 1953.

VAN WARMELO, N. J.: "Notes on the Kaokoveld (South West Africa) and its People", Government Ethnologist. Republic of South Africa. Department of Bantu Administration. *Ethnological Publications No. 26,* Government Printer, Pretoria, 1962. G.P.S. 8706503. 1961/62. 500.

VEDDER, H. (Dr.): *South West Africa in Early Times,* Cass & Co., London, 1966.

WALKER, E. A.: *A History of Southern Africa,* Longmans, Green & Co., London, 1964.

WATERS, A. J.: *The Laws of South West Africa,* 1915-1922, Windhoek, 31st January, 1923.

WESSELS, L. H.: *Die Mandaat vir Suidwes-Afrika,* 's-Gravenage, Holland, 1937.

INDEX

119, 136, 250, 252, 253, 255, 256
Boxer Rebellion (Chinese), 143
Brandberg, 54, 55, 71, 74
Breuil, Abbé Henri, 4, 72
British East India Company, 136
British Imperial War Cabinet, 12
Brukkaros Crater, 54
Brutal Mandate, 40
Buitepos, 242
Burke, Admiral, 29
Burnt Mountain, 75
Burundi, 44
Bushmanland, 243
Bushmen, 4, 10, 41, 42, 44, 55, 57, 70, 73, 94—97, 99—101, 107, 110, 112, 113, 243, 247

C

California, 2
Cao, Diego, 67, 103, 113
Cape Cross, 67, 68, 71, 103
Cape Frio, 69, 136
Cape of Good Hope, 28, 104
Cape Province, 53, 54, 82
Cape Town, 30, 107
Caprivians, 98—101
Caprivi, Count Leo von, 53
Caprivi Strip, 26, 53, 58, 96, 101, 159, 243
Carpio, Vittorio, 214
Caribbean, 30
Castro, Fidel, 23
Ceiling, 68
Cattle, 174
Central Africa, 27, 38, 40, 116
Central African Federation, 249
Central African Republic, 52
Chuos, 54
Cloete, Stuart, 64
Coal, 32, 33, 36, 163
Coetzee, Jacobus, 105
Collins, Sam, 79
Coloured Council, 248
Coloureds, 100, 101, 244, 248
Columbus, Christopher, 103
Communism, 195, 221, 252
Communist bloc, 22, 28
Communists, 7, 18
Conference of Independent African States (1960), 209
Congo, 42, 103, 182
Consolidated Diamond Mines

of S.W.A., 77, 82
Counter-Memorial, 19
Crater Lakes, 96
Crete, 4, 72, 73
Cuba, 31, 203

D

Dama, 107, 114
Damaraland, 119
Damaras, 5, 100, 102, 119, 241, 242
Darwin, Charles, 127
De Alva, dr. Martinez, 214
Depression (the 30's), 164, 172
Deutsche Mädchen, 166
Deutscher Südwest Bund, 166
De Villiers, O. P., 204
De Wet Commission, 164
Diamond Coast, 45, 76
Diamonds, 9, 34, 76—82, 146, 147, 176
Dias, Bartholomew, 104, 113
Dias Point, 104
Dinosaur, 3
Dolf Trees, 185
Dunedin Star, 69
Dutch East India Company, 104, 136

E

East Africa, 116
Economic Co-operation, 27
Economy, 4, 171—173, 175—178, 189, 229, 230, 256, 257, 267—269
— Domestic Income, 157
Education, 178—183, 263
Egypt, 4, 72—74
Electoral Districts, 17
Electricity, 32—34, 258, 259, 266
Epukiro, 242, 243
Equatorial Africa, 26
Eriksson's Drift, 258
Erongo, 54
Eros, 54
Ethiopia, 9, 18, 20—25, 27, 39, 62, 63, 182, 191, 193—195, 203—210, 212—216, 218—222, 224, 225, 232, 234, 237
Etosha Pan, 54, 58, 93, 94, 111, 117, 127

F

Far East, 104
Fifth Province, 23
"Finger of God" (Rock), 85
Finnish Mission, 118
Fishing, 31, 64, 65, 80, 81, 175
Fish River, 82, 114, 259
— Canyon, 82, 83
Foot and Mouth Disease, 145, 260
Foreign Affairs, 18
France, 2, 12
Francois, Major Kurt von, 88, 138, 139
Franke, Captain Victor, 142, 151
Free World, 7

G

Galton, Sir Francis, 96, 127, 128
Game, 57—59, 94
Gecko, 70
Geitsigubib, 8
General Assembly, 2, 6, 22, 199, 204, *vide* United Nations
Genocide, 5, 21
Germanium, 9, 35
German Rule, 10, 91, 94, 119, 141, 155, 156
— Troops, 10, 95
— Language, 87, 164
— Protectorate, 80
— Cultural Influence, 87
German Southwest Africa, 12
Germany, 5, 11, 53
Ghana, 28, 39
Gibeon, 140, 242
Gobabis, 127, 247
Gobi Desert, 5, 58
Goering, Dr. Heinrich, 137
Golden Mole, 4, 71
Gordon, Captain Robert J., 106
Gough, John Bartholomew, 272
Grand Canyon, 82
Great Britain, 12, 20
Great Namaqualand, 82
Green, Frederick, 128
Grootfontein, 55, 91—93, 96
Groot Karasberge, 55
Gross, Ernest A., 206, 207
Grundel, 105
Guano, 56, 66, 67

Guerillas, 31
Gunas, 96

H

Hahn, Rev. Hugo, 124, 130, 182
Halifax Island, 107
Hardeveld, 55
Harrigan, Anthony, 28, 30
Health Services *vide* Medical Services
Heibum, 110, 111
Hereroland, 243
Hereros, 5, 10, 37—40, 88, 100—103, 106, 110, 114, 115, 118—120, 122, 124, 126, 129, 132, 134, 136, 137, 141, 143, 144, 146, 170
Heydebrack, General von, 150
Hitler Jugend, 166
Hoacharas, 113
Hoba West, 93
Holland, 52, 104
Homelands, 159, 160, 241, 245, 247, *vide* Bantustan and Self-government
Hoorenkrans, 139
Hoover Institute for War and Peace, 216
Hop, Hendrik, 105
Horse Latitudes, 1
Hottentots, 10, 39, 82, 113
Housing, 178
Hovey, Graham, 192
Huab Valley, 3
Hunsberg, 54
Hydro-Electric Power, 253

I

Ichaboe Island, 66
Imports, 64
Incorporation, 10, 13, 169
— Non-White vote, 168
India, 39, 44
Indian Ocean, 57, 58, 104
Infiltration, 31
International Court of Justice, 2, 49 *vide* World Court
International Law, 11
— Norm, 21, 194
— Community, 21
— Studies Programme, 216
— Labour Organisation, 220

279

Investment, 185
Iron Curtain, 46
Islands, off-shore, 66
Italy, 2
Itzawisis, 243

Makololo, 101
Malagasy Republic, 253
Malaria, 99
Malawi, 44, 250—253
Mambakushu, 98
Mandate, 11—16, 19, 25, 46, 166,
    197—200, 203, 204, 206, 223,
    240
Manning, Professor Charles, 217
Mariental, 242
Marble, 146
Marine Diamond Corporation,
    79
Marshall, General S. L., 29, 215
Marula (fruit), 261
Masubiya, 98
Mbandero, 121, 123
Mbukushu, 116
Meat Industry, 175, 262
Medical Services, 178, 179, 265,
    266
Metals, 34, 35, 91, 176
Meteorites, 93
Militarising, 10, 21, 213—215
Minerals, 9, 33—35, 176
Mining, 33, 92, 141, 146, 176
— Deep Level, 9
Minority Groups, 5, 222, 270, 271
Morrel, Captain Benjamin, 66,
    105
Mossamedes, 118
Mozambique, 251
Multi-National Society, The, 39

N

Naga Rebellion, 39
Namaland, 130, 136, 142, 243
Namaqua, 82
Namaqualand, 83
Namas, 5, 8, 38, 39, 55, 75, 86—88,
    100, 103, 105—107, 110, 111,
    113—115, 121—123, 125, 126,
    128, 130, 132, 136, 137,
    139—141, 145, 146, 159, 242,
    243
Nameless Land, The, 2, 52
Namib Desert, 3, 55—57, 61, 65,
    67, 68, 70, 76, 77, 79, 185, 189
Namutoni, 93, 95
Naras, 70
Narrow Bay *vide* Angra
    Pequena, 104
NASA, 93

Natal, 62
National Geographical Society,
    58
National Socialism, 166, 167
Native Reserves Commission,
    160
Naturalisation, 165
Naute River, 258
Nautilus, 135
Nazism *vide* National Socialism
Ndonga, 117
Negroid, 114
New Guinea, 11, 12, 14
New School for Social Research,
    217
New York University, 217
New Zealand, 11, 12
Nicodemus, 140
Nigeria, 53, 62, 63, 182
Nkrumah, 28
North West Cape Province, 101

O

Oceanographic Museum, 103
Odendaal Commission, 47, 223,
    229—232, 239, 241, 244, 248,
    256—258, 260, 264, 266, 267,
    269
Odendaal, Frans H, 228
Odendaal Programme, 48
Odendaal Report, 239, 262
Ohopoho, 75
Oil, 35, 163
Okaukeujo, 93
Okahandja, 122, 142
— Maherero Treaty of, 130
Okavangoland, 17, 40, 57, 58, 60,
    97, 159, 243, 260
Okavango River, 58, 60, 62, 97,
    116, 128, 266
Okavangos, 5, 40, 93, 100,
    115—117, 120, 258
Olifants River, 106
Omahangu (plant), 259
Omaheke, 111
Omaruru, 142
Omaruru River, 259
Omatako Peak, 54
Omatako-Waterberg, 259
Omataku-Otjituo, 259
Ondangua, 119
One-man-one-vote 18, 42, 195,
    232

281

Vogelsang, Heinrich, 135
Volcano, 8
Vorster, John, 252

W

Wages, 177
Wall Street Journal, 32
Walvis Bay, 30, 54, 55, 59, 62—67,
92, 103, 107, 108, 127, 134,
141, 147, 149
— Annexation of, 133
Warmbad, 107, 114
Water, 9, 47, 57, 86, 96, 98,
183—188, 266, 267
— Conservation of, 5, 187
Waterberg East, 242
Waterberg Mountains, 143
Waterberg Plateau, 90
Welwitsch, Friedrich, 69
Welwitschia (plant), 3, 6, 9
Weslyan Missionary School, 108
White Farmlands, 241—244
White Lady of the Brandberg,
4, 71—73
Whites, 43, 49, 101, 102
Wilhelm II, Kaiser, 103, 129
Wikar, H J, 105
Wilson, President of the USA,
12—15
Windhoek, 54, 55, 59, 61, 63, 67,
82, 84, 85, 87, 88, 90, 93, 122,

123, 141, 142
— Museum, 104
Witbooi, Chief Hendrik, 86,
134, 137—140, 144, 145
World Court, 2, 6, 7, 9, 10, 15,
19, 20, 22—25, 27, 29, 171, 174,
190, 192, 193, 196, 197, 199,
204, 205, 207, 209, 210, 212,
214—216, 219, 220, 224—228,
231, 232, 234, 237 *vide* International Court of Justice
World Press, 2
World War I, 147, 149, 151,
152, 157
World War II, 8, 18, 68, 87, 92,
165, 167, 168
Wright, Quincy, 11

Y

Yugoslavia, 39

Z

Zambesi River, 53, 97, 116
Zambia, 26, 44, 53, 250, 251, 253
Zaris Mountains, 54
Zebra Mountains, 54, 60
Zimbabwe, 74
Zulu, 116
Zululand, 99

What is this territory of South West Africa that has featured so prominently in the world press the past year, contending for headlines with Vietnam, China, the Middle-East and other troubled areas of the globe? It has been referred to as a "threat to world peace" and, according to the Afro-Asian world, the entire future of the United Nations now depends on what happens to South West Africa. It has been the subject of a five year dispute before the International Court of Justice — the World Court — and at the beginning of 1967 a United Nations Committee was debating whether to recommend to the world body that South West Africa's disputed international status be settled by force, by persuasion or by negotiation.

Yet of all the regions in Africa, South Wes Africa is the least known and its socio-political structure the least understood.

A good book on South West Africa for American readers has been beyond expectation. Only two books have been written on this subject in the past ten years, and neither one has provided the background so badly needed. Most Americans know practically nothing about this territory, which covers an area the size of Texas. Yet it has been front-page news in almost every newspaper in the United States in recent months. South West Africa can no longer be ignored.

Why has this little known land suddenly been catapulted onto the world scene? Why is it one of the most controversial issues before the UN today? What should be done about it? This is the book that provides the answers. Few, if any, authors are so well versed on the subject as Dr. Rhoodie.

— Father Daniel Lyons, S. J.
Author of **Vietnam Crisis.**